Understanding Korean Webtoon Culture

Harvard East Asian Monographs 459

Understanding Korean Webtoon Culture

Transmedia Storytelling, Digital Platforms, and Genres

Dal Yong Jin

Published by the Harvard University Asia Center
Distributed by Harvard University Press
Cambridge (Massachusetts) and London 2023

© 2023 by The President and Fellows of Harvard College
Printed in the United States of America

The Harvard University Asia Center publishes a monograph series and, in coordination with the Fairbank Center for Chinese Studies, the Korea Institute, the Reischauer Institute of Japanese Studies, and other facilities and institutes, administers research projects designed to further scholarly understanding of China, Japan, Korea, Vietnam, and other Asian countries. The Center also sponsors projects addressing multidisciplinary, transnational, and regional issues in Asia.

Cataloging-in-Publication Data is on file at the Library of Congress.

ISBN 9780674291317 (cloth) | ISBN 9780674291324 (paperback)

Index by the author

∞ Printed on acid-free paper

Last figure below indicates year of this printing
32 31 30 29 28 27 26 25 24 23

For Kyung Won (Eustina) Na

Contents

	List of Tables and Figures	ix
	Preface	xi
	Acknowledgments	xv
	List of Abbreviations	xvi
	Introduction	1
1	Evolution of Webtoons in the Digital Platform Era	21
2	Platformization of Korean Webtoons	48
3	Webtoons' Digital Sphere: Snack Culture and Binge-Reading	78
4	Transmedia Storytelling of Webtoons in Big-Screen Culture	100
5	Webtoons' Transnational Transmediality	132
6	Sociocultural Perspectives on Webtoonists	160
7	Webtoons' New Perspectives	181
	Notes	195
	References	201
	Index	223

Tables and Figures

Tables

2.1 Top 15 Dream Jobs among Elementary Students in Korea, 2009 and 2020 — 53
2.2 Naver Webtoon's Estimated Annual Earnings in Billions of Won, 2018–2021 — 54
2.3 KakaoPage's Estimated Annual Earnings in Billions of Won, 2017–2021 — 55
2.4 Types of Webtoon Platforms — 63
4.1 Selected Webtoon-Based Dramas Aired on Korean Television, 2014–2021 — 110
4.2 Selected Webtoon-Based Films Released in 2006–2021 — 120
5.1 Exports of Korean Cultural Products, 2010–2020, in Millions of Dollars — 138
5.2 Webtoons in Global Markets in December 2018, by Selected Platforms — 140

Figures

1.1 A *manhwabang* of the 1970s — 24
1.2 Number of webtoons, 2014–2019 — 26
1.3 Number of webtoons by platform — 27

1.4	Webtoon genres in the early 2000s and 2013, by percentage of all webtoons	29
1.5	Kang Full's *Sunjeong* manhwa: "Part I. Elevator"	36
1.6	Art from the second episode of the webtoon *Misaeng: Incomplete Life*	41
2.1	Webtoonists' annual income in 2018 in 10,000s of won and with percentages of webtoonists by income level	57
2.2	Kakao: Vertical integration in content production as of 2020	65
2.3	Art from the webtoon *They Say I was Born a King's Daughter*	74
4.1	Art from the webtoon *Navillera: Like a Butterfly*	104
4.2	Art from the webtoon *Itaewon Class*	112
4.3	The movie and webtoon versions of *Along with the Gods*	123
6.1	Yoon Tae-ho working on a new webtoon	162
6.2	Art from Yoon Tae-ho's *Moss*	168

Preface

Webtoons were already everywhere. When K-pop began to penetrate global music markets in the early 2010s, Korean webtoons also started to knock on the door of Western countries. Unlike K-pop—which Psy gave a huge boost to starting in 2011 in the Global North with the hit song "Gangnam Style"—Korean webtoons at first left only a small footprint in several Western countries, including the United States and France, as well as in Asian countries like Japan and Indonesia. I began reading several webtoons in the late 2000s, and I immediately believed that webtoons would be the next driving engine for the Korean Wave due to their fascinating storytelling and diversity in genres. Consequently, I started to conduct research on webtoons and published an article about them in 2015, which might be the first academic article on the topic published in English. Ever since, many scholars in several fields have paid attention to webtoons from diverse perspectives, such as cultural studies, literature studies, political economy, and transnationality.

Webtoons are a latecomer to my research agenda. However, they have become a perfect storm mainly due to their distinctive characteristics, wherein popular culture and digital technologies converge. Since I have also focused on three related research areas—the Korean Wave, digital platforms, and globalization and transnationalization since the early 2010s—the webtoon has been a great research topic, in which I can benefit from my knowledge of these three research fields. As Korean youth, followed by some global youth, are increasingly interested in webtoons,

I wanted to expand the scope of my research interests to include this distinctive digital youth culture.

More specifically, my interest in webtoons has been growing because of several significant developments. To begin with, unlike older components of audiovisual culture such as television programs, K-pop, and films, webtoons not only have a textual format but also often spin off other audio-visual content, such as films, television dramas, and digital games. Due in part to transmedia storytelling, the webtoon industry has become one of the most significant sectors in the Korean cultural sphere. Second, since their inception, webtoons have been produced and circulated by the two most significant contemporary digital technologies—namely, digital platforms and smartphones. Third, webtoons are gaining global recognition after establishing popularity in Korea. Either as separate cultural products or as sources for transmedia storytelling, webtoons have continued to expand their transnationality, which means that they are riding the Korean Wave (in Korean: Hallyu) to become one of the major cultural products in the Hallyu tradition—referring to the rapid growth of local cultural industries and the demand for Korean popular culture and digital technologies around the globe. Whether people read webtoons or not, they are deeply influenced by webtoon culture as they unwittingly enjoy webtoon-based cultural content like television dramas and films.

Webtoons are still unfamiliar to many global media outlets and cultural consumers. As I have continued to study the Korean Wave and digital platforms, I have had many opportunities to talk about the growth of Korean cultural industries to both Hallyu audiences and representatives of the media in many parts of the globe. One of the primary questions from audiences and reporters is "What will the next major cultural industry in the Korean Wave trend be?" I answer that this will be the webtoon sector. For those who are confused by this unexpected response, I try to explain that webtoons have proven their great potential as parts of new youth culture and digital culture, while transforming the cultural industry's paradigms.

This does not mean that the future of webtoons will be rosy, as several challenges must be resolved in the near future. The platformization of webtoons demonstrates their effect on late capitalist society. A handful of negatives, including violations of intellectual property rights, should be carefully dealt with as well, while developing webtoons' exceptional form of digital youth culture. I therefore hope that this book will be considered by future researchers and students not only of webtoon and manhwa, but also of transmedia storytelling. I also expect that many webtoon fans, cultural creators, cultural policy makers, and cultural corporations will continue to advance webtoon-driven cultural production in the early twenty-first century.

Acknowledgments

I would like to express my sincere gratitude to the people who worked hard within such a short period of time to provide permissions for the various images used in this book. I was lucky enough to have a sabbatical in the fall of 2021 and the spring of 2022, which I spent in Seoul so that I could directly contact the permissions holders. At the same time, I learned a great deal about the Korean webtoon sphere. I also want to thank to the reviewers of the book proposal and the manuscript. They heartily accepted my approach and encouraged me to develop the direction of the book with greater clarity. I have been always grateful for such wonderful colleagues, anonymous academic friends who make the journey to publication both enjoyable and meaningful.

Finally, I want to acknowledge two previously published journal articles that I drew upon for this book. One is "Snack Culture's Dream of Big-Screen Culture: Korean Webtoons' Transmedia Storytelling," which was published in the *International Journal of Communication* 13 (2094–2115) in 2019. The other is "Korean Webtoonist Yoon Tae Ho: History, Webtoon Industry, and Transmedia Storytelling," which also appeared in the *International Journal of Communication* 13 (2216–2230) in 2019. The original articles have been substantively updated and reinterpreted in this book.

Abbreviations

AI	artificial intelligence
AR	augmented reality
BL	Boys' Love
KBS	Korea Broadcasting System
KOMACON	Korea Manhwa Contents Agency
LGBTQ	lesbian, gay, bisexual, transgender, and queer
MBC	Munhwa Broadcasting Corporation
OSMU	one-source multi-use
OST	original sound track
OTT	over-the-top
PC	personal computer
PPS	Page Profit Share
PR	public relations
SBS	Seoul Broadcasting System

INTRODUCTION

Since the early twenty-first century, South Korea (hereafter Korea) has emerged as one of the most significant non-Western centers for the production of transnational popular culture and digital technologies. While the influence of Western popular culture, in particular from the United States, has continued in global cultural markets, Korean cultural industries have developed and globally exported various cultural products, such as television programs, films, popular music (K-pop), and digital games (e.g., online and mobile games). Specifically, Korea has developed an innovative type of popular culture known as webtoons, comparable to webcomics in the United States.

Webtoons are a latecomer to the Korean cultural scene, which is becoming part of the global cultural scene. However, the rise of webtoons has been peculiar in the Korean cultural market due to various distinctive elements, such as the convergence of cultural content and digital technologies (e.g., smartphones and digital platforms), the growth of transmedia storytelling (referring to the flow of a story or stories from the original text to different cultural forms like films and television dramas and involving the expansion or compression of the original story to fit into the particular digital platforms' unique attributes), and the Korean Wave (the rapid growth of local cultural industries and the export of Korean cultural content to global markets)—which are all interconnected (Freeman, 2017; Jin, D. Y., 2019a). Webtoons are cementing their place as a new component of digital technologies, with interest in this niche comic form—now evolving into a major comic form—increasing across a range of platforms (Yecies et al., 2019).

Webtoons have become part of a digital culture enjoyed by many people in their teens and early twenties as well as young adults, both Millennials and members of Generation Z.[1] According to one survey conducted in 2017 (*Yonhap News*, 2017), about 83 percent of webtoon readers in Korea were Millennials or members of Generation Z. More specifically, youth in their teens consisted of 32.1 percent of the readers, followed by people in their twenties (29.5 percent), thirties (21.4 percent), forties (11.7 percent), and fifties and above (5.3 percent). In 2019, 61 percent of the readers of webtoons were still people in their teens and twenties (Korea Creative Content Agency, 2020c). However, since the webtoon boom started about ten years ago, many people now in their forties and older continue to enjoy webtoons. Webtoons are also popular among members of Generation Z in North America. In the case of Line Webtoon (now called Webtoon), which manages the American market, in the late 2010s users under the age of twenty-four made up about 75 percent of the users in North America. Sixty-five percent of them are female (Salkowitz, 2018; Park, J.H., 2020). Webtoons are among the most popular forms of digital culture among Generation Z members and Millennials, who have turned away from outmoded print manhwa in favor of reading on their smartphones.

Korean webtoons have been gaining global fans among comic readers based on their soaring popularity among viewers in Korea, just as Japanese anime and manga have penetrated global cultural markets over the past several decades. In fact, *CBR* (a popular online magazine formerly known as *Comic Book Resources*) discussed the recent development of interest in webtoons globally in a 2020 article: "Japanese manga has long dominated the Asian comics market so completely that, for decades, very few Westerners were even aware of the existence of similar comics being created anywhere else. In the United States, manga and anime are still thought of as being inherently Japanese. However, just as the continued digitization of our world is changing the landscape for American comics, it's beginning to have an impact on the manga industry as well. Demonstrative of this is the increasing readership of Korean manhwa [meaning webtoons] around the world—including in Japan" (Burrowes, 2020). *Quartz Weekly Obsession* (2019) also claimed that webtoons have "broken through enough to threaten the drawn-content kingpin that is Japan's revered manga industry, and gained enough global traction to join K-pop and Korean beauty products on the list of South Korea's burgeoning soft power exports."[2] Webtoons have gradually become one of the major cultural forms that many Korean youth—and now some youth in North America, Europe, and Asia—enjoy anytime and anywhere (Han, C. W., 2013; Lynn, 2016; Kim, S. J., 2019; Cho, H. K., 2021).

Korean webtoons also attract cultural creators and entertainment companies in both the Global North (in countries such as the United States, France, and Japan) and the Global South (including China and Indonesia). Global entertainment firms and cultural creators that have already enjoyed Korean cultural content such as Korean films, television dramas, and K-pop now see webtoons not only as a new form of popular culture but also as a source of transmedia storytelling for their own films, television programs, and digital games.

To sum up, many global fans enjoy Korean webtoons, either purely as webtoons or as webtoon-based big-screen culture, which indicates the worldwide popularity of Korean webtoons and their importance in the global manhwa sphere.

What Is a Webtoon?

The word *webtoon* is a neologism that combines *web* and *cartoon*. A webtoon is a manhwa-style webcomic that is typically published in chapters (called episodes in the webtoon world) online (Kwon, O. S., 2014). The term *webtoon*, used as a form of new youth culture, appeared for the first time in Korea in the late 1990s. Since then, Korean youth and young adults began to enjoy webtoons in tandem with the advent of digital technologies, in particular smartphones; digital platforms (called internet portals) such as Daum, Kakao, and Naver; and smartphone applications (apps). These platforms are not only distributors but also producers and creators that control the entire process of webtoon cultural production. Webtoons rely on the visual storytelling of manhwa and have combined digital technologies and cultural content to become a distinctive form of youth culture (Jin, D. Y., 2015a and 2020; Zur, 2016).

While webcomics are common in many parts of the world, the term *webcomic* is not common in Korea. Koreans instead use the term *webtoons* for webcomics, although in fact webtoons differ from webcomics. It is not easy to clearly define webcomics or digital comics, but webcomics are mainly digitalized (scanned) versions of print comics published online (Yecies, 2018). Webcomics also include comics that are designed for the web but are not too long or vertically arranged short cartoons (Korea Creative Content Agency, 2016). Similarly, a digital comic refers to "a print-born comic that has been adapted into digital format" (Aggleton, 2019, 397).

In contrast, webtoons usually are created first for the web and made by independent cartoonists who produce no original print version and have no financial support. Webtoons consist of vertically arranged images, which allows readers to scroll from top to bottom, usually on a smartphone. In other words, webtoons scroll vertically, as opposed to traditional manhwas in Korea and even webcomics in the United States and manga in Japan, all of which are read horizontally.

In this light, Burrowes (2020) points out two major reasons for the steady rise of webtoons in global markets. First, webtoons are fundamentally suited to being read in digital formats. Second, webtoons are made in color instead of black and white. These two factors make webtoons incredibly appealing to people around the world who are accustomed both to reading on their smartphones and to watching anime in full color. Combining these features with ease of access has made the webtoon one of the most significant forms of global youth culture (Burrowes, 2020). Webtoons' vertical mode of presentation allows webtoonists to show one large image on the screen at a time, making it less restrictive in terms of the layout of images—which is critical for storytelling (Harvey, 1996; Kim, J. H., and Y, Yu, 2019). Although the webtoon is often considered as another and nascent form of manhwa, it is arguably not the same as manhwa.

While Korea is not the only country whose citizens enjoy webcomics, it was the first to create webtoons, a new manhwa format, by using major characteristics of digital technologies in production, circulation, and consumption. The production and later global circulation of webtoons initiated and advanced by various digital platforms (including Naver, Daum, and Kakao) have diversified and facilitated participatory fan practices and digital youth culture, including snack culture and binge-reading (consuming many webtoon chapters with little to no interruption). In the midst of a changing media ecology surrounding digital technologies, webtoons have also become new products that cultural industries have to develop, both nationally and globally.

Major Features of Webtoons

The emergence of webtoons has been one of the most remarkable breakthroughs in the Korean cultural scene in the early twenty-first century. With the increasing role of webtoons, the local manhwa industry has strategically altered its business norms, and youth in their teens and twenties have increasingly included reading webtoons in their cultural activities. In fact, the revenue of the Korean manhwa industry soared from $270 million at the end of 2015 to $1.6 billion in 2020 (Korea Creative Content Agency, 2021). One research report predicted that webtoons would make up about 70 percent of the manhwa industry in 2019, up from only 7.1 percent in 2010 (KT Economic Management Institute, 2015). According to a newspaper report, the share of webtoons in the Korean manhwa market in December 2019 was actually 50 percent, although the report did not specify how it arrived at this particular number (Park, J. W., 2020). Compared to the prediction made in 2015, the 2019 data show that webtoons did not reach the expected industry market share. However, these two different data points certainly proved the growth of webtoons in the manhwa industry. The Korea Manhwa Contents Agency (KOMACON; 2018b) stated that webtoons were largely responsible for the development of the entire manhwa industry in the 2010s.

There are a handful of significant features that explain the growth in popularity of Korean webtoons, culturally and technologically. First, webtoons have a huge fan base among "digital native youth who are increasingly shunning the traditional print formats in favor of titles read on apps" in many countries—including Japan, in which manga and anime are some of the most popular cultural content for youth (Osaki, 2019). Webtoons can be read anywhere and anytime, such as before going to sleep. Webtoons are usually a quick read, so it is no wonder that hundreds of them are uploaded every day. This contributes to the evolution of so-called snack culture, which is the habit of consuming information and cultural resources quickly rather than engaging with them at a deeper level (Miller, 2007; Jin, D. Y., 2019a; Kim, S. J., 2019).

Second, the advent of smartphones, relevant apps, and high-speed internet services have spurred the rapid takeoff of webtoons. This trend shows a great evolution of media convergence—not only in terms of the merger of popular culture and digital technologies, but also in terms of the creation of a new form of digital culture. When Jenkins (2006) talked about media convergence, he primarily described the flow of culture and news in digital technologies so that people could enjoy already created television programs and news on their computers and later mobile devices. However, media convergence for webtoons has been unique, as webtoons themselves constitute a new digital culture. There is no print-first format in this case, in contrast to webcomics or digital comics.

Third, webtoons have developed new youth cultures embedded in digital technologies. In conjunction with the development of digital platforms, webtoons have advanced binge-reading culture as Netflix and over-the-top (OTT) service platforms in general brought about the development of binge-watching culture. Webtoon readers may enjoy their favorite webtoons for free, if they can wait, but many of them pay to read webtoons earlier. Webtoon platforms also provide binge-reading sections consisting of similar genres and themes. Therefore, people can easily binge-read webtoons.

Fourth, webtoon-based transmedia storytelling is a key aspect of webtoon production and culture. As various television dramas and movies—such as *Secretly, Greatly* (2013), *Misaeng: Incomplete Life* (2013), *Cheese in the Trap* (2016), *My ID Is Gangnam Beauty* (2018), *Itaewon Class* (2020), and *All of Us are Dead* (2022)—were created from webtoons and achieved notable success, many film directors and television producers pivoted to developing webtoon-based cultural content. Just as manga and anime have become significant sources for Japanese movies and television dramas—and later for many other countries' cultural products, including American animation (Daliot-Bul and Otmazgin, 2017)—webtoons have become transmedia platforms that act as a new source in which webtoon characters and stories can move into television dramas, films, and digital games (Chae, 2018; Hwang, 2018; Park, K. S., 2018). Cultural creators first in Korea and later in many other countries came to prefer webtoons to other original sources like animation and novels because webtoons often feature various new topics, and they are addictive.

Webtoons become transmedia platforms that create a virtuous cycle in which manhwa and/or cartoon characters and stories are able to be transformed into big-screen cultural content. Compared to snack culture, big-screen culture refers to popular culture that people spend more time enjoying. For example, watching a movie takes around two hours, and audiences have to use around sixty to ninety minutes to finish an episode of a drama series. Meanwhile, digital gamers in online gaming need a few days or even a few weeks to finish a massively multiplayer online role-playing game. The distinction between snack culture and big-screen culture in this book is not based on the size of the screen that people are watching as they enjoy popular culture. Exhibition platforms are also dramatically shifting. Television monitors at home are getting bigger, while people can watch films on Netflix using their smartphones or notebook computers. The size of a device or screen is not the main point that divides snack culture and big-screen culture. Rather, the distinction is based on the characteristics of each culture's content.

This new media environment will likely continue, as webtoons represent a treasure trove of original stories. They come with an established fan base, and the format is a narrative and visual map that the filmmakers and drama producers can use as a foundation. In fact, many cultural creators are eager to work with well-made webtoons. They can easily adapt webtoons' sophisticated information for movies and digital games from the original detailed visuals (Jin, D. Y., 2019a).

Last but not least, webtoons have become a new trend in the Korean Wave, contributing to a unique transnational cultural phenomenon. As of December 2019, Korean webtoons were being exported to more than 150 countries, in both the Global North and the Global South. Along with Line Webtoon, Naver Webtoon provided its webtoon service in 150 countries during the same period (Kim, I. G., 2020). Although other countries have entered global markets with print comics, Korea is the first and so far the only country to massively export webtoons to advance a new form of transnational culture. Webtoons have created a new Korean Wave (in Korean: Hallyu) meaning that while global youth enjoy Korean webtoons, cultural creators such as television producers and film directors in other parts of the globe, as well as OTT platforms like Netflix, pay attention to webtoons to boost big-screen culture. Webtoons have influenced global manhwa markets. Transnational cultural flows have mainly happened from the Global North to the Global South. However, webtoons are an example of a new transnational model, in which the cultural products of a small and non-Western country (in this case, Korea) are successfully competing in the global markets.

Major Goals of the Book

Over the past few years, numerous media scholars, sociologists, cultural anthropologists, and Korean studies scholars have explored webtoons, and several books and quite a few academic journal articles have addressed terrain somewhat similar to what is covered in this book. These works are valuable resources, as they offer intriguing case studies of and/or theoretical discussions about webtoons. Unfortunately, there has been little research in book format on webtoons—and, in particular, very little written in English. Keane, Yecies, and Flew (2018) included two chapters on webtoons in an edited volume. My recent edited volume (Jin, D. Y., 2020), which focuses on transmedia storytelling, also included two chapters on webtoons. In some of the latest academic work on webtoons, Yecies and Shim (2021) delve into the dynamic relationships between serialized content, artists, agencies, platforms, and global readership, in particular in East Asia. As I discuss below (mainly in chapter 1), a few books written in Korean (Han, C. W., 2013; Lee, S. J., 2016; Park, S. H., 2018) provide various interesting perspectives on webtoons, including their history and transmediality, and review the early stages of webtoon development. However, these publications do not discuss the most up-to-date topics, such as platformization, binge-reading, snack culture, new media ecology, IP-based transmedia storytelling, and the Korean Wave. These relevant yet fragmented discussions of webtoons show the lack of comprehensive and systematic studies of this emerging cultural content. Therefore, this book offers a critical understanding of webtoons as a transnational media phenomenon, focusing on digital youth culture, platformization, and transmedia storytelling.

First, the book documents the evolution of local popular culture according to the surrounding digital media ecology, driving the continuity and change of the manhwa industry (which now focuses on webtoons) over the past twenty years. As a major part of this analysis, the book maps the history of webtoons by discussing crucial elements in the evolution of the webtoon world. The book discusses a variety of new concepts and ideas, and it includes the history and context of these concepts as they align with current trends. Thus, readers can easily understand the evolution of webtoons from a historical perspective and contextualize the advent of webtoons in a broader and shifting sociocultural media environment.

Second, this book examines a new form of digital convergence, as digital platforms play a major role in the production, circulation, and consumption of webtoons. The advent of webtoons is closely related to the development of digital technologies, and that development has become a driver for webtoons and webtoon-based transmedia storytelling, as many new artists and creators in the realm of popular culture have quickly started to use media convergence between digital technologies and content to develop a new type of culture. With the arrival of smartphones in the early twenty-first century, people's lifestyles and consumer patterns have substantially shifted, and webtoons have flourished in this new media milieu. Interestingly, digital platforms have controlled the entire circle of webtoon's cultural production. By analyzing various business models, infrastructural transformation, and IP-based global reach, I discuss the ways in which a few mega digital platforms have dominated the webtoon sphere. In other words, I discuss how digital platforms have capitalized on new digital culture and webtoon readers through the platformization process, and I provide a critical lens for readers to use as they journey into the webtoon world.

Third, this book analyzes webtoons through the lens of emerging digital cultures and discusses relevant cultural perspectives. In particular, as Millennials and members of Generation Z enjoy popular culture on their personal mobile gadgets and streaming services, the book shows that snack culture and binge-reading are two of the most recent forms of digital culture that webtoon platforms capitalize on to capture people's shifting cultural consumption. I discuss snack culture in tandem with speed culture in the digital platform era. Since people's shifting consumption habits in this era are quite different from those of previous eras (even the early digital media era), the analysis of snack culture in the realm of webtoons provides a new theoretical framework for interpreting the crucial role of digital technologies in the cultural sphere. Also, by comparing binge-reading with binge-watching in OTT platforms like Netflix, I examine the ways in which webtoon fans have changed their habits to enjoy webtoons. As webtoons are a major cultural form that has introduced binge-reading into the entertainment industry, this book addresses the reasons why people practice binge-reading. It especially focuses on the two forms of digital culture (binge-reading and speed culture) that digital platforms develop to investigate whether this is a contemporary capitalization of popular culture.

Fourth, this book analyzes the development of webtoons as an underresearched process of cultural transnationalization (discussed in chapter 5), in which transnational media technologies and youth cultures are articulated to generate new media practices. The book acknowledges that the consumption of webtoons is an emerging cultural trend, produced by Korean cultural industries' extensive use of local culture, and arguably not an appropriation or hybridization of Western cultural conventions that can be easily seen in other major cultures like films, television programs, K-pop, and digital games. Nonetheless, it argues that webtoons reveal a transnational momentum that signals a new way of cultural circulation, moving beyond geocultural contexts and the Western-centric framework of media industries. The global success of webtoons has interestingly relied on their Koreanness. Unlike American manhwa, which focuses on heavy and serious action and thriller stories as well as superheroes, Korean webtoons emphasize people's daily activities embedded in local mentalities in various genres (Lim, K. U., 2018). This book presents an engaging analysis of the evolution of webtoons as a transnational process of digital content production, circulation, and consumption and how this evolution affected the lived experiences of webtoon fans around the world.

To achieve these goals, the book adopts the two different, yet connected, approaches of political economy and cultural studies, and it thus reveals the dynamics between structural forces and the textual engagement in global media flows. In other words, it brings together political economy (through the use of historical and institutional analyses) and cultural studies (through the use of textual analysis of major webtoons, social media posts, and in-depth interviews with webtoon artists such as Yoon Tae-ho). The book details the various stages of webtoon production as a form of transmedia storytelling, global circulation as part of the Korean Wave, and cultural processes, and it thereby describes a transnational embedded system for globalizing commodified culture. It sheds light on current debates about people's shifting habits of cultural consumption and a new form of capitalization in the cultural industries. The book's political economy approach discusses the role of technology as an integral component in all stages of cultural production, circulation, and consumption, and its cultural discussions of audience's engagement with webtoons contributes to advancing transnational cultural studies. To historicize the evolution of webtoons and transmedia storytelling, the book also employs underused documents, including yearly white books published by the Korean government and the Korea Creative Content Agency and industry reports from webtoon platforms and various research institutes. These documents help contextualize various interviews and connect them to broader cultural policy processes in the realm of webtoons and/or manhwa.

Overall, this book pushes the empirical and theoretical boundaries of existing studies of digital culture, transmediality, and transnational culture, as it investigates the cultural production of webtoons across boundaries in cultural forms as well as across national borders. I attempt to develop an evidence-based, critical framework for understanding the complexities in cultural production in conjunction with webtoons, and I hope that the outcomes of future debates will result in the enhancement of solid theoretical implications in critical media studies and cultural studies.

Understanding Digital Transmedia Storytelling and Media Convergence

As webtoons are an emerging and comprehensive culture, encompassing written texts, drawings, and digital technologies, as well as the convergence of popular culture and digital technologies, it is not easy to use any particular existing theoretical framework. Furthermore, the unique nature of webtoons requires us to use diverse theories, such as those related to transmedia storytelling, platformization, and transnationality. Transmedia storytelling in the realm of webtoons is one of the most significant theoretical frameworks that connects secondary relevant theories, such as media convergence, platformization, and digital culture.

Storytelling is as old as human history, and it has been a significant and effective way to distribute knowledge and information and preserve cultural heritage from generation to generation (Yilmaz and Cigerci, 2019). Transmedia storytelling is also not a new form of distributing knowledge and information. Since the early twentieth century, transmedia storytelling has gradually become a major strategy in cultural production, as evidenced by the transformation of novels into radio and film versions in early uses of the concept. However, transmedia storytelling has greatly appealed to cultural creators in the twenty-first century. Webtoons especially have opened the door to a new form of transmedia storytelling, both nationally and transnationally. As transmediality is the driver and heart of webtoons, both theoretically and practically, this book emphasizes some major characteristics of webtoon-based transmedia storytelling that differentiate it from older forms of storytelling.

First, one of the major characteristics in understanding transmedia[3] phenomena is that a transmedia story is told through multiple media and platforms. For example, the Superman story began in comic books in the United States in 1938, continued in a television series, expanded into full-length feature films, and incorporated new interactive adventures in video games (Daniels, 1998). *Superman* moved to radio and television in the 1940s and ended up being shown on the big screen for the first time in 1978 (Scolari, 2014, 70). Transmedia storytelling was initially theorized as "a process where integral elements of a fiction get dispersed systematically across multiple delivery channels" (Jenkins, 2007), and it is understood for the most part as a coordinated system of convergence-driven media production that establishes a "new synergy amongst media companies and industries" (Hay and Couldry, 2011, 473). Transmedia storytelling is a prominent technique in the cultural industries, as "doing transmedia means to make the project's content available on different technological platforms, without causing any overlaps or interferences, while managing the story experienced by different audiences" (Giovagnoli, 2011, 8). In particular, it has offered new opportunities for increased diversity and meaningful participation in cultural industries (Baker and Schak, 2019).

The major characteristics of the notion of transmedia storytelling have continued to change due to a shifting media ecology. As Freeman (2018) points out, media and cultural industries are defined by ever-changing conditions, and as these conditions have shifted over time, the models of transmedia storytelling have been reconfigured accordingly. It is true that contemporary media convergence has led transmedia storytelling to become more urgent in the present moment, as media creators make use of a host of internal corporate interconnections and digital platforms (Freeman, 2018). However, this urgency has not necessarily resulted in a media landscape in which stories always unfold fluently as continuities "across multiple platforms, with each medium making distinctive contributions to our understanding of the world" (Jenkins, 2006, 336). As Fast and Örnebring (2017, 637) argue, rather than limiting conceptions of transmedia storytelling to "planned, strategic aspects of creation," it is equally important to "emphasize the many disjunctions and contradictions that almost inevitably follow when extending transmedia worlds across/between media."

Second, in the early twenty-first century, in contrast to old forms of transmedia storytelling as exemplified by the Superman story, contemporary transmedia storytelling in the realm of webtoons is deeply related to digital media, including platform technologies, which continue to grow and change. Unlike other forms of transmedia storytelling, webtoon-based contemporary transmedia storytelling can be categorized as digital storytelling, referring to "a two-to-four-minute multimedia story in which photographs, film and drawings are used to convey a personal story, personally narrated by the storyteller" (Hancox, 2017, 53), and therefore as digital transmedia storytelling. This characteristic of digital storytelling is exactly what webtoons represent as snack culture. Transmedia storytelling is also the practice of telling a single story across multiple platforms and formats, but in the case of webtoons, there is a particular focus on using digital technologies (Ram, 2016). As Freeman (2017, 32) aptly puts it, "it is digital platforms that most emphatically and most frequently build fictional story worlds across media; online promoters exploit digital tools like social media and film websites to plant in-universe artifacts about a given story world."

In fact, storytelling has developed with the progress of digital technologies into digital storytelling (Yilmaz and Cigerci, 2019). Digital storytelling is a way of adapting traditional storytelling through the use of digital media together with images, music, voice, and narrative to create media-rich stories. Digital storytelling is brought to life using computer-based tools and delivered via a huge variety of multimedia formats, including smartphones and social media platforms. Digital storytelling distinguishes itself from classic storytelling in that it "represents the democratisation of the modern world, where anyone with a computer or mobile device can tell their story, using any number of social media, podcast or other online platforms" (Bryne, 2019).

The dependence of global youth on the smartphone, mainly due to its mobility and intimacy, is a crucial element in the growth of youth culture—particularly snack culture and binge-reading, two of the most significant cultural trends that come mainly from Korea and represent the Korean cultural scene in the early twenty-first century. While digital storytelling as a technique dates back to the early film era, its widespread use exploded in the age of smartphones. With a camera and editing apps at people's disposal, anyone could become a photographer or videographer. Choices among media, devices, and platforms have proliferated, providing people with various options. But in the end, it is still about telling a story (Bryne, 2019). For example, many people upload their videos to YouTube, and these become sources for transmedia storytelling.

However, webtoons have become unique, since cultural creators rely heavily on them for big-screen culture. The webtoon is a perfect entity: both part of contemporary popular culture created with digital technologies and possessing the potential to be transformed to fit big-screen culture. Webtoons as a component of snack culture developed on digital technologies have become major sources of big-screen culture, and they are deeply interconnected with the increasing role of digital storytelling. In the global cultural industries, many audiences have enjoyed popular culture on digital technologies. Once novels, manhwa, and animation came out as forms of written texts, audiences have enjoyed them either as they are or via digital technologies, such as digital platforms and the internet. While these texts have various characteristics, convergence here is about the combination of cultural content and digital technologies to maximize the benefits to both cultural creators and audiences in the digital media era.

Third, as a continuation of the previous discussion but in a different way, transmedia storytelling is closely related to media convergence, mainly referring to the merger of old and new media. Transmedia storytelling is perhaps "the most aesthetically theorized component of media convergence" (Freeman, 2015, 215). In this regard, Jenkins (2006, 2–3) argues that one of the major characteristics of media convergence is "the flow of content across multiple media platforms." Thus, the term *platform* that Jenkins (2006 and 2007) employs is used to designate media as a channel or medium through which cultural content can be delivered and circulated. When Yecies (2018, 135) analyzed the spread of Korean webtoons in China, he also seemed to understand platforms as channels to intermediate marketing and globalization processes: "Suffice it to say that this 'webtooniverse' is sufficiently capacious to contain online and mobile spaces and interfaces and all of their contents, including webtoon agencies, artists (amateurs, intermediates, and stars), platforms, apps, technological innovations, and devices, as well as policy makers, translators, and national and international readers. While the size of the expanding webtooniverse is still an unknown quantity, the ways in which this new digital screen medium is taking its place as part of a new wave of media globalization is now becoming evident." However, these descriptions alone do not suffice to articulate the social, cultural, and generic parameters within which transmedia storytelling operates. In fact, a digital platform is often conceptualized in one of three ways: "as technology, as industry, or as culture or content" (Beddows, 2012, 11–12). The notion of platform and, therefore, media convergence in this book should be much different from the original one (see chapter 1).

Likewise, transmedia storytelling in webtoons needs to be understood not only as the flow of a story from the original text to different platforms, but also as the expansion and/or compression of the original story to fit into a platform's unique attributes (Scolari, 2017; Jin, D. Y., 2019a). As a few scholars (Suzuki, 2019; Steinberg, 2012) have pointed out, transmedia storytelling involves not only text but also characters and visual images. This implies that the previous focus on the adaptation of a textual story is limited, and it reflects the contemporary emphasis on visual images. It is crucial to understand that transmedia storytelling is not a simple adaptation from an original text to another cultural form: rather, it necessitates expansion to fit into each cultural form's visual attributes (Jin, D. Y., 2019a).

The old form of media convergence—the mix of traditional and new media—fails to fully explain webtoon culture, since webtoons are an integrated combination of written texts and digital technologies. Instead of writing the text and/or drawing pictures first, and then showing them on digital technologies, webtoonists treat their productions as digital forms from the beginning. Therefore, from production to circulation and then to consumption, both webtoonists and audiences produce, distribute, and enjoy webtoons through digital technologies. Webtoons are not a simple example of media convergence, but rather a new form of media convergence. With webtoons, Korea has developed a new type of transmedia storytelling. Cultural firms have paid attention and adapted webtoons to their own cultural forms. As Stavroula (2014, 28–29) points out, "technology advancements have created new forms for stories," and "a digital story is a short form of a digital production narrative. Digital stories combine moving images with voice, music, sound, text, and graphics." Webtoons are a nascent, and the most significant, form of Korean transmedia storytelling.

Meanwhile, webtoon-based transnational transmediality has been growing. As a comparative perspective that would suggest significant implications for Korean webtoons, based on manga and anime, Japan developed transmedia storytelling as many Japanese film directors and television producers adapted media products into big-screen productions. In light of the term *media mix* (see Steinberg, 2012), it can be seen that the impact of Japanese anime or manga as source materials in global cultural markets, including in the US entertainment sector, has been quite noticeable (Daliot-Bul and Otmazgin, 2017). Japanese manga have long been the center of transmedia practices in Japanese cultural industries (Joo, Denison, and Furukawa, n.d., 17–19). Compared to Japanese manga, webtoons have only recently become popular. Many Korean cultural industry corporations have developed their cultural products based on webtoons in the early twenty-first century, and cultural creators have considered adapting webtoons in this way. For them, webtoons as original source content are easy to adapt, and therefore transmedia storytelling based on webtoons has blurred the boundaries between genres, platforms, and even between types of entertainment (Jin, D. Y., 2019a). In Korea, transmedia storytelling has become the norm in cultural industries, as both popular culture (particularly webtoon culture) and digital technologies have expanded greatly.

Webtoons have indeed changed the culture of transmedia storytelling. In the cultural industries, webtoon-based transmediality has become the new norm because it goes beyond the traditional one-source multi-use (OSMU) scheme or cross-media storytelling, which is a remediation of cultural content that has already proven successful in another type of cultural genre (Kim, M. R., 2015; Kwon, M. S., 2020). When cultural creators used to consider books and comics as source materials for their big-screen culture, they read these written materials after they were published. What makes webtoons different from this established cultural content pattern is the introduction of simultaneous planning and production of various cultural products. Many digital platforms and webtoonists consider multiple production approaches from the beginning. When they start to publish new webtoons, they are already considering the productions' adaption to film or television and therefore closely tie webtoon production to the film and television industries.

Several cultural creators in various countries have also rapidly developed their cultural content based on Korean webtoons. Webtoons, again, often become a rich supply of stories for other forms of popular culture. In the Korean manhwa industry, some experts believe that webtoons are even threatening Marvel in the United States with their many unique characters and stories (Choi, I. J., 2020). Webtoons come with an established fan base, and their formats are narratives and visual images that Korean and overseas cultural creators are easily able to use as a foundation. Many film producers and corporations are keen about well-made webtoons because they can leverage their very detailed texts and pictures for their own movies, television programs, and animation. Transmediality has seemingly become the norm in cultural production, both nationally and globally (which is related to both production and consumption culture), and webtoons are becoming a new standard in contemporary cultural industries. However, due to the comprehensive role of webtoon platforms in transnational transmedia storytelling, transmediality has been designed and influenced by digital platforms.

Organization of the Book

The organization of the book is as follows. Chapter 1 documents the development of webtoons, separating the history of webtoons into four different eras (based on the development of webtoons, their role as a source of transmedia storytelling, their relation to digital platforms, and the shifting trend of webtoon genres) and discusses the main characteristics of each period. The first era is best represented by artists who drew characters on their home pages between the late 1990s and the early 2000s. The second era started between 2003 and 2008, when webtoonists began posting webtoons on internet portals. The third era began with the introduction of smartphones: it started in 2009 and lasted until the mid-2010s. The fourth era started around the mid-2010s, when webtoons became a major part of the Korean Wave and, therefore, transnational youth culture. This chapter discusses the reasons why local webtoons have become such significant transnational cultural products in comparison with Japanese anime, which exhibited a downward trend during the same period.

In chapter 2, I discuss the political economy of webtoon platforms in the Korean webtoon industry. Regardless of new webtoon platforms, the majority of webtoonists still prefer posting their webtoons on Naver Webtoon and KakaoPage, including Daum Webtoon. Therefore, many webtoon readers have to access these platforms to enjoy webtoons. Consequently, a handful of mega webtoon platforms have greatly expanded and intensified their dominant roles in the webtoon industry through various business strategies, including webtoon production, infrastructural transformation, the establishment of in-house companies, and IP-based transmedia. This chapter therefore examines webtoons from a platformization perspective.

Chapter 3 mainly discusses new youth culture relevant to webtoons. In particular, it discusses snack culture and binge-reading as new forms of commodified digital culture. In the early twenty-first century, global youth enjoy popular culture mainly on smartphones, consuming bite-sized content that takes minimal time to engage with—which contributes to the development of snack culture. Millennials and members of Generation Z also enjoy webtoons through binge-reading. As some readers often cannot wait until a new episode appears on a webtoon platform, they pay fees to review the episodes ahead of other readers. Many readers also wait for the release to enjoy webtoons, which indicates that webtoon platforms use snack culture and binge-reading as part of their business model. This chapter therefore examines the ways in which webtoon fans have transformed their routines to enjoy webtoons. Since the webtoon is arguably the first major cultural form to introduce snack culture and binge-reading, the chapter investigates the reasons why people enjoy webtoons in tandem with snack culture and binge-reading. Then it discusses the ways in which webtoon platforms capitalize on these new cultural perspectives as their most profitable business model.

Chapter 4 analyzes webtoon-based transmedia storytelling, which has been one of the crucial characteristics of the emergence of contemporary entertainment industries. Traditional Korean entertainment industries, including the broadcasting and film sectors, were suffering from their ongoing lack of appealing content. They thus began to pay attention to webtoons. Webtoons are great resources for content producers, as the original messages and episodes are typically already strong, and it is easy to add dramatic elements to them. Many film and television producers are interested in well-made and popular webtoons because they feature colorful and detailed pictures that can be leveraged for use in movies or television shows. This chapter investigates the recent emergence of webtoons as a prime source of transmedia storytelling for Korean cultural sectors. It also analyzes webtoon genres and recurring themes that have been reimagined for big-screen culture over the past fifteen years to identify major trends and characteristics of digital transmedia storytelling.

Chapter 5 investigates webtoons' global reach. It discusses the digital Korean Wave, not as a separate Hallyu trend but as a new and significant component of the entire Korean Wave. After achieving huge success in Korea, both the manhwa industry and digital technology corporations have strategically penetrated other Asian and Western markets. With a slew of successful titles with original stories and characters (many of which have been made into other forms of entertainment, such as films and television dramas), webtoons are currently considered a type of next-generation content that may appeal to overseas comic book readers and fans. In the 2010s, some emerging cartoonists also established studios in the United States to attract foreign investment while expanding their presence in foreign markets. As the global reach of webtoons expanded, Korean manhwas have become a source of Hollywood movies, and webtoonists target not only the webcomic market but also the movie and drama markets by using localization strategies.

Chapter 6 discusses webtoon artists' career progression and trajectory, training processes, and typical working conditions. It also includes a conversation with the renowned webtoonist Yoon Tae-ho and describes his unique experiences in the manhwa industry disciple system before he became an independent webtoon artist. Unlike other webtoonists, he also founded a webtoon company (Nulook Media) and is well positioned among other highly read webtoon artists to contextualize the industry. The chapter delves into Yoon's engaging and interesting perspectives on webtoons, their creators, and webtoon culture gleaned through in-depth interviews, which are categorized into key dimensions for readers.

Chapter 7 summarizes the major characteristics of the new phase of webtoons in the era of digital technology. By revisiting the two dimensions of webtoons—digital transmedia storytelling and transnational youth culture—this chapter examines how transmedia storytelling and transnational cultural flows can be theorized and how the webtoon phenomenon contributes to this theorization.

CHAPTER 1

Evolution of Webtoons in the Digital Platform Era

Since the mid-1990s, when Korea began to develop information and communication technologies including broadband services, internet portals, cable channels, and smartphones, the country has been widely known as the most wired nation in the world. Korea developed rapid advancements in high-speed internet technology(becoming the leading country in terms of internet penetration rate in the 1990s), and it also developed new smartphone technologies (becoming the largest gadget maker in the world). The advent of smartphones has substantially altered people's daily activities and markedly impacted youth culture. These cutting-edge technologies have had numerous significant impacts. In particular, digital platforms and smartphones have become vehicles for webtoon artists to make themselves known to a wide audience, as the technological convergence between digital technologies and cultural content continues to be a steady trend. Webtoons have been able to flourish within this shifting media environment in the early twenty-first century (Song, J. E., Nahm, and Jang, 2014). Therefore, it is critical to understand the evolution of webtoons based on the shifting sociocultural media ecology over the past two decades.

This chapter documents the history of webtoons by discussing crucial elements of the evolution of the webtoon world. It divides the history of webtoons into four different eras and discusses the primary characteristics of each era based on a few major features, including the growth of webtoons, their role as sources for transmedia storytelling, their relation to digital platforms, and changes in major genres of webtoons. The chapter therefore historicizes the evolution of Korean webtoons since the late 1990s, based on the surrounding new media ecology. By identifying various breakthroughs in history, it discusses the ways in which webtoons have managed to become one of Korea's signature forms of youth culture in the digital era.

The Advent of Digital Culture: From Manhwa to Webtoon

Comics have been one of the major cultural genres that many people, in particular youth around the globe, enjoy. Comics (called manhwa in Korea) are a medium that is used to express narratives through images, usually combined with text. In other words, they are a medium that interweaves words and images and thus requires its audience to practice "both visual and verbal interpretive skills" (Eisner, 2008, 2; see also Cho, H. K., 2016). McCloud (1993) also defined comics as pictorial and other images that are juxtaposed in deliberate sequences. For the most part, comics take the form of a sequence of panels of images. As the comic is the original cultural source of webtoons, I first document the brief history of manhwa in a local context. This prehistory of webtoons provides the foundation for the study of webtoons, in particular for understanding the transformation of the manhwa industry and evolution of manhwa artists into webtoonists.

A BRIEF HISTORY OF MANHWA

The history of manhwa begins with the first satirical cartoon published in one of Korea's early newspapers in June 1909. As a text-based cultural form, newspapers and other periodicals that were launched in the late nineteenth or early twentieth century used comics and cartoons to appeal to readers. The newspaper cartoon strip was the first form of manhwa that functioned as part of mass media (Sohn, S. I., 1999). One newspaper, *Daehan Minbo*, began publication in 1909, and on June 2 it included a cartoon by Lee Do-young on the front page. This was a one-panel manhwa conceived as a form of satirical cartoon and illustration. Since its content and expression were what manhwa were generally intended to provide, it is considered the first manhwa in Korea (Bang, 2018). In 1925, another newspaper, *Dong-A Ilbo*, began to publish a series of four-strip comics by Ahn Suk-Joo, while a third newspaper, *Chosun Ilbo*, which had recruited the cartoonist Kim Dong-sung in 1924, also began to publish various types of comics and cartoons dealing with contemporary issues. However, these satirical and enlightening comics were banned by the Japanese colonial government in the late 1920s and disappeared. At the same time, "comics culture began to flow from Japan to the Korean peninsula during the Japanese colonial era" between 1910 and 1945 (Chie, 2013, 87). When Korea was liberated from Japan in 1945, the U.S. military occupied Korea and carried on many of the policies set by the Japanese. Then the Korean War erupted in 1950, lasting into 1953. During this period, comics were used as a medium for propaganda, while manhwa directed at children as a way to comfort them and distract them from war were also published. Called *ddakji* manhwa or *ddegi* manhwa, they were thin booklets of poor quality, but they were full of adventures and fantasies (Park, I. H., 2006).

Newspaper comics also had to endure political oppression. From the mid-1950s through the mid-1960s, shops called *manhwabang* (*bang* means *room* in Korean) appeared, offering with stacks of comics for rent (fig. 1.1). *Manhwabang* were the forerunners of so-called bang culture in modern Korea, which is unique. Various types of bang arose in tandem with the development of new aspects of popular culture, such as the *nolaebang* (karaoke), PC bang (internet café), and video bang. *Manhwabang* spread throughout the country, as manhwa were among the most enjoyable entertainment products and were extremely popular. At the end of the 1960s, there were about twenty thousand *manhwabang*, which was comparable to the boom in PC bangs in the 2000s. However, due to the rise of digital technologies and webtoons, the number of *manhwabang* had shrunk to just 690 in 2018 (Hong, J. M., 2012; Korea Creative Content Agency, 2020a).

Against this backdrop, Korean comics began to branch out into diverse genres that suited the tastes of a diverse and growing readership. And in the 1980s, they began to expand into a new visual culture. As they became linked with the artwork styles of the 1980s, Korean comics became rich in external appearance (Park, I. H., 2006). Although manhwa

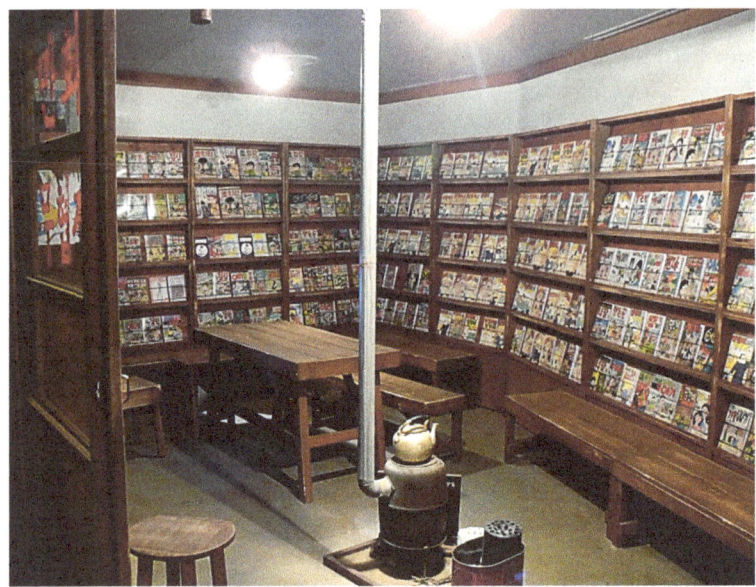

FIGURE 1.1   A *manhwabang* of the 1970s. Source: Provided by the Korea Manhwa Contents Agency in October 2021.

has never been considered highbrow or educational, it had evolved into a unique literary genre of its own, defined by an unusual flair and narrative (*Korea Times*, 2009). The Korean manhwa industry marked its hundredth anniversary in 2009, and the Korean Ministry of Culture, Sports and Tourism implemented a 140-billion-won (about $100-million) plan designed to expand and connect manhwa with various cultural and information technology sectors, including films, animation, television dramas, and games (*Korea Times*, 2009).

Manhwa had become one of the major popular cultural sectors by the late 1990s. Not coincidentally, the history of Korean webtoons also goes back to the late 1990s. Webtoons are the latest Korean cultural form (more recent than K-pop), and they started to become popular in the mid-1990s. Conventional manhwa seemed to be giving way to a new generation of webtoons, and the rapid growth of webtoons enhanced the status of the manhwa creators. They are "no longer low-profile, underground artists" in the Korean cultural industries but rather "attention-grabbing celebrities" who receive relatively decent incomes and public acceptance:

"Traditional artists who began their careers in the 1980s and '90s endured long and hard apprenticeships from their mentors who ruled the industry in the 1960s and '70s. Their rise took time. In the case of web cartoonists, some rose to stardom overnight with an immediate response from Internet users. Thus, their way of expression and content are different from the conventional medium. While conventional comics put more emphasis on the art of drawing, web cartoons might be less artistic but are story-oriented and palatable to the public taste" (Chung, A.Y., 2014a). Manhwa has rapidly turned into webtoons, and manhwa artists have also transformed their identity to that of webtoonists. Thus, some significant elements—including the market structure, webtoon platforms, and webtoon genres—can be identified in the evolution of webtoons.

UNDERSTANDING THE SHIFTING WEBTOON INDUSTRY

In 2018, comics earned $3,862 million in Japan (the largest market in the world), followed by the United States, China, Germany, and France, in that order. In Korea, the sixth largest market, they earned $1,052 million (Korea Creative Content Agency, 2019a and 2020a). Korea has rapidly developed its domestic manhwa industry, and its webtoon industry is now the largest in the world. Globally, print manhwa have lost their momentum, and their market size in terms of revenue has continued to decrease—partially due to the emergence of digital or web comics. Webtoons are a distinct form of comics separate from print manhwa in both style and distribution practices.

Korean print manhwa have experienced a similar setback, but the country has rapidly adapted to the shifting media ecology and developed webtoons as a new popular youth culture. As people live with digital technologies, especially smartphones, the webtoon has rapidly become a major form of youth culture. The creation of webtoons has continued to grow since in 2009, when the iPhone and Galaxy kicked off the smartphone era in Korea. In the early stage of webtoons in the 2000s, only a few were published each year, but their number soared in parallel with the introduction of smartphones. In 2010, just 163 webtoons were published, but 2,767 webtoons were introduced in 2019 (Korea Creative Content Agency, 2020b) (fig. 1.2).

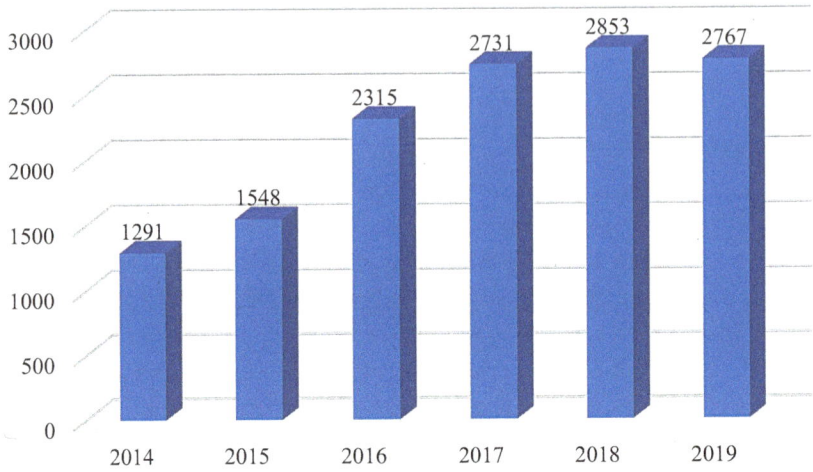

FIGURE 1.2   Number of webtoons, 2014–2019. Source: Korea Creative Content Agency (2020b).

While there are various reasons for the evolution of webtoons, the advent of webtoon platforms has been a major driver. In the early stage of webtoon development, two major internet portals, Daum Webtoon (later Kakao) and Naver Webtoon, played key roles in providing space for webtoon publication and consumption. In the late 2010s, there were about sixty webtoon-specific platforms—including Lezhin Comics, BomToon, and Justoon—that produced many webtoons (Korea Creative Content Agency, 2019a) (fig. 1.3). For example, unlike the 2000s and the early 2010s, when Naver and Daum were the two major webtoon platforms, in 2018 the largest webtoon platform, BomToon, published 277 webtoons, followed by Daum Webtoon (201), Naver Webtoon (197), TOPTOON (177), MrBlue (159), TOOMICS (149), and KakaoPage (144) (Korea Creative Content Agency, 2020c).

However, it is critical to understand that a handful of webtoon platforms, such as Naver Webtoon, KakaoPage, and Daum Webtoon, have continued to be dominant players. Daum Webtoon and Kakao Corp, the operator of Korea's mobile messaging service KakaoTalk, merged to become Daum Kakao in 2014, which was renamed just Kakao in 2015 as part of an effort to solidify its identity as a mobile platform provider (Lee,

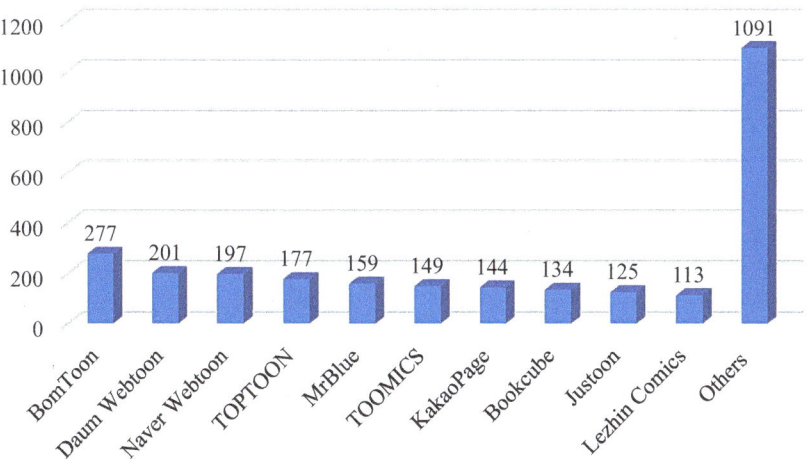

FIGURE 1.3 Number of webtoons by platform (2019). Source: Korea Creative Content Agency (2020a).

S. Y., 2014; *Korea Herald*, 2015). Kakao had already established KakaoPage in 2013 as a digital content marketplace, allowing brands and individuals to create and distribute visual, audio, and written content (including manhwa and genre fiction). It later added Daum Webtoon as part of the platform.

Although many webtoon platforms have regular publications and readers, these three major platforms are the largest in terms of both user visits and page views—the two most significant indicators of popularity from the users' perspective. Naver Webtoon accounted for 56.6 percent of user visits in 2018, and KakaoPage and Daum Webtoon collectively accounted for 19.9 percent, meaning that these three mega platforms controlled 76.5 percent of user visits. Meanwhile, Naver Webtoon accounted for as many as 67.7 percent of page views, while KakaoPage and Daum Webtoon collectively accounted for 14.5 percent: therefore, these three major platforms controlled 82.2 percent of page views (Korea Creative Content Agency, 2019b). This implies that these earlier platforms are still more important than newer webtoon sites. Thus, subsequent chapters focus on the Naver Webtoon/Line and Kakao Page/Daum platforms rather than more recently developed ones.

Meanwhile, as these platforms have developed numerous webtoons with various themes, webtoon genres in the twenty-first century are continuously changing, which makes it complicated to describe these genres. In the early stages of webtoons, *sunjeong* (meaning *pure love* in Korean) was a major genre, but later diverse genres, including BL (for *boys' love*), emerged. *Sunjeong* was introduced in the Korean manhwa world in the 1950s. In the post–Korean War era, Korea experienced significant poverty, and the suffering of marginalized groups in society (such as women and children) was extreme. Under these circumstances, *sunjeong* manhwa was introduced as a comic genre to comfort the population; it was especially popular among women and children. The stories of *sunjeong* manhwa gave many readers comfort by telling them that being a warmhearted, kind person would help others (Yoon, Y. W., 2001, 22–23).

Since then, webtoon genres have multiplied, with approximately thirty-five identified in the mid-2010s, including drama, gag or comedy, fantasy, *il-sang* (meaning *daily activities*), action, thriller, BL, sports, and adult or mature. Drama was the largest genre, with 478 out of 1,928 webtoons (24.8 percent) published between the early 2000s and 2013. This was followed by the gag (18.1 percent), fantasy (12.7 percent), cartoon (6.7 percent), and thriller genres (5.6 percent) (KOMACON, 2015) (fig. 1.4). The top three genres—drama, gag, and fantasy—accounted for 55.6 percent of webtoon content. Webtoons (in particular, epic webtoons) often weave several plots together. Therefore, it is not easy to identify a single genre for each. Some webtoons are simply classified as dramas based on their subject, which is why drama is the largest webtoon genre (Kim, S. J., 2019). Of course, the shares of the major genres have rapidly changed over time. Compared to Korean films, where the top three genres (drama, action, and comedy) accounted for as much as 75.5 percent between 1971 and 2016 (Jin, D. Y., 2019b), Korean webtoons show a comparatively more even distribution among genres.

Although a few popular webtoon genres lead the webtoon market, many specific genres portraying contemporary Korean society exist. Korean webtoons in the digital era have continued to diversify their themes and genres to become sources for big-screen culture, both nationally and globally. With these key developments in mind, in the following sections, I historicize the evolution of webtoons according to key factors: digital technologies, transmedia storytelling, and major genres.

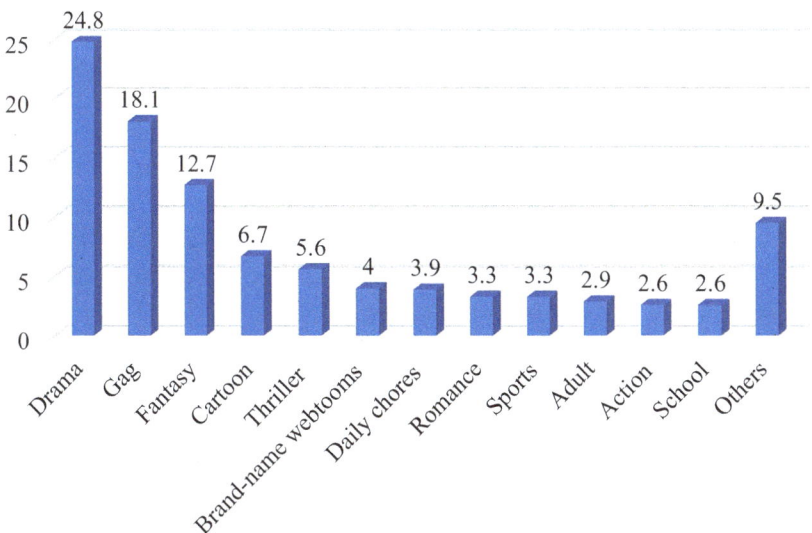

FIGURE 1.4   Webtoon genres in the early 2000s and 2013, by percentage of all webtoons. Source: Korea Manhwa Contents Agency (2015).

The First Generation of Webtoons: The Dawn of Webtoons, between 1997 and 2002

Due to the relatively short history of webtoons compared to other cultural forms such as films, television programs, and K-pop, we might expect to find very clear historical evidence about the beginning stage of webtoons. However, there is no academic consensus about the starting point of webtoons, in contrast to the case of manhwa. Although many scholars and government documents have discussed the history of webtoons, these discussions are not consistent, and some repeatedly rely on misinformation. Therefore, it is critical to determine when the term *webtoon* was first used, related to which concepts and in what circumstances.

The advent of webtoons and webtoon phenomena are discussed in a few academic works published in Korean (Yoon et al., 2015; Kim, K. A., 2017; Park, S. H., 2018) or English (Yecies, 2018; Jeong, J. H., 2020; Park, H. S., 2021; Yecies and Shim, 2021). Among these, S. H. Park (2018) argues that the term *webtoon* appeared first in 2000 when newspapers, including *Chosun Ilbo*, and the internet search engine Chollian used the term for the first time. KOMACON (2015) claims that the term appeared first on April 28, 2000, when *Chosun Ilbo* published an article titled "[Moving Image Manhwa] Webtoon Unfolds a New Genre." Yecies and Shim (2021) also claim that the term *webtoon* was used for the first time in a Korean context in *Chosun Ilbo* in April 2000. Meanwhile, K. A. Kim (2017) claims that the word appeared first in popular media in July 2000.

However, based on my newspaper archive research, the term *webtoon* appeared in *JoongAng Ilbo* on June 22, 1999, to indicate "newly created manhwas for the web" (Chung, H. M., 1999). The article used the term *webtoon* to explain "manhwa books that people can read on the internet."[1] In another newspaper article published on January 22, 2000, I. H. Bae (2000) also stated that a new form of internet manhwa service, webtoons, had been transforming the online manhwa market. Based on these reports in popular media, it is not necessarily incorrect to argue that there were significant developments in the advent of webtoons in the late 1990s, although the concept was a bit different from the contemporary notion of webtoons.

Due to the complexity in identifying the first webtoon, I believe that it is worth documenting the early history of webtoons through four different developments: the rise of newspapers' web pages, internet manhwa broadcasting companies, personal home pages, and the old internet service engine form. These early forms of digital technologies certainly became the foundations for the development of webtoons.

The first form of webtoons dates back to the late 1990s, when personal web pages were launched and when a handful of newspapers developed their web pages and a new form of cartoon. Korean manhwa were published in newspapers and then became part of the mass media. Similarly, the first generation of webtoons appeared on newspapers' web pages between the late 1990s and the early 2000s—when the initial stage of transmedia storytelling also appeared. In other words, the history of webtoons started with the opening of newspapers' dot-com era. Back then, Korea drove the development of digital technologies, and a handful of major newspapers (including *Chosun Ilbo*, *JoongAng Ilbo*, and *Hankook Ilbo*) developed their online services in 1995, followed by *DongA Ilbo* in 1996. These news sites saw advantages in content creation via web pages as they published news and information daily.

These major newspapers commonly developed manhwa that consisted of ten panels on average (compared to four-panel newspaper cartoons) and used full-color formats (unlike the previous black-and-white print manhwa). Although color manhwa cost approximately 30 percent more than black-and-white ones, they were popular with readers and eventually influenced the establishment of webtoons, almost all of which were in full color (Jang, S. Y., 2018). Park Kwang-su's *Kwang-su Thinking*, published in *Chosun Ilbo* in April 1997, became the first digital cartoon, and it was transformed into a play with the same title in November 2006 (*Yonhap News*, 2009).[2] This online cartoon was considered one of the earliest webtoons, since some early internet users shared it on their home pages, emphasizing its digitally mediated nature.

In addition to the growth of the internet in the late 1990s, the 1997 financial crisis—the worst economic recession in Korean history—became another major historical backdrop for the advent of webtoons. Many Koreans experienced severe setbacks at that time, as unemployment was high and job loss was common. When newspapers began to focus on web page development and tried to find new content for their new websites, the International Monetary Fund crisis provided a new opportunity for them, and newspaper companies attempted to develop a new form of manhwa to portray people's everyday stories and struggles that could be published on their web pages. As PC bangs began to open, primarily during the economic crisis of 1997, cyber manhwa (manhwa viewed through the internet) began to appear. PC bangs were often used for online gaming, but they were also visited by readers who enjoyed webcomics or digitalized (scanned) versions of print comics (Kim, J. Y., 1998; Song, T. H., 1999). Since a large amount of the manhwa available online in this era consisted of published print manhwa that had been scanned for digital consumption, only two pages of a manhwa were visible on a monitor at a time, and turning to the next two pages required time to load them—making it difficult to read them through telephone modem services at home. This incentivized readers to go to PC bangs equipped with high-speed internet (Song, T. H., 1999). Many manhwa artists immediately started to develop manhwa for the web to reflect the socioeconomic ordeals of Koreans and to solve the problems with reading digital comics during this period. At the beginning of webtoon production, "the main contents of webtoons were social issues from everyday life, such as poverty, cyberbullying, suicide, youth unemployment, and domestic violence. Amateurs made episodes found in everyday life and attracted sympathy from viewers. These works became a new genre called *il-sang-toon*, meaning webtoons dealing with everyday life stories. The spread of webtoons contributed to changing negative prejudices against manhwa in print and to boosting the Korean comics industry" (Jang, W. H., and Song, 2017, 175).

The second form of early webtoons came with broadcasting, when AniBS Broadcasting System—one of the internet manhwa broadcasters, established in April 1999—developed what it called *webtoons*, meaning manhwa that people enjoyed via the internet (Chung, H. M., 1999). Of course, this early form of webtoons used animation manhwa or web animation, which was developed with flash software (Yoon, K. H., 2014; Park, S. H., 2018). *ETnews*, Korea's oldest online newspaper, published an article on February 1, 2000, that described webtoon service as digital moving images developed from previously published print manhwa that used flash software (Bae, I. H., 2000). By adding color, moving images or animation, and voice-overs, internet broadcasters introduced a new type of multimedia manhwa service, known as webtoons—the same term as that used today but with a slightly different meaning. Several characteristics of these early features embedded in webtoons developed by a few internet manhwa broadcasters were adopted in the smartphone era, as webtoonists and webtoon portals sought to add new features (e.g., moving images) to attract young readers beginning in the early 2010s. This certainly implies that we have to include these early webtoon formats as part of the historical development of webtoons.

The third form appeared back in the late 1990s, when the term *webtoon* was first used, and Korean comic artists began publishing on the web (Marshall, 2016). C. W. Han (2013), a manhwa and webtoon expert and professor at Sejong University, argues that webtoons started in the midst of the boom in personal web pages. Luckily for webtoon creators, the expenses of production on the web were not as high as they were with magazines, and independent manhwa artists could also create new works based on their own ideas (K-Studio, 2012). In fact, from the late 1990s until the very early 2000s, many cartoonists-turned-webtoonists created their own web pages to showcase their work instead of trying to debut through magazines. These comics evolved from picture diaries on personal home pages that attracted viewers who often commented on, modified, and circulated them (Jin, D. Y, 2015a).

For example, *Papepopo Memories* by Shim Sung-hyun, *Snow Cat* by Kwon Yoon-ju, and *Marine Blues* by Jeong Chul-yeon were notable big hits at that time (Age of Webtoons, n.d.; Bae, S. M., 2017). Each was published online by its author rather than through magazines or editorials (Yun, J. H., 2019). Kwon Yoon-ju—a comic artist of the new generation— created *Snow Cat*, an endearing comic about the diary of a white cat. (In February 1998, when the comic began, Kwon used Cool Cat as a pen name on her homepage, but she changed it to Snow Cat in August 2000.) Unlike previous print manhwa that emphasized a long epic story, *Snow Cat* was a single-panel manhwa, published on her personal web page as her diary. It portrayed daily chores with a very short form of online manhwa, reflecting an early characterization of contemporary snack culture.

Last, but not least, there was another breakthrough when the webtoon, not in animation form but in manhwa form, with new traits, started in August 2000. At that time, Chollian, an old-form internet service engine, established what it called Chollian Webtoon to provide webtoons to readers. As Ok (2011) correctly puts it, young people—in particular, youth in their teens and twenties—were the main users of this online space. Their activities in this online community became the central focus of digital youth culture, meaning that webtoons were closely related to youth culture from the beginning. Chollian used the term *webtoon* in its service platform, and *Invincible Hong Assistant Manager* (*Daeri*), created by Hong Yun-pyo, became the first webtoon on this service (Lee, K. W., 2000). In 2000, a Korean web portal managed by Chollian created a new site for internet comics. Most of the comics appearing on this site during this time that were identified as webtoons followed conventional print formats, not animation formats (Cho, H. K., 2016).

Thus, webtoons as both a term and practice had already been in development in the late 1990s due to the rapid progress of the internet and served as the foundations of many internet sites and magazines (known as webzines, a combination of the words *web* and *magazine*), which were key to the early digital manhwa era. Although Chollian Webtoon could be considered the first platform to use the term *webtoon* in 2000, a few newspapers, webzines, and internet broadcasters not only developed an earlier form of webtoons but also used the term before the platform was developed. The late 1990s were very important in Korean history due to the 1997 financial crisis and the advent of the internet era, both of which were part of the context for the emergence of webtoons. It is always important to pinpoint the first person and/or medium to use a certain term. However, it is equally significant to understand that these sociocultural and technological backgrounds worked together to build the current form of webtoon.

Meanwhile, early webtoons, including *Marine Blues*, were well on their way to becoming famous among the Korean public, which played a role in their use as transmedia storytelling sources. *Marine Blues* is about the everyday life of Sea Urchin Boy and is composed of short, unconnected stories that capture different moments in his life. The webcomic, which started in 2001, was met with great acclaim, becoming one of the most successful webtoons in the 2000s. There have been more than a few transmedia releases based on Sea Urchin Boy's story, including an online game released in 2006 and an Android game released in 2012 (Lee, D. W., 2012). Although they had some limitations, these early forms of webtoons as snack culture became a new source for diverse cultural productions (Kim, Y. S., 2016). These early forms can be categorized as digital storytelling because the creators developed cartoons for a multimedia story in which drawings were used to convey a personal story on web pages (Hancox, 2017). As early webtoons featuring digital storytelling opened a door to a transmedia storytelling format, Korean webtoons have remained new resources for many cultural forms.

The Second Generation of Webtoons: The Rise of Webtoon Platforms

The second generation of webtoons started between 2003 and 2008, when webtoonists began to post webtoons on internet portals. In the first generation of webtoons, they were mainly published in newspapers and on personal web pages. In the second generation, with the help of mega internet portals, the number of webtoons rapidly increased, and they became one of the largest cultural sectors in Korea. Webtoons also developed new features, as they were mostly published as long vertical strips. They were also mainly published in color because, unlike the previous manhwa, which were printed in black ink due to the cost and time required for coloring, webtoons were posted online, where there was no extra cost to coloring (Jin, D. Y, 2015a). In fact, during the 2000s the sociocultural milieu surrounding the Korean manhwa industry changed substantially due to the development of digital technologies. This period greatly contributed to the development of the webtoon era, and the webtoon sector could no longer be considered a small-scale cottage industry.

Most of all, the creation of webtoon platforms by the largest internet portals in Korea became a major turning point in the growth of webtoons. In 2003, Daum created its own webtoon portal called World in Manhwa and recruited cartoonists to publish webtoons on it. Following Daum, Naver established an in-house start-up for webtoons in June 2004. According to the platform's official history, "Naver Webtoon is dedicated to innovative storytelling that changes with the world by developing a platform where creators can truly meet their audience" (Naver Webtoon, 2018). Meanwhile, Daum began its mobile webtoon service in 2008, one year before the Korean smartphone era started (Daum Webtoon, 2020). Interestingly, as many webtoonists published their works on internet portals, some webtoonists started to receive a writer's fee, although these were relatively small (Park, S. K., 2013; Seo, C. H., 2017). While quite a few famous webtoons were published during this period, Kang Full's *Sunjeong Manhwa* reached the milestone of attracting an average of two million viewers per day (Lee, M., 2008). Kang Full developed a new template for using the computer screen without panels or page divisions, combined with eccentric, humorous, and warm romantic comedy stories (Lynn, 2016) known as the *sunjeong* or romance genre, as discussed above in this chapter. This genre was especially important, as it was posted on the webtoon portal with a vertical layout, an epic story, and transmediality, thereby possessing several of the major characteristics of contemporary webtoons (fig. 1.5). In fact, when it was published on Daum with a vertical display in October 2003, it was considered to be the first contemporary webtoon in the manhwa industry (Korea Creative Content Agency, 2016).

Kang Full combined epic narratives with a vertical scroll method unlike previous digital comics, which consisted of only a few episodes. These included *Kwang-su Thinking, Snow Cat*, and *Marine Blues*, early *il-sang* toons that portrayed short stories of everyday life within only a few panels

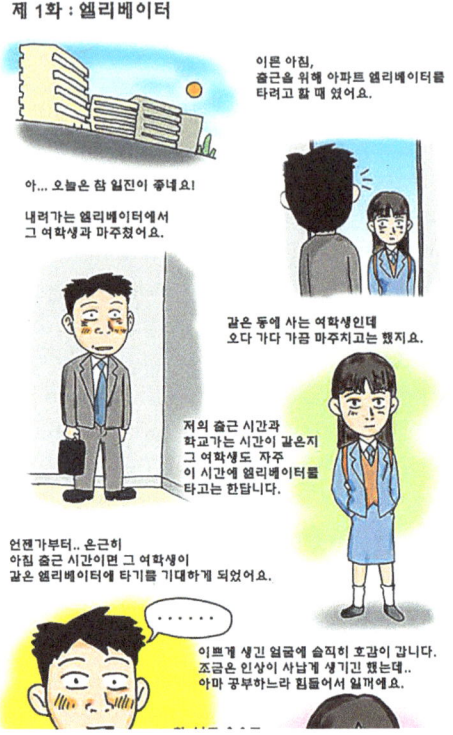

FIGURE 1.5   Kang Full's *Sunjeong* manhwa: "Part I. Elevator." Source: Kakao.

(Lee, S. J., 2016). Kang Full opened up the new possibility of running feature stories for extended periods of time (Seo, E. Y., 2018) and publishing them on a portal site (Korea Creative Content Agency, 2015).

At this historical junction, the webtoon was defined as manhwa created to be posted on the web with web-focused attributes, such as a vertical layout, the use of color, quick production, and rapid consumption (Han, C. W., 2013; Seo, C. H., 2017; Park, S. H., 2018). The webtoons in this initial stage already possessed numerous key features of contemporary webtoons. The most important characteristic of webtoons is their vertical layout. This is important because comic writers who published their works on internet portal sites such as N4 and Comics Today in 1999–2000 created horizontal pages that were designed to fit the landscape layout of a computer screen before the emergence of vertical-layout webtoons.

Since the vertical layout was introduced, it has been adopted by many webtoonists and has become the dominant webtoon format (Cho, H. K., 2016).[3]

The use of vertical layouts in webtoons (to fit the smartphone's vertical screen shape) creates diverse expressive effects that separate them from print comics, which are mainly horizontal (Cho, H. K., 2016). Webtoons emphasize verticality in cultural consumption as many people enjoy their vertical layout. Webtoons were originally created and consumed on personal computers (PCs). However, to read them on mobile devices, the user had to connect to the internet to access webtoon platforms, and the reading format for PCs was no longer optimal. Therefore, webtoon distributors began developing apps allowing webtoons to be consumed on mobile devices that allowed readers to enjoy them regardless of location (Korea Creative Content Agency, 2013). During this evolution process, webtoonists had to enhance verticality to optimize their creations for smartphones and webtoon apps.

The biggest difference between webtoons and conventional comics is their panel division. Because smartphones have limited screen sizes, overlapping panels would be hard to read on them. In the webtoon world, panels are arranged in vertical order, with more space between them, to accommodate the smaller display sizes. In Japanese manga, the shape of the panels and the placement of characters and dialog are arranged according to page size. However, webtoons make use of a long page format and arrange these elements with more space in between them. Large spaces can be used to indicate scene changes as a whole. Unlike in traditional comics, in webtoons the area surrounding a panel is not limited to white. Black or a theme-based color are quite common (Art Rocket, n.d.). Webtoons consist of vertically arranged images so that readers scroll from top to bottom when reading. *Medium* clearly identifies this major differentiating aspect of webtoons: "If you're used to Japanese manga, reading these South Korea–born webtoons might require a bit of an adjustment. For one, there are no black-and-white grids—nearly all webtoons are in full color. There's no flipping of pages or reading from right to left either. Webtoons are formatted *vertically*, so you'll have to scroll down to read. Developed with digital natives in mind, webtoons are optimized for smartphones, so you can read your favorite series even when you're on the go" (V, 2020). Webtoons' vertical mode of presentation allows webtoonists to show one large image on the screen at a time, making it less restrictive in terms of image layout—which is critical for storytelling (Harvey, 1996; cited in Kim, J. H., and Yu, 2019).

Kang Full's *Ba:Bo* (November 2004–April 2005), one of the earliest webtoons, clearly illustrates the introduction of the vertical layout. The first panel in the first episode, titled "Neighborhood," is almost ten times longer than other panels (Kakao Webtoon, n.d.).). The panel shows the homecoming to Korea of the main character, Jiho, after studying abroad for ten years. The panel starts with the words of the song *Twinkle, Twinkle, Little Star* and has a beautiful shining night as a background. It ends with Jiho saying, "I always want to come to the place where I lived with the background of a sky-blue air alongside soft clouds."

Such an extended scene, shown through an extremely long vertical panel, delivers a sense of time and space that cannot be expressed in print comics because to do so would require a number of pages in that format. Webtoons are "distinguished not only by the language and the site of production, but by the use of the web format to alter, at least in many cases, presentation, through vertical scrolling and use of multimedia visual and sound effects such as flash animation, sound, and touch reaction buttons" (Lynn, 2016, 1). In very recent years, webtoonists have posted new webtoons on social media that cannot use the vertical layout. However, since the majority of webtoons are published on webtoon platforms and viewed via smartphones, verticality is still one of the most significant cultural characteristics of webtoons.[4]

Webtoons' optimization for verticality certainly reflects people's habits, as smartphone users hold their phones upright almost all the time, and they typically consume cultural content without having to rotate smartphones ninety degrees. Before the arrival of smartphones, almost all video content was horizontal and optimized for larger screens, because of the way people enjoyed the content. With the advent of smartphones, cultural content creators, social media designers, publishers, marketers, and advertisers were incentivized to change the content format to better conform to users' consumption (Slade-Silovic, n.d.). Smartphones have dictated people's cultural consumption habits, and webtoons shrewdly produce digital content consistent with some of the major cultural characteristics of smartphones.

The Korean webtoon industry began to expand as a source of transmedia storytelling, a key feature of which is spreadability, or the spreading of a narrative across platforms (Jenkins, Ford, and Green, 2013). As Stavroula (2014, 34) points out, "transmedia is especially contextualized from a film perspective because films are key components of transmedia productions," and therefore many film producers pay special attention to webtoons. Unlike novels, webtoons consist of visual images supported by text, so they are good potential sources for filmmakers. For example, after its debut in 2003, the sweet and wistful webtoon *Sunjeong Manhwa* became a pop culture phenomenon, generating countless internet hits. In 2008, this webtoon was adapted into a film titled *Hello, Schoolgirl*. The film deviated significantly from the original webtoon. However, it kept the webtoon's main themes intact as the director of the film, Ryu Jangha, preserved the webtoon's key story line—the gradual development of love regardless of age differences (Soh, J., 2008). Another of Kang Full's webtoons, *Ba:Bo* (which debuted in 2004), was also adapted into a film in 2008. And *Dasepo Naughty Girls*, which also began in 2004, was made into a drama that aired in 2006–2007 on the cable channel Super Action, to lukewarm success.

The adaption of Korean webtoons in this later period was still limited to a few famous webtoons, and the movie versions did not achieve great commercial successes. In part, this reflects the difficulty of transmedia storytelling. Webtoons are sometimes too simple and, at other times, too complex, which requires film directors and television producers to expand or constrict the original stories. During the process, some webtoon-based films and television programs lose the originality of the webtoons, which leads to controversies among fans of the original webtoon and those of the webtoon-based film or television drama. During this period, films based on webtoons were not box office successes (Ha, 2016). However, they certainly provided opportunities for webtoonists and big-screen creators to work together. As I discuss in the following section, lessons learned from these early adaptations of webtoons in transmedia storytelling later led to huge successes in adapting webtoons published in the 2010s as films and television dramas.

Since the mid-2000s webtoons have played a pivotal role in transmedia cultural production while being circulated and re-created across multiple platforms. Webtoons have also become sources for transmedia tie-ins, in which media features converge to produce innovative aesthetic effects and new cultural genres (Cho, H. K., 2016). Between 2003 and June 2016, Daum published more than 500 webtoons, and 280 of them have been adapted for other cultural forms—including films, characters, and manhwa books (Daum Webtoon, 2020). Webtoons became popular not only as part of a new youth culture but also as a new source of transmedia storytelling during this period.

The Third Generation of Webtoons: The Boom of Local Webtoons in the Smartphone Era

The third generation of webtoons began with the introduction of smartphones in 2009 and lasted until the late 2010s. This era is characterized by the close convergence between webtoons and smartphones, which drove the popularity of webtoons and webtoon-based transmedia storytelling. Locally branded smartphones, including Samsung Galaxy, were first sold in Korea in 2009, and Apple's iPhone was also first imported in the same year. There is no doubt that the growth of smartphone use and Korea's world-class high-speed internet spurred the rapid development of various forms of popular culture in the country, including webtoons.

Timely support from the Korean government also played a role in creating this generation of webtoons, although it was not a major factor. In May 2014, the government started to spotlight webtoons as one of the fastest-growing cultural industries, and between 2014 and 2018 it announced new public subsidy and investment programs to support and promote webtoon authors (Ministry of Culture, Sports, and Tourism, 2014b). For example, many people were able to read the webtoon *Misaeng: Incomplete Life* on their smartphone, using an app subsidized by the Korea Creative Content Agency, two weeks in advance of publication by paying fees, while anyone could read a free version of the same webtoon on Daum two weeks later (Daum Webtoon, 2012).

To respond to the needs of busy digital users, media content providers in the 2010s released more webtoons, web novels, web dramas, and other web-entertainment materials short enough to be enjoyed in under ten minutes on smartphone devices. Snack culture is a result of digital users' desire to enjoy cultural content quickly on the go rather than spending more time on cultural consumption activities (Baek, B. Y., 2014c). This decade also marks the boom era of webtoon-based transmedia storytelling.

Compared to previous webtoons, many webtoons published during this period were long enough to become direct source materials for film directors and television producers. Thus, webtoons published in the smartphone era have been important sources of material for big-screen creators. Yoon Tae-ho, the author of a number of famous titles such as *Moss* (2008–2009), *Inside Men* (2010), and *Misaeng: Incomplete Life* (2012–2013), became the most influential webtoonist of that time. Many of these titles were turned into highly successful films and television dramas. For example, *Misaeng: Incomplete Life*, a webtoon about the office life of a fictional trading company that portraying a hopeless office intern (fig. 1.6), was released as a drama on the cable channel tvN in 2014. The television series was a sensational hit. Following its initial success, it was adapted into successful movies and additional drama series.

Webtoon platforms and webtoonists have also developed various formats to attract audiences. Webtoons have become optimized for

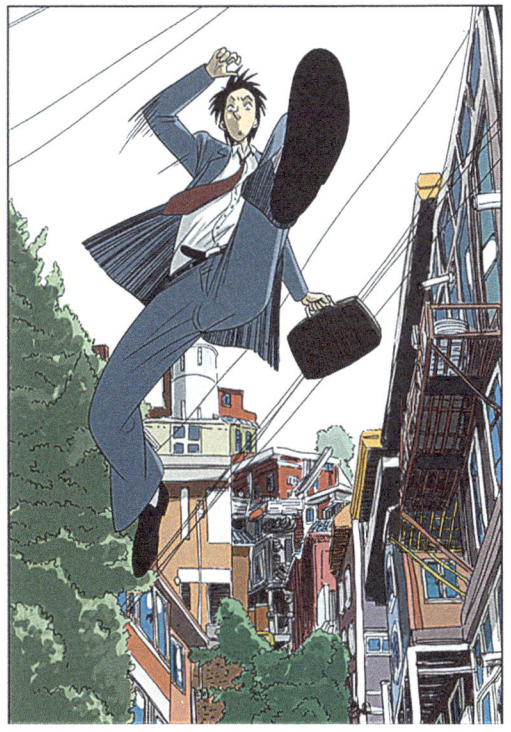

FIGURE 1.6 Art from the second episode of the webtoon *Misaeng: Incomplete Life*. Source: ©Supercomix Studio Corp.

smartphones, from a prototypical webtoon with pictures and quotes on a vertical display to versions that include special effects such as sound, background music, and vibration (Lee, S. Y., 2016; Cho, H. K., 2021). For example, in 2015, to add an extra depth to its new releases, LINE Webtoon adopted the use of HTML5 in several series to create sound effects and moving images (Acuna, 2016). Some webtoons also have features such as animation or music that play while readers scroll through new episodes. As Yecies (2018, 125) points out, webtoons were "enhanced with color, vibration, music, sound effects, and animation effects" as well as with augmented reality (AR) images. One offshoot, the smart toon, is designed for smart-device screens: it uses a touch-screen function for viewing and offers novel ways of framing each panel. These developments facilitated a rapid surge in the popularity of webtoons in the cultural market.

Meanwhile, one of the major characteristics of the third generation of webtoons is the diversification of genres and themes, which has become a key reason for big-screen creators' paying increasing attention to webtoons. As mentioned above, one of the latest webtoon genres that has become popular is BL, which has been developed as a webtoon genre since the mid-2010s. Webtoon platforms such as MrBlue and BomToon focus on this genre and publish many popular BL webtoons. MrBlue, created in 2003 as an online comic and webtoon content service platform, has also focused on teenagers as its major audience base. As of April 2020, MrBlue published 725 webtoons, 608 of which are completed series. BL was the largest genre of these webtoons (315, or 43.4 percent), followed by romance (138, or 19.0 percent), adult (121, or 16.7 percent), drama (71, or 9.8 percent), and action (29, or 4.0 percent) (MrBlue, 2020). On Bom-Toon, which mainly targets teenage girls and young adult women, about 60 percent of webtoons released are in the BL genre. BL is considered "a Japanese genre of homoerotic manga" (Kwon, J. M, 2019, 3), and it has continued to grow as a share of the Korean webtoon sector. As of March 2019, seven of the top ten webtoons on Lezhin Comics, including *A Man Like You* (which debuted in 2016 and ranked second in March 2019) and *Star X Fanboy*, were in the BL genre.

As explained above, Korean BL webtoons are rooted in the Japanese genre of manga and anime that features love relationships between young men. In Japan, the BL genre generically describes what was termed in the 1970s as *Yaoi*. BL as a genre in Korea seems closely linked to two big social movements that have crossed the globe in recent years: the gender equality and LGBTQ (lesbian, gay, bisexual, transgender, and queer) rights movements (Kawano, 2019). In the Korean context, feminism, gender, and LGBTQ matters have recently become major sociocultural issues. After the feminist resurgence in the mid-2010s, female narratives proliferated in various media, and feminist female narratives are being created in webtoons. The major consumers of BL content, including webtoons, are female readers who are in their teens and twenties (Kim, H. W., 2019). In addition to the sociocultural issues mentioned above, women in their teens and twenties often enjoy this particular genre of webtoon, as BL content may fulfill romantic fantasies similar to those addressed in *sunjeong* genre webtoons (Kim, H. W., 2019).

Korea is a highly conservative country, and Koreans were generally not accustomed to enjoying this type of cultural content. However, with the shifting social milieu, BL has become a key webtoon genre. In particular, since Yoo Hajin's *Totally Captivated* had a huge success in 2006, many webtoonists have adopted the newer BL formula and attracted much attention from readers. The success of Yoo's work led eComix to include more BL content. In the 2010s, the status of BL culture in the webtoon industry became more solidified (Kwon, J. M, 2022). While the *sunjeong* manhwa genre may fulfill female audiences' romance fantasies, so may BL. Therefore, the number of fans preferring BL to others has continued to grow (Kim, H. W., 2019).

Third-generation webtoons have continued to expand their themes and genres, and, unlike the webtoons that were popular in the first and second generations, many are long enough for webtoon fans to spend hours consuming various episodes. Due to their diversity in terms of subjects, lengths, genres, and themes, webtoons have solidified their position in youth culture, while many big-screen creators have focused on webtoons as new source material.

The Fourth Generation of Webtoons: Webtoons Go Global

The fourth and most recent generation of webtoons started in the mid- to late 2010s, when webtoons became a part of the Korean Wave and, therefore, transnational youth culture. This generation overlaps with the third one as webtoons continue to become increasingly popular abroad—not only as independent cultural forms but also as sources for transmedia storytelling in a few countries outside of Korea. During this period, a number of major dimensions have characterized webtoons, including the convergence of webtoons and social media, the continued diversification of webtoon themes, and the transnationalization of webtoons. These three major elements are closely connected in the continuing development of webtoons as a popular culture product.

The diversification of webtoon genres and themes has been achieved partially due to convergence with social media. Webtoonists who could not publish through traditional outlets now can post their webtoons on Facebook and Instagram. Therefore, they have shifted the notion of webtoons once again, using social media as a means of gathering an audience. For example, *Star X Fanboy*, mentioned above, was originally posted on Twitter, and Lezhin Comics officially invited the creator, Kim Cheomji, to its platform after that webtoon's grassroots success. Meanwhile, Soo Shin-ji, known as min4rin on social media, published her webtoon *Myeoneuragi* (meaning *daughter-in-law*) on Facebook and Instagram between May 2017 and January 2018 (Instagram, 2020).

Myeoneuragi was very popular on social media: it had 220,000 followers on Facebook and saw regular engagement on Instagram. It portrayed significant sociocultural issues, including LGBTQ and feminist issues, which were in the headlines in Korea at that time. Due to its popularity, Kakao TV—the mobile television platform owned by Kakao—created a webtoon-based drama of *Myeoneuragi* (known as *No, Thank You* in English) and released its twelve episodes in November 2020.

Myeoneuragi received high praise for dealing with the conflicts between a woman and her daughter-in-law. The webtoon aroused interest from many businesswomen in Korea, who often struggle to balance work and family life. It revolves around a businesswoman named Min Sa-rin, who lives with her husband and his family. Min tries to get along with her mother-in-law, but she is uncomfortable with the older woman, who believes that women should do more chores than men (Baek, B. Y., 2017). The webtoon explores common issues in family life through the eyes of Sa-rin. For example, in one episode featuring a traditional holiday, Sa-rin is shown in the kitchen preparing meals while the men watch a baseball game. *Myeoneuragi* casually comments on patriarchal norms through a women's perspective without providing explicit explanations and leaves room for readers' interpretations and judgments. The intention behind this webtoon is quite clear, and it has been successful: readers hope Sa-rin will be freed from her restrictive life (Lim, H. B., 2019). The television version of the webtoon used its characteristics but transformed it, revealing family life through the perspective of a female narrator that had not been shown in previous *il-sang* toons (Koo, 2019).

Some webtoons on social media have further shifted webtoon trends. Unlike previous webtoons that used the vertical layout format, these could not be published vertically. In the case of *Myeoneuragi*, for example, the webtoonist posted only several panels and, due to the limitations of social media, could not use a vertical layout. *Myeoneuragi* thus reflects a shift back to a format optimized for social media that was used during the earlier era of webtoons.

As webtoons have diversified their genres and themes, they have been well received in many parts of the world, both as webtoons and as sources for transnational digital storytelling. After achieving huge success in Korea, both the manhwa industry and digital platforms have penetrated markets both in the West and in Asia outside Korea. Webtoons are currently considered next-generation content that can appeal to overseas comic book readers and fans. The rise of Korean webtoons in global cultural markets is noticeable, in contrast to Japanese anime and manga—which have exhibited a downward trend during the same era (Daliot-Bul and Otmazgin, 2017; Korea Creative Content Agency, 2020c). As I discuss in chapter 5, in the Korean Wave phenomenon the webtoon sector has been a lesser-known industry than other cultural sectors like film, K-pop, and dramas until the mid-2010s. However, thanks to numerous systematic efforts by the Korean government, webtoon platforms, and webtoonists, as well as a growing webtoon fandom in other countries, webtoons have become a major form of transnational cultural content beyond Korea's borders. Webtoon platforms especially have greatly emphasized international markets.

Naver Webtoon has broadened the spectrum of new entertainment content and provided new opportunities to amateur artists worldwide. The Spanish version of Line Webtoon was introduced in November 2019, and the French version was released in December 2019. Naver Webtoon continuously provides "content which is suitable for the local market and plans to increase readership with the help of consistent marketing" (Park, I. J., 2020). Regardless of the piracy of webtoons in foreign markets and the growth of adult content, among other issues, the webtoon world has become a significant form of youth culture in Korea and beyond. Within a relatively short period, the webtoon sphere has improved its status as a new cultural icon and business model.

Conclusion

This chapter has presented a history of the evolution of webtoons. A historical perspective on webtoons is important, mainly because it "invalidates the question of whether local pop cultures are either imitations or subversive appropriations of American pop culture" (Cho, Y. H, 2017, 21). Understanding the history of local pop culture not only contributes to our knowledge of that culture "based on our empirical experiences, but also generates alternative frameworks for the many debates and discussions that those experiences engender" (Cho, Y. H,, 2017, 21). While manhwa has had a long history, webtoons first appeared only about two decades ago. Unlike other cultural sectors such as broadcasting, film, and music, webtoons are considered as a form of snack culture, and many people (in particular, those in their teens and twenties) enjoy this new type of culture with no time and space restrictions. Digital natives are part of the generation that is always on smartphones and other mobile gadgets, as well as social media that are regularly at hand, and they can enjoy webtoons at any time and in any place. Although the history of webtoons is brief, it has become one of the major cultural products for both youth culture and foreign trade in Korea.

Notably, the webtoon has evolved concurrently with digital technologies, including computers, the internet, and smartphones, while manhwa artists advanced new genres portraying shifts in Korean society—including people's struggles after the 1997 financial crisis and sociocultural topics surrounding LGBTQ and feminist issues. Although the early form of webtoons appeared first on newspapers' websites and on personal home pages, webtoons were quickly developed for publication on and delivery through digital technologies, from Chollian to internet portals. Webtoons have combine popular culture and digital technologies to become a new form of digital culture. Unlike manhwa and novels, which typically appear first in printed text formats and later are converted into digital formats, webtoons appear first as digital formats and sometimes are later published as printed books.

The genres and themes of Korean domestic webtoons have shifted, having formerly emphasized *sunjeong* and now including the growing BL genre. Originally, webtoons mainly featured simple, lighthearted stories about personal experiences and everyday life. Later, as webtoons began to be published on internet portals such as Daum and Naver, the stories became increasingly narrative-driven and dramatic, with more sophisticated pacing (Park, J. Y., 2019). The BL market in Korea is still in the early stages of being incorporated into the general media market. Given the widespread use in Korea of mobile devices, through which young fans consume online BL content, the commercialization of BL in webtoons is growing quickly (Kwon, J. M, 2022). Like the producers of Japanese manga, Korean webtoonists have tried to develop new genres to attract diverse audiences. Korean webtoons feature a variety of subjects and themes and have notably included nontraditional genres that cannot be seen in other cultural forms. Although webtoons are still driven by their niche market, the attempt to expand webtoon genres and themes will eventually influence other cultural forms, including literature and audiovisual cultural content. With their emphasis on new themes and genres, Korean webtoons have gradually become one of the major local cultural products that are penetrating global cultural markets.

CHAPTER 2

Platformization of Korean Webtoons

As webtoons have become one of the most significant symbols of digital culture, digital platforms have played an increasingly pivotal role in the cultural industries. Since the late 2000s, many webtoonists have used digital platforms to publish webtoons. Consumers buy and enjoy the particular cultural content of print manhwa in book format. However, they have to read webtoons on platforms, mainly through smartphones. Webtoon platforms and smartphones have played crucial roles in the evolution of webtoons, and they deeply influence many people's cultural activities, in terms of both production and consumption.

A number of major digital platforms, such as Daum (now part of Kakao) and Naver began to develop webtoon platforms in the early 2000s. These platforms have continued to play a major role in the webtoon sector ever since. Regardless of the emergence of newer webtoon platforms, the majority of webtoonists continue to post their webtoons primarily on Naver Webtoon and KakaoPage, which includes Daum Webtoon. Therefore, many webtoon readers access and enjoy webtoons on these platforms. These companies have formed a collection of mega webtoon platforms that have expanded and intensified their dominant positions in the webtoon industry. The companies have also developed various business strategies, including webtoon production, infrastructural transformation, the establishment of in-house companies, and the use of IP-based transmedia. Their webtoon platforms have advanced platformization and manage all stages of the webtoon industry, from production and circulation to consumption.

This chapter uses the analytical framework of the platformization of cultural production and discusses the political economy of webtoon platforms and cultural production in Korean cultural industries. First, I critically analyze new business models that are aligned with the creation of new forms of cultural content by mapping the dominant role of digital platforms in webtoon production. Second, I discuss the infrastructural transformation of webtoon platforms through an analysis of their vertical integration. Third, I investigate the increasing role of digital platforms in tandem with advances in IP, focusing on the distinctive role of IP in the capitalization of webtoons. In so doing, I discuss the implications of platformization, such as the power relationships between webtoon platforms and webtoonists and the capitalization of webtoon culture.

Platformization in the Korean Webtoon Industry

Many Koreans already began to enjoy webtoons on their mobile phones (also known as feature phones) before the introduction of locally produced smartphones by Samsung and LG in 2009, while Daum and Naver provided venues initially for manhwa artists and later for webtoonists. As I briefly explained in chapter 1, in 2003 Daum, then the second-largest Korean internet portal, created a webtoon portal. Daum also started a mobile webtoon service in 2008 (Daum Webtoon, 2020). In 2004, Naver Webtoon began as an in-house startup at Naver, the largest Korean internet portal. These digital platforms play a key role in cultural production, which refers to "the social processes involved in the generation and circulation of cultural forms, practices, values, and shared understandings" (Oxford Reference, 2019). Webtoons as new digital cultural products started to play a central role in the Korean cultural market in the mid-2000s while they were being distributed and re-created through multiple platforms. Therefore, cultural production in the realm of webtoons can be broadly understood as consisting not only of the production of webtoon content but also of the overall process, including the production, distribution, and consumption of media content and popular culture.

As major digital platforms, Naver and Daum have steadily increased their power in the manhwa industry and, therefore, in Korean cultural industries. As van Dijck clearly points out, in general digital platforms are greatly increasing their power in global cultural markets. According to van Dijck, a digital platform acts as "a mediator rather than an intermediary," because "it shapes the performance of social acts instead of merely facilitating them" (2013, 29). Digital platforms do not simply convey cultural products from producers to consumers: they strategically control, manipulate, and design the entire process to maximize their power and revenues. Nieborg and Poell (2018, 4281) also argue that cultural creators—in this case, webtoonists and later big-screen producers—are "impelled to develop publishing strategies that are aligned with the business models of platforms." A platform is a discrete and dynamic digital technology defined by a specific combination of technical, sociocultural, and capitalist business practices (Jin, D. Y., 2015b) that requires platformization—a holistic analysis of the overall ecology relevant to digital platforms.

Platformization in the cultural industries is a strategy used by cultural firms that focuses on the value of the digital platform ecosystem and seeks to facilitate and expand integration, orchestrate resources, compose services, and encourage joint creation among relevant actors. In particular, it is the basis of digital technologies that allow cultural creators and customers to "share data and processes, expand digital capabilities, and combine services and business models" (Gimenes, 2018). The purpose of the technology platform is to allow a corporation "to create value from business ecosystems," and platformization requires the ability to provide resources such as data, algorithms, and processes to connect new partners and other ecosystems (Gimenes, 2018). Companies maximize profits while creating value for participants or stakeholders in the platform's ecosystem. As Nieborg and Poell (2018, 4276) argue, platformization can be defined as "the penetration of economic, governmental, and infrastructural extensions of digital platforms into the web and app ecosystems, fundamentally affecting the operations of the cultural industries." Through a case study of social media, Helmond (2015) points out that platformization is the rise of the platform as the dominant infrastructural and economic model of the social web and the consequences of that rise. Platformization therefore affects the production and circulation of cultural content; the evolution of media ecology as a result of structural changes in contemporary society; and the development of business models used by companies and other social actors that create, control, and use various platforms.

More specifically, platformization transforms existing cultural products or content and creates new forms of cultural production (Steinberg, 2020). By analyzing the development of LINE in Japan, Steinberg describes platformization as a threefold process. First is the formatting of cultural goods for exchange on platforms, which is the foremost objective of the platformization of cultural production. Here the emphasis is on the shift from existing production of discrete and linear commodities to the production of the contingent cultural commodity, a distinctly platform-ready form of content. Unlike other cultural content, such as films and television programs, webtoons as a form of convergence between cultural content and digital technologies are a platform-ready form of digital content. Second, platforms create new cultural markets and sites of exchange for these newly formatted cultural goods. Webtoonists and webtoon readers alike use digital platforms such as Naver and Daum as the marketplace for production and consumption. Third, platforms encourage new cultural producers and consumers to participate in these markets. The most common example of this is the rise of the entrepreneurial self. Platforms are increasingly central forces in the webtoon sector, bringing producing and consuming subjects into being—a process that should be scrutinized when considering the platformization of cultural production (Steinberg, 2020, 2–3).[1]

Along with newly emerging business models, production methods, and consumption habits, the platformization of webtoons serves to drive traffic to Naver, Daum, and Kakao, which monetize webtoons through display or banner ads featured at the end of each webtoon episode. Webtoons are a highly interactive form of online content, with a strong communication channel connecting readers and authors through real-time comments (Yoon et al., 2015). In most cases, typically one or two new episodes of a webtoon are uploaded per week. Underneath each episode is a section where readers can post comments. Readers can also rate each episode on a scale of one to five stars, like the rating system for films. The ratings and the number of clicks on an episode provide immediate feedback to both webtoonists and portal platforms. These measures serve as gauges for webtoons' potential adaptation as television dramas and films (Sohn, J. Y., 2014). The appropriation of webtoons is a clear example of contemporary capitalism.

In the early twenty-first century, digital platforms are everywhere, and they have mediated the entire process of cultural production, from planning and production to circulation. Webtoons are an increasingly significant digital culture, and digital platforms such as Naver, Daum, and Kakao control the webtoon industry. Therefore, one must understand the various commercial, political, and infrastructural dimensions of digital platforms to determine the critical relationships between digital platforms and users, as both cultural creators and cultural consumers.

A Lopsided Relationship between Webtoon Platforms and Webtoonists

Digital platform companies have developed various corporate strategies to platformize the webtoon sphere. Webtoon platforms are well positioned to benefit from the growing popularity of webtoons around the globe, having extended their purview to include the entire process of cultural production. The increase in the number of webtoons published and "the deepening segmentation of the content creation process (e.g., storyline development, illustrating, coloring, writing, and editing) highlight the importance of production management and planning. To achieve higher quality, writers are likely to team up with content providers (versus working alone)" (Park, J., 2020, 9). With a few exceptions, the work of webtoonists is mainly managed by mega digital platforms.

The asymmetrical power relationship between webtoon platforms and webtoonists has been systemic. Many young Koreans wish to become webtoonists, but only a few digital platforms dominate the webtoon industry. In 2020, when the Korean Ministry of Education conducted a survey among elementary school students about what they wanted to pursue when they grew up, webtoonist ranked ninth (table 2.1). Although many youngsters still want to become doctors, educators, and professional

Table 2.1 Top 15 Dream Jobs among Elementary School Students in Korea, 2009 and 2020

Rank	2009	2020
1	Teacher	Sports player
2	Doctor	Medical doctor
3	Cook	Teacher
4	Scientist	Creator (e.g., YouTuber)
5	Singer	Pro Gamer
6	Police officer	Police officer
7	Baseball blayer	Cook
8	Fashion designer	Singer
9	Football player	Webtoonist
10	Actor/actress	Baker
11	Dentist	Computer graphics designer
12	Lawyer	Lawyer
13	Kindergarten teacher	Hair stylist
14	Pianist	Model
15	Pro Gamer	Pet groomer

Source: Ministry of Education (2020).

athletes, this certainly demonstrates a shift in the job market. The fourth most desired job category was content creator, including YouTuber, followed by pro gamer. Thus, these young students are highly interested in a few professions in the field of digital culture (Ministry of Education, 2020). In a similar survey in 2009, neither webtoonists nor manhwa artists were ranked, which is not surprising given that webtoonist is a relatively new job category. Unlike high school students, who are generally more realistic, and tend to select very plausible future jobs, elementary school students seem to choose jobs that reflect current trends and dreams. The results certainly show that webtoonists are among the popular job categories that young teens are eager to consider.

As webtoons rapidly gained popularity and many young Koreans decided that they wanted to become webtoonists, webtoon platforms have significantly increased their traffic. Due to the increase in the number of webtoon readers, these platforms have also increased their revenues. For example, in 2005, just ten thousand people enjoyed webtoons per day on Naver Webtoon. However, as of August 2014, on average 6.2 million people visited Naver Webtoon per day, and there were as many as 8.0 million at

Table 2.2   Naver Webtoon's Estimated Annual Earnings in Billions of Won, 2018–2021

	2018	2019	2020F	2021F
Total earnings from content (series on Naver Webtoon)	60	128	203	292
Earnings in Korea	60	92	120	142
Earnings in the United States	0	20	48	91
Earnings in other countries	0	16	35	59
Earnings from other sources	12	33	43	48
Total earnings from above categories	72	161	246	340
Earnings from Line Manga	85	118	122	135

Source: Naver Webtoon (2019); Park, J. (2020), 8.
Notes: Other sources of earnings include advertising and IP use. Estimates for 2018 and 2019 are for calendar years. Estimates for 2020 and 2021 are for fiscal years.

the end of 2018 (Naver, 2014; Lee, S. G., 2019). In 2019, Never Webtoon's revenue was 161 billion won, a 124 percent increase from the previous year (Naver Webtoon, 2019). As can be seen in table 2.2, the revenue of Naver Webtoon was projected to continue to grow rapidly, from 72 billion Korean won in 2018 to 339 billion won in 2021. In 2019, the revenue from webtoon content was 161 billion won, accounting for 79.5 percent of the total.

KakaoPage has shown a similar trend, earning 257 billion won in 2019, a 37 percent increase from the previous year (Kakao, 2019). KakaoPage, which includes Daum Webtoon, manages digital content, including webtoons and music. KakaoPage is Kakao's main content platform for webtoons, novels, and movies. As table 2.3 shows, KakaoPage's revenue has increased quickly, and it is expected to grow further in the near future. Due in large part to the significance of IP-based transmedia storytelling, transmedia storytelling in particular is expected to grow as a major commercialization model.

The two largest platforms have developed different mechanisms to use webtoon artists. Webtoon platforms source webtoon content through in-house studios or by contracting with individual authors or other content providers. In recent years, webtoon agencies have become new players that act as mediators between webtoon platforms and webtoon artists. Initially, Daum Webtoon mainly worked with established webtoonists

Table 2.3 KakaoPage's Estimated Annual Earnings in Billions of Won, 2017–2021

	2017	2018	2019	2020F	2021F
Total earnings (including Daum Webtoon and advertising)	118	188	257	299	346
Earnings from the domestic platform	110	168	198	231	270
Earnings from global IP distribution	8	20	28	34	38
Earnings from advertising and other sources	10	21	31	34	39

Source: Kakao (2019); Park, J. (2020), 8.

Note: Estimates for 2017, 2018, and 2019 are for calendar years. Estimates for 2020 and 2021 are for fiscal years.

after signing contracts with them. Later, Kakao attempted to secure a steady content supply by making equity investments in major content partners. Other webtoon platforms such as World in Manhwa on Daum and Dojeon Manhwa (Challenge manhwa) on Naver Webtoon have recruited a few thousand artists to post their webtoons on them. The Dojeon Manhwa section invites anyone to upload content to the platform, and popular series in the section are given an opportunity to be published on the main webtoon platform. Naver Webtoon has launched a similar service called Canvas in the United States. In 2019 alone, this service was responsible for adding about 580,000 amateur and 1,600 professional webtoonists to the global webtoon ecosystem (Choi, J. W., 2020). Naver, which operates an open platform centered on user-generated content, focuses on forging contracts with individual writers, artists, and other creators.

The major platforms have continued to diversify their strategies to create webtoons as the growth of the webtoon market has soared. The current structure of profit generation in the platform context has raised some criticism, which holds that such a competition-based model benefits only a few winners in the top tier at the expense of the time, labor, and passion of a much greater number of webtoonists from the lower tiers (Kim, J. H., and Yu, 2019, 5). Other platform operators—mostly small and mid-size webtoon-dedicated platforms, such as Lezhin Comics and MrBlue—"secure content through in-house creators (with employment contracts), outside sourcing (with revenue sharing), or partnerships" (Park, J., 2020, 9).

More specifically, two major trends have emerged in the new recruitment system since around 2010. One is the development of webtoon agencies, which play roles in planning, managing webtoon artists at their agencies, and dealing with IP. Until 2010, webtoon artists worked directly with webtoon platforms, either with or without contracts. Editorial teams for webtoon platforms conducted planning, managed artists, and circulated their webtoons. With the rapid development of webtoons as one of the most significant cultural forms in Korea, webtoon agencies jumped on the bandwagon and started to work as intermediaries between webtoon platforms and artists. Thereafter, webtoon artists typically received contracts with webtoon agencies instead of working with and signing contracts directly with webtoon platforms. The revenues of these agencies increased from 1,377 million won in 2017 to 2,048 million won in 2018 (Korea Creative Content Agency, 2019b). Webtoon platforms have also created their own webtoon agencies and invested in existing agencies. For example, KakaoPage established its own agency, Yeondam, in 2010 to develop webtoons and web novels. In January 2020 KakaoPage secured 25 percent of the shares of another webtoon agency, ToYou's Dream. Naver Webtoon invested in YLAB, which was created in 2010, and secured a 5.6 percent share of the company in 2019.

These new trends have made webtoon artists' status in the new webtoon ecosystem even weaker than before. Previously, webtoon platforms and artists shared income. However, with the arrival of webtoon agencies, webtoon artists' shares of revenues are getting smaller: the artists typically get only 10–20 percent of the total revenues. In the new system, webtoon platforms take 30–50 percent of the revenues, while webtoon agencies take 30–70 percent of the remainder. Webtoon platforms prefer to use new webtoons produced by their own webtoon agencies, instead of webtoons from other agencies. Thus, the new webtoon ecology negatively impacts webtoon artists who work for small independent agencies (Park, J., 2020). While the industry scene has changed, mega webtoon platforms have continued to control the entire industry.

Webtoon platforms have successfully aggregated creators, procuring both professional cartoon artists and amateurs, who have "combined to make up a greater labor pool" (Kim, J. H., and Yu, 2019, 4). Artists have continued to provide their work to mega digital platforms, while hoping to increase their income and job security. Their incomes have continued to improve, but this does not mean that they have decent incomes or job security. According to a survey on the current status of webtoonists conducted by the Korea Creative Content Agency (2019d), in 2018 the average annual income of the 409 webtoonists who responded to the survey was 47.6 million Korean won, equivalent to $38,600. Moreover, their median income was much lower: 30.0 million won for male webtoonists and 24.3 million won for female webtoonists. If we exclude the 11.1 percent of male and 7.9 percent of female webtoonists who earned more than 100 million won, the typical income would be even lower (fig. 2.1). In other words, although a few famous webtoonists make large incomes, the majority of webtoonists suffer from various hardships, including insufficient income, low social status, and job insecurity.

These data clearly indicate that while a few webtoonists are able to earn good incomes, the majority are still earning significantly less. It is also important to note that the data are only for 409 webtoonists who were relatively established, meaning that they were able to make some money. Thus, despite the fact that major digital platforms have rapidly increased their revenues, many webtoonists have not been able to earn a living wage. In fact, another survey conducted in 2017 showed that 68.7 percent of the 761 webtoonists surveyed earned less than 30 million

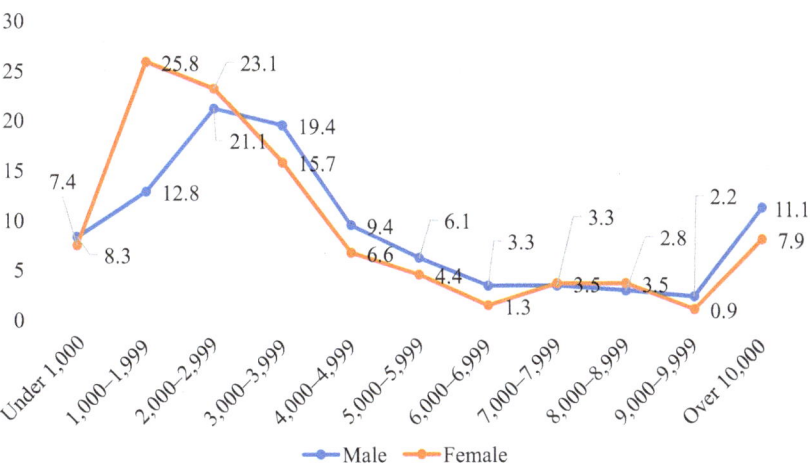

FIGURE 2.1 Webtoonists' annual income in 2018 in 10,000s of won and with percentages of webtoonists by income level. Source: Korea Creative Content Agency (2019d).

won annually, and their average annual income was 1.66 million—much less than the first survey indicated (Korea Creative Content Agency, 2018). In Korea, there were 5,802 webtoonists in 2019, which implies that the average income of the entire webtoonist population is even lower than that shown in the 2017 survey.

Since the mid-2010s, webtoon platforms have developed several mechanisms as ways to try to enhance webtoonists' earnings, responding to increasing demand for their art and criticism from many people, including the webtoonists themselves. In particular, in 2013 Naver introduced the Page Profit Share (PPS) model, consisting of freemium models (explained below; see also chapter 3), advertisements, and licensing fees for merchandising. Naver intended to share these earnings with webtoon artists (Bloter, 2013). However, this diversification of payments has not increased webtoon artists' earnings. For example, digital platforms using the PPS model connect artists with advertisers. The advertisers then pay the artists directly for their brand-name webtoons and product placements, while the platform receives publishing fees from the advertisers. This implies that the financial resources available to webtoon artists have been diversified (Cho, H. K., 2021). PPS also includes visual ads that use a webtoon's art and characters to promote a product. These ads are featured alongside of or at the end of a webtoon episode. Although webtoon artists receive some payments from these types of ads, the remainder goes to the platform provider (Lee, S. W., 2013). From the platforms' perspective, webtoons are a perfect way to lure customers to regularly visit their internet portals, which is crucial for attracting advertisers.

However, the caveat here is that these new business models have been made unidirectionally by the webtoon platforms, "without any explanation to artists or to the management companies or agencies that manage groups of artists. Except for a small number of well-established webtoon artists, most artists find they have little choice but to accept the platforms' constantly changing regulations, monetization systems, and even unfair contracts, while also fashioning their artwork to work with those operations" (Cho, H. K., 2021, 9–10). As discussed above, the percentage of advertising revenues received by webtoonists in the new systems is still very small. Therefore, except for a few well-established webtoonists, most are not able to receive relatively decent annual earnings.

As Caves (2000) points out, webtoon artists sacrifice much to devote themselves to their creative work, with typical incomes lower than those of workers in nonartistic fields. Webtoonists engaged in full-time creative work generally earn lower wages than others in "humdrum occupations but equipped with the same basic ability and stock of human capital (education, training, and experience)" (Caves, 2000, 78). This confirms the large income gap between a few famous webtoonists and the majority. In this regard, Gian 84, a famous webtoonist known for his appearances on numerous television programs, stated that there are many webtoon platforms, but that only a few of them treat webtoonists fairly well (Lee, S. G., 2019). While digital platforms and smartphones gave cartoons a second life, most manhwa artists, including webtoonists, believe that "things were better in the old days" (Baek, B. Y., 2014a). Webtoonists are eager to publish their webtoons on big webtoon platforms, but the majority of them have not been treated fairly by the digital platforms—although their working environments have improved slightly.

Diversification of Business Models

Digital platforms such as Netflix, Spotify, and YouTube have continued to act as major drivers of cultural production. These platforms have developed their own business models, including subscriptions (Netflix), advertisements (YouTube), or both (Spotify). In contrast to these global digital platforms, Korea-based digital platforms in tandem with webtoons have advanced unique business models, which strongly influence the cultural production of webtoons and cultural industry firms in general. Unlike the global platforms mentioned above, on Korea's digital platforms, webtoons and web novels generate income from a combination of various business models, including user payments, advertisements, corporate sponsorships, and licensing fees based on IP use, with user payments being the initial driver of market growth and the largest contributor to earnings.

Several platforms, including Naver Webtoon and KakaoPage, derive their earnings mainly from payments for content. While the contributions of advertisements and IP use remain limited, they could become important engines for revenue growth in the future, given the increasing sophistication of advertisements and the growing use of IPs, both nationally and globally (Park, J., 2020, 11; Kim and Lee, 2022). As I discuss further in chapter 3, user payments are closely related to people's reading habits—in particular, binge-reading.

The first way digital platforms make money is through banner ads. Daum and Naver initially monetized their content via display and text advertising. The addition of webtoons would drive traffic to Daum and Naver, both of which "indirectly monetized [content] from display or ads featured at the bottom of each webtoon episode" (Lee, S. W., 2013). Digital platforms share ad revenues with webtoonists, and the use of banner ads is still one of the major business models that adds revenues to such platforms: "Webtoon ads are growing more sophisticated, evolving from simple banner ads to content-relevant ads, including product placements, branded webtoons, and character-based ads. Significantly, content-relevant ads can generate income for content providers. Indeed, platform operators are adopting profit-sharing models for content-relevant ads exceeding a certain number of impressions [images or manhwa cuts]" (Park, J., 2020, 12). In addition, webtoonists earn royalties on published books and other merchandise and copyright fees for secondary works such as games and novels (Korea Creative Content Agency, 2019d).

Second, platforms develop brand-name webtoons ordered by corporations. Many big corporations such as Samsung and Hyundai desire to develop their corporate brands and promote their new products and services, and webtoons have become a new avenue for large corporations and public relation (PR) agencies to use. Corporations may provide basic stories and characters to digital platform companies and request webtoonists to create relevant webtoons.

Third, webtoon platforms have recently developed IP-based transmedia, both nationally and globally, which I discuss in the section titled "Platformization of Webtoon's IP" in this chapter. Many webtoons are leveraged into big-screen content, such as television programs, films, and games. Digital platforms have strategically developed webtoons for transmedia, starting with the planning stage. In addition to developing a new form of digital culture, webtoon platforms have greatly advanced IP-based transmedia as a new business model.

Last but not least, digital platforms have developed freemium models, which have become one of their largest revenue segments. Compared to global digital platforms, Korea-based digital platforms working in tandem with webtoons have created unique user payment models. Again, platforms such as Naver Webtoon and KakaoPage derive much of their revenue from direct user payments for content. Such payments will likely continue to rise sharply, helped by ongoing traffic growth. Digital platforms have been creating fee-based webtoon services since the 2010s, though in the early stage of the digital webtoons they did not charge fees. Back then, Daum and Naver used free webtoon systems to increase traffic to make money via ads, so readers were able to subscribe to many webtoons for free. When webtoons were considered a subculture, people did not want to pay to read them, in contrast to other cultural forms such as movies and television dramas. However, now that webtoons are becoming a major digital culture, more people are willing to pay fees to enjoy them. The new model is not entirely fee-based, of course. Webtoons are increasingly operated under a freemium model, in which readers who want early access to episodes must pay for it (Listly, 2019). In other words, episodes are generally free. But if people fail the infamous "marshmallow test" because they cannot delay gratification, more recent episodes (called fast-pass episodes) can be unlocked using money or the app's currency. In the United States, for example, a fast-pass episode can cost 3–5 coins (10 coins go for $0.99) (V, 2020).

The freemium model in the cultural industries has been used primarily by digital game companies, which influenced the webtoon sector. The freemium model, also known as the free-to-play model in digital games, means that the game can be downloaded at no cost from an app store. While there may be no initial acquisition cost with freemium games, players need to pay a premium fee in the form of real money to access certain content. This concept is reflected in the name *freemium* (Ramirez, 2015). Digital game firms that develop freemium games rely on the monetization of virtual items, currencies, or services to generate revenue and permit the initial free distribution of their product (Wohn, 2014, cited in Ramirez, 2015, 118). As Evans (2016, 564) points out, "initially available for free but exploiting in-game commercial strategies, many such games are becoming incredibly financially successful."

KakaoPage developed a freemium model for its webtoon business after learning about the model's possibilities from Anipang, a mobile game released in Korea in 2011 (Park, M. J., 2020a). Cultural norms play an important role in social game-playing practices. Like its counterparts in the social puzzle genre, Anipang costs nothing to play, but it deducts a heart for each round. A heart is automatically filled up every eight minutes, but users can also receive hearts from their friends (Jin, D. Y, 2017b). If they do not have friends to send them hearts, they can buy some to continue playing and win the games.

The freemium model has taken hold in the webtoon industry, gaining wide acceptance among users. Under this business model, platform operators first attract users by providing a certain number of initial episodes for free, and then they generate revenue by charging for additional episodes. A webtoon series is typically updated once a week, like regular TV shows. A few series are divided into seasons (again, just like regular TV shows), and "they can go on breaks in between" (V, 2020). Unlike subscriptions, this kind of partial monetization charges users based on how many episodes they view. The use of microtransactions (viewing an episode costs 500 Korean won or less), which are adapted to lower the psychological resistance to monetization, also contributes to the long-term development of platform transactions (Park, J., 2020). For example, as of May 2020, to binge-read (a phenomenon discussed in chapter 3) *Itaewon Class*, a finished webtoon, after reading fifty-three free episodes, people pay 6,600 won (200 won each) to read the thirty-three remaining episodes—an amount equivalent to $6.00.

Web novels touching on light, fun themes have become one of the major forms of snack culture in the smartphone era (Kim, S. G., 2016). Web novels are driven by the same digital platforms as webtoons and often use the same freemium model. Like webtoons, web novels use a business model with divisions and paid previews. In most cases, one novel is divided into around a hundred small pieces. After reading a few free pieces, people need to pay 100–300 won per piece to read more. The growth in the readership of web novels started right after the introduction of domestic smartphones in 2009.

Another major payment model adopted by web novel or webtoon platforms is partial monetization, or the pay or wait approach (table 2.4). Notably, adult content and popular concluded series are usually fully monetized. The degree of monetization is often determined by the item's popularity, user retention rate, and number of episodes. In the Korean webtoon market, monetization is quickly gaining traction as a growing number of users become accustomed to paying for content (Park, J., 2020) in other cultural industries—in particular, digital games. In many online

Table 2.4 Types of Webtoon Platforms

Type	Name	Major business model	Additional business models	Main genres
Portal based	Naver Webtoon KakaoPage Daum Webtoon	Free	Pay or wait	General
Webtoon dedicated	BomToon Lezhin Comics MrBlue TOPTOON TOOMICS	Pay per view (only initial episodes are free)	Subscription	Adult or general

Source: Park, J. (2020).

and mobile games, to upgrade their levels, players can buy and immediately receive some game items instead of waiting for certain times or earning them by playing.

Digital platforms have diversified their business models. Major webtoon platforms owned by the two largest platform corporations have developed a variety of monetization strategies to maximize their power and revenues. The platformization of the business model in relation to webtoons clearly shows that webtoon platforms have developed multiple business models closely connected to corporate strategies to maximize profits.

Structural Transformation of Webtoon Platforms

Webtoon platforms have dramatically transformed the structures of their corporate ownership, which acquire relevant companies and establish new subsidiaries, both nationally and globally, to handle the entire webtoon industry. For example, Kakao has rapidly restructured its webtoon business. Ever since it established the first webtoon platform in history (back when it was known as Daum), the company's strategies have constantly evolved. Kakao launched KakaoPage to monetize content optimized for mobile devices in 2013. After merging with Daum, Kakao established a new subsidiary, Daum Webtoon Company, in 2016, separating its internet cartoon platform service under KakaoPage.

Kako has also developed a globalization strategy, which included establishing its Japanese comic app platform, called Piccoma, under Kakao Japan in April 2016. Piccoma's number of annual transactions jumped nearly fourteenfold from 2016 to 2017. Transactions continued to grow at a rapid clip, rising 156 percent in 2018 and 130 percent in 2019 (Kakao, 2020).

Kakao's advances in the webtoon sector have been concentrated in Korea and Japan. However, its expansion plan includes penetrating the Indonesian market and eventually other markets in Southeast Asia. As a result, Kakao acquired Indonesia's leading webtoon platform, NeoBazar, in December 2017 and relaunched it as KakaoPage Global in 2019 (Kim, Y. W., 2018). Kakao is set to further expand its services in Asia, including in Taiwan, Thailand, and China (Park, J. Y., 2020).

In China, Kakao works closely with Tencent DongMan, China's largest webtoon and animation platform. In 2017, Kakao collaborated with Tencent and introduced over twenty KakaoPage and Daum Webtoon items—such as *I Hate Love* (I hate *yeonae*), the fantasy and action thriller *Shaman Girl* (Sonye-o Shinse-on), and the romantic comedy *What's Wrong with Secretary Kim?* (Gimbise-oga wae ge-ure-olkka?)—to Chinese readers. Kakao has been able to extend its collaboration with Tencent to include sharing business models and platforms as well as content (Shin, 2017). The two companies plan to expand their collaboration to IP business fields, including secondary content and videos. "Tencent DongMan not only has profound amounts of commercialization experience in the digital cartoon and animations field, but also has succeeded in managing the publication rights of premium IP and the management of following enterprises." Lee also stated that Kakao is trying its best to "successfully introduce the 'Wait then Free' model in the Chinese market and thus help Tencent DongMan grow its influence in the market" (Shin, 2017).

Kakao plans to create a synergistic effect via vertical integration (as exemplified by the merger of Disney and Marvel) in global cultural industries (fig. 2.2). Disney acquired Marvel Entertainment (the parent company of Marvel Comics) for $4 billion in 2009, and since then has earned more than $18.2 billion at the global box office from Marvel movies (Whitten, 2019). Kakao eventually wants to create an in-house entertainment

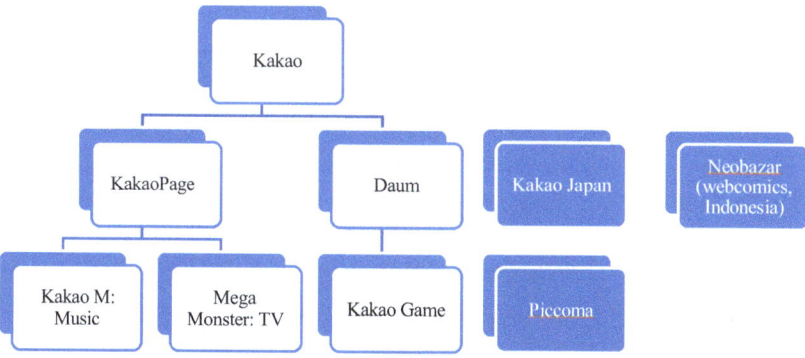

FIGURE 2.2 Kakao: Vertical integration in content production as of 2020. Source: Kakao (2020); Park, J. (2020).

production department, achieving synergistic effects by controlling relevant cultural content companies (Nam, D. Y., 2020). Kakao has expanded its business from cartoon platform operations to investment, joint production, and global copyright businesses related to works derived from cartoon content. The major goal is clear: to strengthen the profitability of the webtoon business by applying advertisement and commercialization models used for the mobile publication platform service KakaoPage, and eventually to establish a virtuous cycle of content (Yoon, S. W., 2016). In one recent development, KakaoPage and Kakao M merged in 2021 to form Kakao Entertainment. Kakao stated that the merger would complete a value chain in the entertainment business that includes the intellectual property of story lines, artist management, production, and platforms on which the created content can be played. Kakao Entertainment adopted a company-in-company structure, in which the two entities carry on their businesses independently as "Page Company" and "M Company"—therefore, KakaoPage continues to exist as a platform (Song, K. S., 2021).

Naver also has plans for corporate integration, which is vital for the growth of the company. It has established two major webtoon-related subsidiary companies: Naver Webtoon and Line. Naver Webtoon has focused on the national and global markets, excluding Japan, and Line has focused on the Japanese market. Line was developed by Naver Japan, Naver's Japanese subsidiary, as part of the second generation of chat apps.

As Steinberg (2020, 1) aptly puts it, "LINE is a chat app turned social media platform launched and dominant in Japan. While debuting as a chat app, it has become a full-fledged social media platform, as well as an integrated services provider. From allowing voice calling (VoIP) and video conferencing, to providing freemium games, ordering taxis, having indoor maps of shopping malls, becoming a hub for news in Japan, offering music and video streaming services, and affording direct-to-user advertising—there is little that LINE cannot do. It has become one of the do-everything apps particularly prevalent in East Asia." Line also established Line Manga in Japan in 2013, which is an "extended service and a separate app from the Line messaging app which allows users to read manga while on the move, available both on iOS and Android" (Wee, 2013).

Naver Webtoon established Studio N to focus on IP-based transmedia storytelling in 2018. Its main emphasis is to produce television dramas and films based on stories from its library of Korean webtoons and web novels. Studio N serves as a bridge: "By supporting the production and screen release of original work, it operates as a co-producer of film and drama series together with existing production companies. The aim of the subsidiary is the virtuous cycle of webtoon content from Naver, which has been nurturing the digital comics industry. The company intends to combine webtoons and web novels with the mediums of movies and TV dramas to expand their customer reach and diversify income resources for writers" (Top, 2018). Studio N was formed with 100 percent funding from Naver Webtoon. As Mi-kyung Kwon, Studio N's chief executive, stated, "We will find the best way to express the original work of webtoons in films and dramas and differentiate our works to embody the webtoons' unique characteristics and diversified stories on the screen. . . . As an IP bridge company that collaborates with existing film and drama production companies, we will create a new win-win model and various success cases to explore our potential in the global market" (quoted in Top, 2018).

Naver Webtoon has successfully introduced its pioneering self-publishing platform to the global marketplace, creating a vibrant webtoon ecosystem of 58 amateur creators and 1,600 professional artists, while Canvas (the self-publishing platform of Line Webtoon US) is seeing the number of published works on its site more than double every year. Naver

Webtoon also unveiled plans to bolster its video streaming service through its media production affiliate Studio N, with the aim of making the latter a full-scale entertainment company (Lee, Y. I., and Kim, 2019).

One of the most interesting and potentially significant business activities is related to Naver's new focus on artificial intelligence (AI). Cultural sectors—including film, music, and broadcasting—have rapidly developed their AI-supported cultural production systems (Jin, D. Y., 2021), and webtoon platforms also plan to use AI in their content production. Naver already created an AI-supported webtoon, called *Came Across* (*Majuchyeotda*), in 2017. In the second episode, for example, AI technology inserts the webtoon customer's face in place of that of the main character of the webtoon. When the customer takes a picture of himself or herself with a smartphone, the AI transforms the customer's face into the webtoon's style (Song, B. G., 2018). Naver is now very confident about the future of the AI-supported webtoon era.

Domestically, Naver Webtoon acquired V.DO, a local AI start-up, in January 2020 (Oh and Choi, 2020). For $600 million, Naver Webtoon also purchased Wattpad, a Canadian digital storytelling app company that uses data-driven machine learning technology—one of the major AI technologies (Vlessing, 2021). Of course, one primary reason for the deal was the potential synergy between these two companies in developing new original stories, while simultaneously advancing IP-based revenues. Since AI has become a significant digital technology for many cultural creators and cultural industry firms, it will play an increasing role in the webtoon sphere as well. Naver Webtoon has continued to pursue its interest in converging digital technologies (in this case, AI) and popular culture. However, because only a handful of webtoon platforms are expected to be able to jump onto the AI bandwagon, Naver Webtoon's inclusion of AI as part of its cultural production is expected to intensify the asymmetrical balance of power between mega webtoon platforms and small and mid-size platforms and webtoon agencies.

The platformization of webtoons demonstrates that over time webtoons have dramatically changed their relationship with digital technologies, including the web, smartphones, apps, and AI—changes driven by digital platforms such as Daum and Naver, in an unprecedented development.[2] The proliferation of smartphones and webtoons has created another form of app-centric global marketplace, ushering in the app economy (Jin, D. Y, 2017b). This term refers to the range of economic activities surrounding mobile applications (MacMillan and Burrows, 2009). In tandem with webtoons, the app economy has also advanced a new form of cultural economy based on digital technologies. As Manovich (2013, 7) argues, "platforms, such as Google, Facebook, iOS, and Android, are in the center of the global economy, culture, social life, and, increasingly, politics." In this regard, it is important to view the growth of smartphones and apps and their implications through a nuanced perspective (Jin, D. Y, 2017b). In the case of Korean-based platforms, webtoons have entirely orchestrated the platformization of popular culture and digital technologies.

Meanwhile, on May 28, 2020, Naver announced that, as part of its globalization strategy, it plans to make its US-based Webtoon Entertainment the head office for online webtoon businesses (Choi, M. Y., 2020). According to Naver Webtoon (2020a), California-based Webtoon Entertainment purchased the majority of shares of Line Digital Frontier, Naver's Japanese internet cartoon unit, and reorganized Korea-based Naver Webtoon. Webtoon Entertainment now controls Naver Webtoon in Korea and Line in Japan, while expanding its services in Europe and South America. Through this structural transformation, Naver is expanding its webtoon service to the entire global market, while its IP business is closely working with Disney and Netflix. In other words, Naver is reorganizing and relocating its webtoon business to its global head office to accelerate outreach to English-speaking readers. Webtoon Entertainment now oversees Naver's entire webtoon business and intends to take Korean digital cultural content to more countries, including those in Europe and South America. Naver expects webtoons to ride the Korean Wave fever (Hong, S. Y., and Lee, 2020). It is premature to analyze Naver's 'Webtooniverse dream' (Yecies, 2018), but it is certainly a grand dream for a local-based digital platform. In fact, it is a very ambitious plan, as no other major cultural industry corporation in Korea has its headquarters in the United States. It signals the potential for eventually shifting the power relationship between local and global forces because it may result in a Korean cultural firm penetrating the markets of the United States and other countries not from Korea, but from the United States.[3]

Naver and Kakao have become vertically integrated, another form of the platformization of cultural production. This is not only an external process in which platforms transform market structures and curate content: it is also driven by digital platform firms that organize production and distribution around platforms. This becomes clear when one examines the ways in which platformization transforms the material infrastructure of the cultural industries, which digital platforms are now a big part of:

> Here, the contingent nature of commodities comes back into view. As cultural producers are transformed into platform complementors, they are incentivized to change a traditionally linear production process into an iterative, data-driven process in which content is constantly altered to optimize for platform distribution and monetization. Over the past decade, digital platforms have initiated a range of services, enticing producers to host, distribute, and monetize their content via their platforms. By offering ready access to APIs, SDKs, and developer documentation, platforms offer news publishers and game developers a seemingly attractive alternative to physical distribution infrastructures, or self-operated digital properties (Nieborg and Poell, 2018, 4287).

Digital platforms have transformed the cultural industries, since the platforms are major actors in the entire process of cultural production. Webtoons are a new form of digital culture, combining cultural products and digital technologies, and with the growth in the webtoon market, digital platforms have increased their roles and maximized profits through the platformization of webtoons.

Both Kakao and Naver, the two largest digital platforms in Korea, have greatly transformed their business structures over the past ten years. They started as tiny in-house webtoon ventures but have turned into some of the largest and most significant digital platforms in the webtoon sector. Both platforms have established new subsidiary companies, acquired small webtoon companies, and collaborated with foreign webtoon platforms. As a result of this platformization, they are able to control the webtoon ecosystem and expand their power as major players in the global webtoon marketplace. As dominant platform operators, they can secure financial benefits. In the webtoon value chain, platform operators have been the first to benefit from market expansion, as they can manage the flow of all content revenue (Park, J., 2020). Specifically, Naver's and

Kakao's industry-leading webtoon service platforms have exhibited rapid earnings growth, supported by robust increases in user traffic in Korea and abroad. Notably, Naver Webtoon is also recording sharp increases in user traffic and earnings in overseas markets such as that of the United States.

However, the concentration of power in the hands of these platforms has resulted in a loss of creativity. Since individual cartoonists must follow the editorial and corporate policies of Naver Webtoon, Daum Webtoon, and KakaoPage, their creative freedom is not guaranteed. Many would-be webtoonists are eager to publish their creations on these two platforms, but their opportunities are limited due to severe competition with other webtoonists. In other words, platformization in the structural dimension not only implies the monopolization of a few webtoon platforms: it also leads to the concentration of webtoonists on a few platforms that focus on commercial webtoons. Webtoonists' creativity and the diversity of their creations cannot be guaranteed in these circumstances. Genre diversity in particular has been negatively affected due to the main focus of Naver, Daum, and Kakao on publishing light humor for teens instead of delicate epics, although they have added serious stories in recent years (Cho, E. A., 2014). Webtoonists who focus on unpopular themes and genres have to find alternative platforms that may be less visible than those of these giants.

Platformization of Webtoons' IP

Webtoon platforms have recently emphasized the significant role of IP, since webtoons as original content sources have migrated into global popular culture. The growing popularity of webtoons require global cultural industries to contemplate the increasing role of IP in the globalization process. Along with the rise of a very successful webtoon-based big-screen culture, including television programs and films, webtoon platforms have recently focused on remakes and/or formats for global audiences. The platforms have increased the significance of original stories as sources for materialization and commercialization.

Digital platforms and content providers can generate revenue by licensing their webtoon content for big-screen content (see tables 2.2 and 2.3). As IP content holders, these providers continue to strengthen their power amid increasing webtoon-based drama or film productions and platform operators' vertical integration for in-house content production. As I discussed above, when webtoon platforms establish their own studios or purchase other companies, one of the major goals is to develop IP. For example, Studio N, established by Naver in 2018, has worked with cultural production companies to develop and release television dramas and films based on the intellectual property of popular webtoons (Sohn, J. Y., 2018). Therefore, many webtoon platforms and relevant companies see IP mainly a new revenue source, since licensing revenue could expand significantly (Park, J., 2020).

However, IP is more than simple intellectual property. As Yecies and coauthors (2020, 42) point out, transmedia flows and participatory culture in the early twenty-first century accompany the extension of this new IP engine: "Its production, distribution, and reception context, including inconspicuous audience data harvested from multiple websites, demonstrate how webtoons are contributing to the creation of an 'IP-engine'—a single source that is transformed across multiple formats, platforms, and products." Li (2020, 226) argues that the concept of IP is not narrowly defined intellectual property: rather, it "refers to transmedia content as original intellectual property for cinematic adaptation, and the notion of IP cultural content describes a trending strategy to attach cultural production to a larger transmedia ecosystem that proliferates various types of content, including films, comics, novels, games, music and television shows, through digital platforms." What Li emphasizes is that IP is not simply about intellectual property but refers to a complex transmedia system that is based on the infrastructure and operation of platforms.

While these scholars' cautious extension of the notion of IP is timely and adequate, they miss one particular aspect of IP-based transmedia storytelling: the potential influence of transmediated big-screen culture on original cultural content, both webtoons and web novels. Once webtoons as original sources turn into big-screen culture, the popularity of visualized content (such as webtoon-based films, television dramas, and games) increases the desire of audiences to consume original webtoons. As an example, after watching *Sweet Home*—a webtoon-based television series that began airing on Netflix in December 2020—many viewers later read the original webtoon on Naver Webtoon's US service platform. Thus, IP in the realm of popular culture should be understood not only as one-way transmedia storytelling, moving content from webtoons to big-screen culture, but also as a collection of reciprocal relationships between original sources and transmediated cultural content. IP provides additional revenue to webtoon platforms and webtoonists, as global audiences look for original webtoons after enjoying webtoon-based big-screen cultural content. Naver's CEO, Han Sung-sook, stated during a media conference in February 2021 that "after the [webtoon-based television drama] *Sweet Home* aired [on Netflix in December 2020], the number of global visitors to Naver Webtoon increased.... We could observe that it leads to consumption of various contents" (quoted in Aju News, 2021). Thus, the notion of using IP in the platformization of webtoons goes beyond traditional concepts of IP. In the realm of webtoons, IP works as a tool in a virtuous circle.

Consequently, Naver and Kakao, which have been expanding their in-house production studios and webtoon agencies and engaging in transmediality, have intensified their power. Naver Webtoon's Studio N jointly produced *Hell Is Other People* (OCN television network) and *Pegasus Market* (tvN television network) with Studio Dragon and CJ E&M, respectively, and Kakao's Mega Monster produced *Touch Your Heart* (tvN) with Zium Content (Park, J., 2020, 18). The programming of webtoon-based dramas on TV channels and OTT (over-the-top) services continues to increase.

Interestingly enough, these platforms have also developed a novel-comic strategy in tandem with IP—meaning that they transform web novels into webtoons, followed by another transformation into big-screen content. In contrast to webtoons, web novels can be produced easily within a short time period because no graphic arts are involved. Once certain web novels become popular on their platforms, the platform companies select famous webtoonists to turn them into webtoons. The first major example of this was *What's Wrong with Secretary Kim?* which was originally a novel published by Kyung Yoon Jung in 2013. KakaoPage invited Jung to create a web novel with the same name on KakaoPage. The web novel was released between 2014 and 2017 and was very successful.

It was later produced as a television drama on tvN in 2018. Kakao has continued to develop a novel-comic strategy and transformed some famous web novels into webtoons. For example, it turned *The Legendary Moonlight Sculptor* into a webtoon, followed by a mobile game in 2019. Another example is the famous web novel *They Say I Was Born a King's Daughter*, which KakaoPage published in that format in 2015, followed by a webtoon of the same name in 2016 (fig. 2.3). In the same year the webtoon began to be published in English on Tapas, a US webtoon service platform operated by Tapas Media (Kwon, J. Y., 2017). The progression from novel to comic has become one of the major new business models of mega digital platforms.

Content IP in the realm of webtoons has become one of the major characteristics of transmedia storytelling. IP here is aligned with the participatory nature of fandom to draw audiences further into the story world through increased consumption in ways that allow IP to intensify the value of cultural content and digital platforms (Lee, S. M., 2017). The platformization of cultural industries in the internet era has "profoundly transformed the production and consumption of culture with new logics of content generation, management, and control that are dictated by the technology and political economy of digital platforms" (Li, 2020, 227). Li (2020, 227) further describes the importance of IP in the era of digital platform ecosystems: "the core value of an IP . . . is the monetizable data generated from the networked connectivity among the multitudes of users and contents. As such, the system of IP operates as less a process of textual adaptation than a networked assemblage of transmedia modules, which are often fragmented and highly affective. In other words, the key purpose of an IP is not simply to proliferate contents across different media, but also to assemble and operate these networked modules to generate, enhance, and manage user communication and informational contact for monetization." The platformization of webtoons has continued to increase, and it will change the scope and direction of global trade and transnationalization. Unlike other cultural content, the webtoon has served as an IP engine that has strongly driven the distinctive transnationalization of transmedia.

Several sociocultural issues have emerged, of course, because contracts for webtoonists are less well established that those for creators in other cultural industries, such as films and music—partially reflects the short history of webtoons. Transmedia storytelling is becoming increasingly

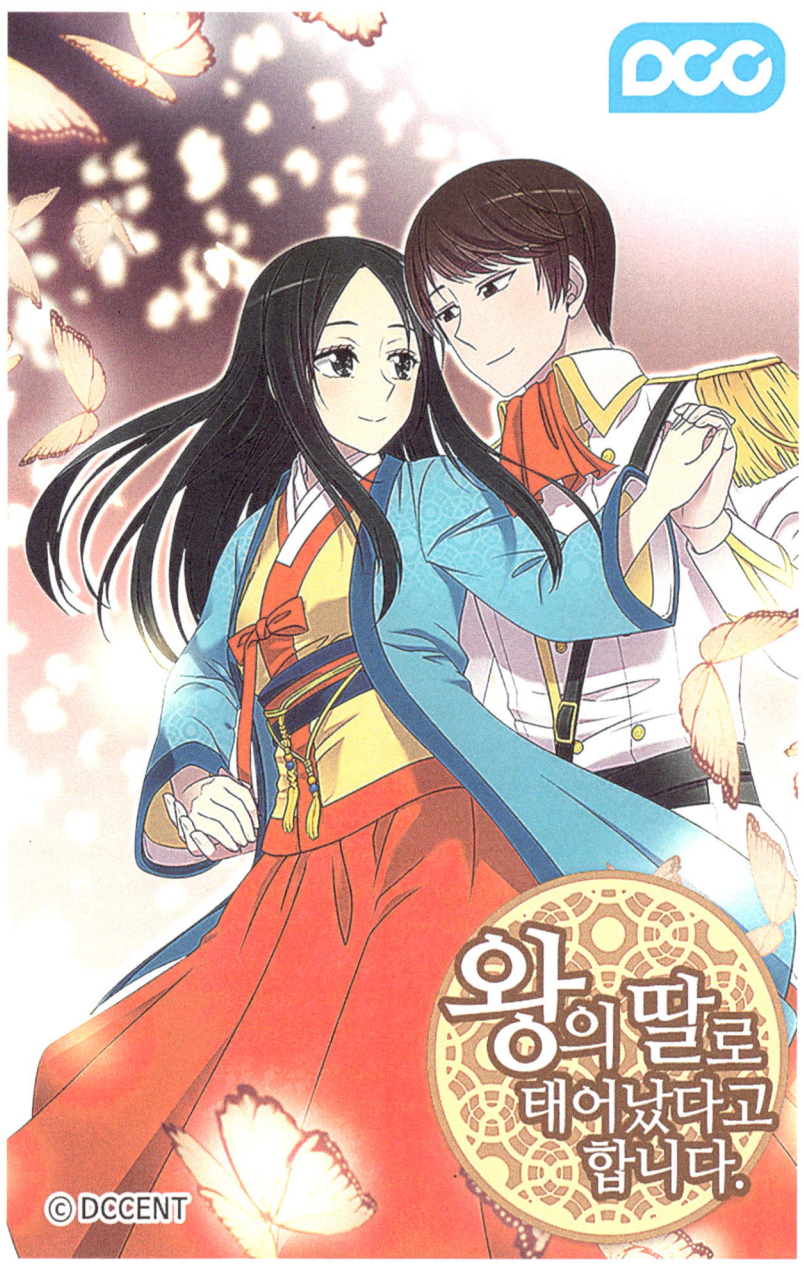

FIGURE 2.3   Art from the webtoon *They Say I was Born a King's Daughter*. Source: Kakao Entertainment.

complex, but webtoon artists generally lack specific knowledge of their contractual rights. In the early stage of their careers, webtoonists are generally not well-known, and it is exceedingly common for them to sign unfair contracts with agencies or webtoon platforms. During the IP process, a few mega webtoon platforms and agencies have contracts stating that they have joint copyright with the authors, even though they do not directly contribute to the creation of webtoons (Lee, E. J., 2021). As webtoon platforms and/or in-house agencies have pursued the rights to use secondary works based on unfair contracts, webtoonists are deprived of the opportunity to benefit from their work on better terms after the publication of their original webtoons. These unfavorable conditions in the IP business imply that webtoonists are losing their rights to make extra money. Regardless of the continuing popularity of webtoons in transmedia storytelling, with some exceptions the majority of webtoonists cannot secure copyright fees as primary sources of income (Korea Creative Content Agency, 2019d). A webtoonist's work needs to be widely known and respected for webtoon platforms to follow that person's development and pay high prices to make use of his or her work (Caves, 2000, 39).

However, webtoon platforms wield great power in dealing with individual webtoon artists because most webtoonists not only desire to publish their work on these major platforms but need to do so to develop large audiences and grow as artists. Furthermore, transmedia storytelling in tandem with IP is multifaceted and unpredictable: thus, most webtoon artists simply leave matters in the hands of mega digital platforms that act as mediators, not simply intermediaries (Gillespie, 2010; van Dijck, Poell, and de Wall, 2018). This uncertainty places webtoonists at another disadvantage in the transmediality process because of their unfamiliarity with the transmedia storytelling system. Like creators in other cultural sectors, webtoon artists may "sell their works outright, with all rights to future use and exhibition passing to webtoon platforms," or they may "subdivide those rights for separate sale, or sell some while retaining others" (Caves, 2000, 280). The real problem is that the majority of webtoonists cannot anticipate the future of their works and cannot properly secure their rights. Webtoons as IP engines bring future benefits for artists. However, webtoon platforms as mediators that control the cycle of cultural production benefit the most from transmedia storytelling in conjunction with IP.

Conclusion

This chapter has critically analyzed the platformization of webtoons. In the early twenty-first century, webtoons have become a symbol of media convergence between cultural content and digital technologies as youth and other consumers enjoy webtoons. Broadcasting and film companies produce cultural products first and circulate them later on the internet. Therefore, media convergence in these industries is generally a combination of two separate entities. However, with webtoons, these entities have been combined since the beginning. Webtoonists create webtoons directly through digital technologies and publish their work on digital platforms.

Although there are several dozen webtoon platforms, Naver Webtoon and KakaoPage (including Daum Webtoon) have greatly expanded their dominant roles in the webtoon sector in recent years, and webtoons and webtoonists are the geese that lay the golden eggs for them. These mega digital platforms have maximized their control of cultural production as producers, circulators, and exhibitors of webtoons, not as separate entities but by controlling the entire process, and they have greatly increased the platformization of cultural production. As mega digital platforms, Naver Webtoon and KakaoPage have created new business models using a pay-per-view approach, advertisement revenue, and IP revenue.

There is no doubt that the balance of power in the webtoon market is tilting toward digital platforms. In global cultural markets, as Steinberg (2020, 8) points out, digital platforms are "not so much a countervailing power—a local site of resistance to global capital—but rather a regional player parlaying regional particularities and cultural soft power into local tech dominance." The mega platforms in the webtoon sector are crucial sites "not for finding the resistance to global capital and its tech giants so much as for grappling with local or regional iterations of the platformization of cultural production" (8). While other global platforms have focused on specific business models—such as advertising on Facebook and Netflix's subscription-based method—webtoon platforms have diversified their business strategies so they can secure maximum profits in the digital cultural market. Digital platforms also technically determine people's consumption habits, meaning that webtoon platforms not only dominate the cultural production but also mediate the process to maximize their own profits (Jin, D. Y., 2015b).

Therefore, the platformization of webtoons has led to a variety of significant power imbalances. In particular, it has intensified the oligopolistic dominance of the webtoon market by a handful of digital platforms. For webtoon artists, digital technologies are a double-edged sword: both an opportunity and a threat. While Naver, Daum, and Kakao compete to get high-profile cartoonists to post on their sites, the majority of artists are compensated poorly, if at all. It is fair to say that the business model of webtoons is based on exploiting artists' desperate desire for exposure, which can be controlled by mega digital platforms (Baek, B. Y., 2014a), although the situation has improved somewhat. Unless the webtoon industry develops a new production model that uses various tools to emphasize the leading role of webtoonists rather than webtoon platforms, the platformization of webtoons will continue—which may eventually have a negative impact on the industry. As Kim and Yu (2019, 10) argue, the platformization of the webtoon industry further entailed "changes in the socio-technical organization of cultural production, business practices, and the nature of the relationship between involved actors, in ways that brought new nuances to the ongoing issues and sometimes enhanced opportunities for creative labor. Failing to consider this broad restructuring of the industry suggests that we lack a basic tool for further analysis of those issues, both existing and emerging within the context of the increasingly platformized cultural production."

Overall, digital platforms have continued to take a leading role in the webtoon industry ever since they played a key role in the early growth of the sector. Naver Webtoon and KakaoPage have developed new business models and expanded their power to capitalize on new digital cultural products in global cultural markets. Since their cultural production relies heavily on users, these digital platforms are not only producing cultural content but also advancing new forms of cultural consumption and marketization through platformization. These locally based platforms' business models and corporate strategies are developing new norms in global cultural markets.

CHAPTER 3

Webtoons' Digital Sphere

Snack Culture and Binge-Reading

Global youth have enjoyed popular culture on their personal mobile gadgets and streaming services in recent years. Unlike previous generations, they find it natural to consume popular culture individually on their smartphones and notebook computers, as they have grown up with such digital technologies. Reliance on digital technologies has deeply changed their consumption habits and advanced a variety of digital cultures. Some of the primary ways in which they engage in cultural activities are snacking and binge-consuming. On the one hand, due to their busy schedules, high usage of technology, rapid consumption of content, and emphasis on individual lifestyles, global youth and young adults typically do not set aside regular times to enjoy popular culture or spend time watching shows with family members in the living room. Rather, many Millennials and members of Generation Z prefer to enjoy popular culture in brief periods of time. On the other hand, they also consume cultural content for many hours at a time when they can which could be considered binge-consuming. Since the mid-2010s, these new forms of behavior—which are seemingly different but in fact are related—have rapidly become notable habits for the digital consumption of webtoons and, in general, in the youth cultural scene.

Snack culture and binge-reading of webtoons are closely connected, and they can be viewed as two sides of the same coin. As I discussed in previous chapters, webtoonists used to post a few new panels of their art once per week on webtoon platforms, which promoted quick reading and the development of snack culture. However, global youth and young adults also consume webtoons through binge-reading, which involves reading multiple webtoons consecutively with little or no break between them, and they may even pay to access chapters early rather than wait for a general release or free access. Webtoons have greatly advanced binge-reading for youth in the age of digital platforms. In addition, webtoon platforms such as Naver Webtoon and KakaoPage have developed freemium models in recent years, which tend to encourage binge-reading.

However, few academics have published research on these practices in the webtoon sector, or in popular culture in general. This chapter discusses snack culture and binge-reading—the two major cultural characteristics of webtoons. First, I analyze snack culture and binge-reading, two of the most recent digital trends that have greatly changed people's cultural consumption habits. I examine the ways in which webtoon fans have transformed their methods of enjoying webtoons in tandem with the rise of speed culture, as snacking on popular culture is a consequence of the busy lifestyle of many people in contemporary society. Second, since the webtoon is a major cultural contributor to the introduction of binge-reading in a digital context, I investigate the reasons why people binge-read webtoons. Third, I map how webtoon platforms capitalize on binge-reading, since this new culture has been mostly designed by webtoon platforms to garner profits by introducing new consumption models.

Webtoons as a New Digital Culture

Digital technologies have developed interesting cultures and transformed youth culture since the invention and broad use of the internet. Given the rapid growth of digital technologies, it is no surprise that there are now more options to enjoy popular culture than ever before. People do not need to leave the comfort of their living room to watch television dramas or enjoy concerts: all that is needed are digital gadgets and connections. The massive use of smartphones has greatly impacted the major characteristics of youth culture, as people now enjoy all kinds of popular culture with mobility on this small gadget. Digital technologies have advanced cultural elements such as openness, participation, and sharing, all of which are characteristics of web 2.0 culture (O'Reilly, 2005). Participation is a part of media convergence, a consumer-driven process that can be "seen largely as an extension of fan culture" (V. Miller, 2020, 101). As Jenkins (2006, 3) points out, the culture of convergence is a participatory one in which "consumers are encouraged to seek out new information and make connections among dispersed media content."

Although webtoons have some commonality with other digital cultures, they have distinctive characteristics that appeal to youth in their teens and twenties. Webtoons' web 2.0 characteristics are different from those of existing digital culture based on the internet, as webtoons developed by digital platforms mainly target smartphone users. For example, webtoons have an advanced and distinctive participatory culture that includes immediate and flexible interactions between webtoonists and readers. Whenever webtoonists post new webtoons or episodes on the web, through online fan websites (including social media) readers can instantly express their feelings and opinions, and even suggest directions for the webtoonist to take. Readers can also give points so that webtoon platforms and webtoonists can quickly see people's reactions to webtoons (Valtysson, 2010). Interaction and distribution are two important features of virtual worlds that web 2.0 has made available to the general public. The streams of cultural information on web 2.0 technologies, including the internet and smartphones, have increased cultural participation, and they have shifted the nature of fans' participation (Valtysson, 2010, 200). Webtoons have a very simple structure that allows webtoonists and readers to communicate easily with each other, and the growth of webtoons in Korea has especially been indebted to mobile culture. As Ok (2011, 330) points out, "most screen-based mobile media services target young people as their primary consumers. For example, [early] 3G mobile multimedia content service was particularly designed to meet and maximize the demands of young people. In order to satisfy young people's appetite, Korean mobile operators have explored mobile-specific content since 2002."

While webtoons have a number of cultural and technological elements, two major aspects of culture—snack culture and binge-reading—reveal their characteristics as constituting a new digital culture, differentiating them from other forms of popular or digital culture. These major cultural elements of webtoons have greatly influenced both people's cultural activities and webtoon platforms' business models, as discussed in the following sections of this chapter.

Webtoons Ride the Snack Culture Wave

Webtoons have greatly increased their identity as a form of snack culture—referring to the habit of quick consumption of information and cultural resources on mobile platforms rather than engaging in a deeper exploration—ever since they appeared in cultural industries (Chung, A. Y., 2014b). Snack culture represents a modern tendency to look for convenient culture that is enjoyed during a short period of time, just as people eat snacks such as cookies within a few minutes (N. Miller, 2007). Pop culture is increasingly packaged like cookies, in bite-size bits for rapid consumption supported by digital platforms (Moura, 2011). From music to mobile games and movies, many people devour popular culture the same way they enjoy candy and chips, "in conveniently packaged bite-size nuggets made to be munched easily with increased frequency and maximum speed" (N. Miller, 2007), and webtoons have developed as a form of snack culture.

Many Koreans started to enjoy webtoons on their notebook computers at home and work on the two largest internet portals, Naver and Daum. Now on the subway, one sees many people, in particular youth and young adults, using their thumbs to scroll quickly on their smartphones. When they are sitting, they can play mobile games with two hands while holding their smartphones horizontally. However, when they cannot find a seat, they cannot use both hands since they have to hold an overhead strap. Many of them use just one hand to read webtoons, using the thumb to scroll while the other fingers hold the phone. One of the major cultural characteristics of smartphones is mobility, and people can consume webtoons with no restrictions imposed by time or space. The internet and the smartphone have become driving engines for the growth of snack culture, and many new creators in the realm of popular culture (including webtoons, films, and television dramas) quickly started to use the convergence between digital technologies and cultural content to develop a new type of culture.

Regarding the nature of snack culture, it is critical to notice the ways in which webtoons are optimized for mobile viewing, distinguishing them from other comic forms. Cultural and social spaces are "not just becoming virtual, but mobile," as new digital technologies—in particular, smartphones—have been "creating new virtual spaces in urban environments" (Moura, 2011, 39). Various elements that optimize cultural production in the digital platform era coincide with the characteristics of snack culture: smartphone-friendly, on-demand, speed, and being small in size. The connection between mobility and snack-ready consumption are some of the most significant dimensions in Korean webtoon culture.

For example, capital of Korea is a large city with one of the highest population densities in the world, and the majority of the residents of metropolitan Seoul—about ten million people as of December 2021—use the subway every day to commute. Webtoons are the primary cultural content that young people enjoy on their smartphones on public transportation systems or elsewhere at their convenience (the primary characteristic of on-demand media). The average commuting time in metropolitan Seoul was eighty-seven minutes per workday in 2019 (Jin, M. S., 2020), and while commuting, people use their smartphones to listen to music, check the news and instant messages (e.g., those on Kakao Talk), play mobile games, and enjoy webtoons.

By comparison, in Japan people can find magazines containing serial manga at almost all train stations and commonly read them during commutes. The major contributors to the development of manga are the weekly and monthly comic magazines, "which carry a collection of about ten or twenty series installments per edition," and it has been common to see Japanese "adults reading manga on a train or at a convenience store" (Matsutani, 2009). These two countries' consumption of comics—manga in Japan and webtoons in Korea—indicate that the connection between mobility or commuting and snack-ready consumption is one of the major reasons for the development of these two cultural formats. However, the webtoon differs from the manga partially due to the platformization of webtoons, as I discussed in chapter 2. This highlights how digital technologies are deeply involved in the production and consumption of webtoons.

More importantly, webtoons have developed a new form of speed culture. Critical theorists (Crary, 2013; Sharma, 2014; Wajcman, 2015) have provided a variety of perspectives on speed culture, which has developed along with the emergence of digital technologies. Instead of applauding the increasing role of digital technologies in today's world (characterized by 24/7, on-the-go culture), which have led to the emergence of snack culture, these authors critically examine how "new technologies and faster-moving capital herald grave political and social consequences" (Sharma, 2014, 6). Wajcman (2015, 183) points out that "the contemporary imperative of speed is as much as a cultural artifact as a material one." For her, digital technologies, including digital platforms, are "integral to our experience of space, time, communication, and consciousness, crystallizing new ways of being, knowing, [and consuming]. They as much reflect our high-speed culture as shape it" (184).

There is no doubt that many Koreans are in a hurry to get to where they are going and complete what they are doing so that they can move on to the next task, and then finish it so that they can move on to the next one (see, e.g., Aizu, 2002; Johns, 2011). *Balli, balli* (meaning *hurry up* or *go faster*) is a common Korean expression and expresses many Koreans' way of life. The country's *balli, balli* culture and Koreans determined perseverance are some reasons for Korea's embrace of digital culture. The country's notable technological advances are also evident in the penetration of broadband, KakaoTalk, smartphones, and now webtoons (Aizu, 2002; Johns, 2011; Jin, D. Y., 2017a).

Korea developed its snack culture partly due to the converging emergence of a cultural genre and smartphones. As one of the most wired countries in the world, it has advanced cutting-edge technologies and has the highest penetration of broadband and smartphones, and such technologies have greatly altered not only people's daily lives but also their habits of consuming cultural content (Jin, D. Y., 2019a). People's daily activities are heavily reliant on smartphones, and cultural content providers have released numerous webtoons, web dramas, and web novels short enough to be viewed in less than ten minutes on mobile devices. Again, smartphones help people endure the tedious commute in big cities such as Seoul, providing a wide range of cultural content. Snack culture is a result of the desire of smartphone users (or digital users in general) to enjoy cultural content briefly on the go rather than setting aside time specifically for cultural activity (Baek, B. Y., 2014c).

Sharma emphasized speed culture's role in hurting democracy rather than enhancing it. She argued that "the contemporary theorist of speed is concerned about how a culture of speed is antithetical to democracy": "They share a similar cautionary tale: Speed is the commanding byproduct of a mutually reinforcing complex that includes global capital, real-time communication technologies [such as the digital platforms discussed in this book], military technologies, and scientific research on human bodies. Democratic deliberation gives over to instant communication" (2014, 6).

Many people in the twenty-first century feel great time pressure, and they consume things quickly due to a lack of time. Reducing the time needed for various activities is one of the most significant challenges for global youth, and they attempt to spend less time or speed up to consume culture. Snack culture has naturally become a global youth trend. However, the connection between snack and speed culture arguably hurts cultural democracy, which emphasizes diversity and deliberation in the realm of popular culture. Snack culture does seem to provide individuals with freedom to access popular culture. However, it does not completely guarantee people's freedom (Moura, 2011) because ultimately a few mega digital platforms (such as Naver and Kakao) control the webtoon world. Snack culture has raised numerous concerns in our contemporary society. As Sharma (2014, 139) aptly puts it, along with new temporal forms of speed culture come are new forms of exploitation: the new snack culture or binge culture certainly "offers new insight into the exacerbation of older, persistent structural inequalities." Webtoon platforms attract contemporary global youth who are busy and digital natives. By targeting their short periods of free time, including commuting time (snack culture) or rest time on weekends (binge culture), webtoon platforms greatly increase their revenues.

As Wajcman (2015, 75) also points out, "we live in a society in which the standard working week, where work was synchronized for a substantial proportion of the population, is no longer the norm. Flexible working hours, 24/7 working time, and contract work creates coordination problems, as working times and locations are increasingly deregulated and scattered." What is significant is that digital platforms, including webtoon platforms (e.g., Naver Webtoon) have replaced traditional means of consumption, constructing one of the strongest hegemonies in the field of popular culture.

Snack culture is about to shift the major element of cultural production, from the production of popular culture to the consumption of cultural content. As readers continue to enjoy webtoons in ten-minute segments on their smartphones, KakaoPage (2021) has introduced a new video-on-demand service, named Free 10 Minute Videos, for films made since 2018. Smartphone users can stream a free ten-minute preview or purchase additional content by splitting it up into segments of five to ten minutes each. Reflecting the popularity of snack culture, KakaoPage has pursued a new strategy to expand its user base: increasing the supply of mobile content. In Korea, smartphone users now consume ten-minute, web-based, cultural content such as webtoons, web novels, web dramas, other web entertainment, and mobile games during their commutes or free time (Chung, A. Y., 2014b). In other words, snack culture—mainly developed in conjunction with the growth of webtoons—has influenced other relevant cultural forms, including films, dramas, and web entertainment. Therefore, webtoon-based snack culture has become a game changer in the cultural industries, as it transforms the ways in which people (in particular, youth and young adults) consume cultural content. Given that snack culture has a handful of major characteristics that allow for the optimization of cultural consumption on people's smartphones, it is expected to grow in the future.

This raises concerns beyond those related to the negative side of speed culture discussed above. In the COVID-19 era, people's time and space often cannot be managed properly due to uncertainty. This new normal, alongside digital platforms, has intensified snack culture and binge culture, because busy schedules lead to a lack of time to enjoy big-screen culture. In addition, people with irregular jobs that require them to stay at home can easily consume snack culture. Under these circumstances, digital platforms—in particular, webtoon platforms—can capitalize on the shifts in working time and space. In the early twenty-first century, customers can when and where they consume culture, and digital platforms have taken advantage of the new digital cultures to maximize their revenues.

The Advent of Binge-Reading Culture

Another major form of youth culture that webtoons have created in the digital platform era is binge-reading. Binging implies the consumption of media culture for hours at a time. While binge-watching is now common due to Netflix, binging is not just for television: some people binge-read books and manhwa during their vacations and holidays. In this section, I discuss binge-reading in relation to history and new business models: the advent of binge-reading in popular culture and the convergence of the business models and cultural consumption habits.

FROM ANIME'S BINGE-WATCHING TO WEBTOON'S BINGE-READING

It is worth discussing the history of binge-watching as a concept, which will help understand binge-reading culture. Binge-watching was first observed as a cultural phenomenon in the 1970s. It was initially called marathon viewing (Rodriguez, 2019), and early examples include marathon-viewing sessions of imported Japanese anime shows on VHS tapes in anime fandom communities. Anime conventions also began in the United States in the late 1970s (Daliot-Bul and Otmazgin, 2017). Back then, Japanese anime was very popular in the United States, and many fans organized clubs and enjoyed anime together while practicing cosplay. However, as has been well documented (McKevit, 2017), anime was rather difficult to access and enjoy. There were no alternatives to broadcast television until videotape became commonly available. Imported videotapes were quite expensive, costing around $70–$100 for a single movie or collection of short episodes. The least costly blank videotapes were about $18 each, and videotape recorders were very expensive as well. Therefore, dedicated anime fans often bought blank videotapes for a friend with a video recorder. Once the week's anime episodes had been recorded, groups of fans would gather and watch a marathon of episodes (Plunkett, 2016).

The term *binge-watching* was popularized in the 2010s with the advent of on-demand viewing, in particular through Netflix. Interestingly enough, Netflix preferred the term *marathon viewing* when the phenomenon was starting to take hold. Todd Yellin, a Netflix executive said, "I don't like the term 'binge,' because it sounds almost pathological. 'Marathon' sounds more celebratory" (quoted in Jurgensen, 2012). The reason for this is that "where the term 'binge' has been associated with excessive drinking, eating, and, generally over-doing it, 'marathon' has more positive connotations of health and accomplishment" (Rodriguez, 2019). Over time, though, Netflix had to embrace the term *binge*, as media outlets frequently used it. Binge-watching has become one of the most distinctive consumption methods in OTT service platforms. However, reflecting its short history in the platform era, there is no agreed-upon definition for it in media studies. A crucial task for television audience researchers is to map "the range of practices currently covered by the label of binge-viewing (also known as binge-watching)" (Turner, 2021, 229), as global youth have shifted their methods of cultural consumption substantially.

Long before Netflix made binge-watching of television popular, binge-consumption had already occurred in the field of literature. Book publishers were "looking to feed readers' craving for sequels to beloved novel series by releasing follow-up instalments more quickly than ever before. Call it binge reading, a concept that, up until now, was only possible with series that already had multiple volumes on bookstore shelves" (Armstrong, 2014). As a common term, though, *binge-reading* appeared in magazines between the late twentieth century and early twenty-first century to indicate intensive period of reading one after another of the works of particular novelists, including Charles Dickens (*Dickensonian*, 2004). *The Millions*, an online literary magazine, used the term in 2011 when Charles-Adam Foster-Simard (2011) wrote an article titled "Henry James and the Joys of Binge Reading." The article referred to binge-reading in explaining people's reading of Henry James's works together within a certain period of time. Meanwhile, Armstrong (2014) used the term to explain novel fans' consumption habits as they devoured such novels as the *Divergent* and *Hunger Games* series. The book industry had also developed the concept of binge-reading: "Historically, books of fiction were often released one chapter at a time, as selections available in magazines. This is known as the serial, a word not coincidentally akin to series. Harriet Beecher Stowe released *Uncle Tom's Cabin* as a serial in *The National Era*. Tom Wolfe released the *Bonfire of the Vanities* as a serial in *Rolling Stone*. Today, if you sit down to read these books from cover to cover in one sitting, you are effectively binge reading. They were intended to be read one chapter at a time, across the course of weeks or months" (Kidd, 2018, 230). The series format for television is also "loosely based on the idea of the chapter book, which strings together a series of stories into one grand narrative" (230).

Of course, it was common to witness binge-reading in the manhwa industry in Korea. As I discussed in chapter 1, starting in the 1960s *manhwabang* were one of the first places where people could go to enjoy popular culture, and many manhwa fans practiced binge-reading of several manhwa series there in the 1970s. I enjoyed manhwa after dinner on weekdays during my childhood, and after lunch on weekends I went to *manhwabang* to read my favorite manhwa for hours at a time. In the 1970s and 1980s, one title typically consisted of three volumes. Later, the length was extended to ten volumes, as in the case of Lee Hyun-se's 1983 *Alien Baseball Team*, one of the most popular manhwas ever, which was also turned into a 1986 film called *Lee Jang-ho's Baseball Team*. It was not unusual for college students to gather at a friend's house or in a public park to read manhwa together.

Similar to binge-reading practices in literature and early manhwa and the binge-watching of television programs, *binge-reading* in this book refers to people's consumption of webtoon series for many hours at a time instead of patiently waiting for subsequent episodes. Binge-reading has been easily adapted to webtoons as people can read webtoons on platforms and smartphones instead of having to purchase physical books, as in the case of literature. Consumers also do not need to go to libraries, bookstores, or *manhwabang*.

It is difficult to identify what constitutes a binge. As Jenner (2018, 110) argues, the number of episodes needed to constitute a binge is not only "subjective" but also "heavily dependent on individual circumstances." In other words, it is not easy to define the notion of a webtoon binge because the episodes are far shorter than in the case of television dramas. In any case, engaging in binge-reading behavior that "blends culture and technology" (Steiner and Xu, 2018, 83) means "prolonging a viewing experience and engagement with a narrative world, as well as emphasizing the story world over the lived experience" (Perks, 2015, cited in Castro et al., 2021, 4). What is clear is that binge-reading webtoons as a new form of youth culture has strongly influenced people's cultural consumption habits, which digital platforms have to pay attention to—requiring platforms to design binge-reading formats.

WEBTOON'S FREEMIUM MODEL AND BINGE-READING

A few webtoon platforms have developed the freemium model, which is closely connected to binge-reading (see chapter 2). In 2014 KakaoPage developed a fee-based service called If You Wait, It Will Be Free.[1] The home page of KakaoPage explains it as "a special way to enjoy the contents available only in KakaoPage. If you wait, you can view over 2,300 works for free." However, this service is aimed not at free users but at fee-paying ones. "If you wait, it will be free" is a core business model of KakaoPage. Users can subscribe to a webtoon and wait a certain amount of time to access an episode for free. KakaoPage allows each user to enjoy the piece with ease. KakaoPage's model, which allows users to read free online comics after waiting twelve or twenty-four hours, has been widely accepted in Korea. Many people who enjoy digital culture cannot wait too long. Indeed, the share of webtoon readers who pay fees increased from 16.3 percent in 2015 to 36.8 percent in 2017 (Lim, H. W., 2018). If they do not want to pay fees, readers need to wait to have access to the content. This means that they increase traffic as people continue to visit the webtoon portal, which also helps the digital platforms. Naver Webtoon has developed a similar service, called It's Free for Only You.

This new form of business model works well for Millennials and members of Generation Z, as they are not used to waiting for cultural content. As can be seen with Netflix, once viewers like a series, they frequently watch episodes one after another: "Netflix is also winning the original content wars, producing shows that are cinematically interesting, with complex narratives, compelling characters, and enough cliffhangers to keep audiences hooked, episode after episode, season after season. As a result, when larger and larger Netflix audiences binge watch *Orange Is the New Black*, *House of Cards*, or *Arrested Development*, there are new implications for television production and promotion going forward. The public's growing preference for back-to-back, commercial-free TV binges is influencing both screenwriting and marketing strategies for new and upcoming seasons of existing shows" (Matrix, 2014, 130–131).

Content viewers today (from Millennials to members Generation Z, many of whom are tech nerds) have "expectations—that every episode of every show is available anytime." They do not know a world where they had to wait for a program (Stelter, 2013). Netflix, Amazon, and other streaming video services are competing ferociously for children's programming (Stelter, 2013).

While the introduction of the freemium model has encouraged people's binge-reading habits, technological breakthroughs have brought about new youth culture as well. As Castro and coauthors (2019, 2) point out, "technology has changed the way people consume TV content, allowing them to orchestrate their own viewing in terms of time, content, location, and devices used. The popularity of Internet-distributed TV services such as Netflix, Amazon Video, and Hulu, together with the production of more complex stories, have contributed to the popularization of a specific mode of TV viewing—so-called binge-watching."

As a result of these business models, digital platforms' revenues have soared. For example, before the introduction of these models, KakaoPage's annual revenue was not significant, but with the new business model, it has continued to soar, as discussed in chapter 2. Although there are other business models, since KakaoPage started to grow rapidly with the introduction of the freemium model, one may conclude that this is one of the most significant and successful business models for webtoon platforms (Lim, H. W., 2018; Kakao, 2020). The commercial structures of webtoons and web novels provide a way to cut through pauses and enforced waiting periods (Evans, 2016). Digital platforms' freemium business models have greatly contributed to the growth of binge-reading among youth and young adults. Partially driven by digital platforms (as is also the case with Netflix), people are increasingly enjoying cultural content through binge-practicing, and webtoon platforms have developed unique tools to advance binge-reading. Binge-reading is both transforming the way global youth enjoy webtoons and shifting the economics of the manhwa industry.

Webtoon Binge-Reading by Themes and Genres

In addition to developing the freemium model, webtoon platforms such as Naver and Kakao have increased the use of binge-reading by combining webtoons that have similar themes and genres. Webtoon platforms categorize webtoons based on themes and genres, allowing readers to binge many different webtoons during their limited free time. For example, Naver Webtoon introduced a section titled Binge Read by Themes that attracts many webtoon fans (Naver Webtoon, 2020b). As of February 9, 2021, this section included twenty-seven themes, including Black Creators, Journey through Space, Strong Female Lead, High School,

Beautiful Boys, and Unexpected Romance. Once people click on a section, they find many famous finished webtoons. For example, the Romance section shows twenty series, so romance fans (including those who did not read the series when they were originally posted) can read all of them together.

Major themes on the platform have changed over time. In June 2020, the section titled Supernatural included twelve webtoon series (which collectively had 44.2 million likes), such as *Rise from Ashes*, *April Flowers*, and *Muted*. Under Beautiful Boys, there were another twelve series (114.4 million likes), including *Lost in Transition*, *Winter Woods*, and *True Beauty*. The High School section included eighteen series (87.2 million likes), such as *Swimming Lessons for a Mermaid*, *Brass & Sass*, and *unOrdinary*. The same platform produced a short clip that promoted binge-reading as follows: "When you remember you have Monday off. Time to binge read some Webtoons and not get any sleep." (Naver Webtoon, 2021).

Due to the recent boom of binge-reading (in tandem with the growth of webtoons and media outlets, both in Korea and abroad), social media in many countries have become venues for webtoon fans to share their binging experiences. Popular media have often reported on binge-reading as a new digital culture. For example, *Korea Daily* (2017) listed "7 Translated Korean Webtoon Recommendations to Binge Read" in May 2017. It mentioned seven famous webtoons: *Cheese in the Trap* (whose genre was "Romance/Drama"), *Tower of God* ("Fantasy/Action"), *My Giant Nerd Boyfriend* ("Slice of Life"), *Something about US* ("Romance"), *Pandora's Choice* ("Drama"), *He Is a High School Girl* ("Comedy"), and *Greetings! Earthling!* ("Comedy/Romance"). *Hankyoreh Shinmun* (2016) also recommended some webtoons that people could binge-read during their Thanksgiving break. The article stated that people's binge-reading used to increase during national holidays and recommended three famous webtoons to newspaper subscribers. Given the similarities between binge-watching and binge-reading, some media articles also simultaneously introduced several American series such as *Game of Thrones* (2011–2019); finished webtoons on webtoon platforms, including *Awl* (2013–2017); and novels for binge-practicing during national holidays (*Weekly DongA*, 2017).

Just as Netflix has become an even more important entertainment hub during the COVID-19 era (notably in the period 2020–2022, as many people had to stay at and work from home), webtoons were increasingly recommended by media as a new cultural form that people could enjoy at home. *MTV News* introduced sixteen graphic novels and webtoons for people to binge-read, including *True Beauty*, *Tower of God*, and *Cheese in the Trap*. According to the article, "in this uncharted period of social distancing and self-isolation, many of us are using this time to dive into something new, whether that's finding distraction in our Netflix queues or in the pages of that book you never got around to reading. But we're here to recommend the colorful world of graphic novels" (Vincent, 2020).

Global webtoon fans' binge-reading is also reflected on social media, including Reddit and Quora. Reddit is an American website with social aggregation, web content ratings, and discussions. Under the section called "Binging Webtoons," many comments and suggestions discuss binge-reading. As A. G. Shim and coauthors (2020, 834) point out, "fan practices in today's digital mediasphere include volunteer translations and user commentary to actively engage with forms of media and popular culture in ways that generate degrees of trust in the user-created content which they produce, share and consume." Webtoon fans gladly share their experiences and opinions in various online communities, including Reddit. One comment on that site asked: "are there any binge-worthy webtoons to read? i enjoy ones with pretty art styles and relatable characters . . . maybe with many chapters/episodes . . . ?" One of the many responses to this question was: "*Days of Hana*, *Lumine*, *Sweet Home*, *April Flowers* and *I Love Yoo* are the ones i enjoyed the most binge-reading. *Freaking Romance*, *Save Me*, and *True Beauty* are also pretty good, but don't have many chapters/episodes yet. If you are into BL/GL stuff i recommend *Ghost Lights*, *Muted*, and *Always Human*." Another response was: "*Cheese in the Trap* for sure. If you watched the drama (which was ruined) and were disappointed, don't worry! The author is changing things up and making it sooo amazing! It's my favorite."[2] As these comments on Reddit clearly show, binge-reading of webtoons has become popular, and webtoon fans often share titles and experiences.

In another comment thread on Reddit, one member stated in April 2020; "I need a BL to binge read. I'm bored and I just binge read *Heir's Game*. I now crave the gay. Send help." There were more than ten immediate responses, including the following:

Hmmm I hope I'm not giving you any that you've already read 😌

Castle Swimmer: beautiful and engaging plot and interesting characters. Softcore BL 🥵 Just a heads up though: the romance isn't the focus of this webtoon so if you're looking for something to read that has BL as its selling point this may not be the one for you.

Stasis: beautiful (listen) BEAUTIFUL art style 👏 This is one of my favorite BL webtoons. It has a really great plot and gorgeous characters. Again though—the BL is ABSOLUTELY there but it's not the selling point of it. Definitely recommend this if you're in the mood to get a great story alongside your romance though :)

Say the Right Thing: great art and cute story line. It has fluff, romance, fantasy, and angst 😌 great read![3]

Meanwhile, on Quora—an American website where questions are asked, answered, followed, and edited by internet users—on December 5, 2019, one person asked, "What binge-worthy webtoons do you recommend?" There were a number of responses. One (which had been liked by more than 250 people as of June 2, 2020) was:

One binge-worthy Webtoon is *unOrdinary*.

The plot, characters, and subtle ideological clashes really make it pop in the eyes of the viewers.

It's not one me, but Nathan Standish and Michael Aquino also! In fact, Michael and I bonded when we first met over *unOrdinary*!

In fact, Nathan Standish just binged through *unOrdinary* in just a couple days! Since he's been caught up, we even have our own space promoting discussion about the Webtoon called *unORDINARY*!

Binge the webtoon, and come join us for stimulating conversation![4]

Naver Webtoon has a supportive fan community, and fans can follow webtoonists on social media (including Facebook and Twitter), like their episodes, leave a comment, and otherwise rate their work. Webtoon fans recommend and share binge-readable webtoons. Whenever a new recommendation for such a webtoon is posted, several hundred Facebook users click on or share this information. As these popular websites certainly prove, binge-reading webtoons has become common, and many webtoon fans participate in discussions and share their ideas and opinions on this topic.

Both traditional and social media show that binge-reading has become very popular in the webtoon sector. Binge-reading through both the freemium model and compilations of webtoons by digital platforms has greatly contributed to people's new cultural consumption. Unlike older generations, who typically wait for cultural content until it appears, Millennials and members of Generation Z have new ways of consuming popular culture: they practice binge-watching and/or binge-reading. According to one survey (*YPulse*, 2019), there is no doubt that binge-watching is young consumers' preferred way of watching television shows: 56 percent of people ages 13–37 would rather binge-watch an entire series at once than watch episodes weekly. Among the members of Generation Z, many of whom do not remember a world without streaming services, this preference is even stronger, with 65 percent choosing to binge-watch a series. It is not surprising that streaming services are their top preference for viewing television content, beating live television by a significant margin. KakaoPage, for example, selectively uses the freemium model and applies it to webtoons that are expected to be popular so that it maximizes profits (Lim, H. W., 2018). With seemingly limitless access to video, Millennials and members of Generation Z have no need to watch a scheduled episode when it airs on television if that is not a convenient time for them (Seemiller and Grace, 2019).

What is interesting is that binge-reading has intensified the personalization of cultural consumption. Personalization is the reason why so many global youth and cultural consumers in general are attracted to digital platforms. As van Dijck and coauthors (2018, 42) point out, "customization and personalization also empower users as consumers and citizens, enabling them to quickly find the most attractive offer and the information they are interested in." Personalization is a major business strategy digital platforms use to garner profits, as well as a major aspect of youth culture, which is now mostly driven by digital platforms. In fact, digital platforms that own webtoon platforms develop bingeable programs for webtoon consumption. Therefore, readers are able to experience individualized consumption of their own niche segment of the culture. As individuals enjoy different genres of webtoons organized by webtoon platforms, nothing is dominant any longer in a medium that was once thought of as popular culture enjoyed by the majority of people.

Critics list several potential dangers of binge-reading, including increased risk of major health issues, addiction, antisocial behavior, and a waste of too much time (Stone, 2022). Global youth are "disembedded from the social and the traditional" as they focus on the individual and liberating aspects of the smartphone as a symbol of global technologies (Yoon, K., 2003, 340). Binge-consuming on smartphones is both the personalization of people's impatience (in particular, that of youth and young adults) and their appropriation of new digital culture. Consumers are further personalizing while reading webtoons and web novels and watching programs. The personalization of cultural consumption implies that people consume individually. It also demonstrates that digital platforms, including OTT and webtoon platforms, have personalized people's consumption habits to maximize their profits.

Critical Understanding of Snack Culture and Binge-Reading in the Webtoon Sphere

Two of the most significant forms of popular culture that are turning into parts of digital culture are snack culture and binge-reading driven by webtoon platforms and smartphones. While there are some differences between snack culture and binge-reading, experts researching contemporary viewing practices in popular culture focus on how design choices have helped bring us to where we are today, as well as on the consequences of the control that digital platforms have over people's cultural consumption habits (Pitre, 2019). As Jenkins (2006, 2–3) points out, one of the major components of media convergence is the migratory behavior of media audiences, whose members can go anywhere in search of new entertainment experiences. For global youth, in particular, "appointment viewing might seem old-fashioned, a vestige of the dark days before DVRs [digital video recorders] and video on demand" (Blake and Villareal, 2019). As Pitre (2019) argues in the case of binge-watching, "Television's traditional linearity has been upended via home video, on-demand, and most significantly, streaming, with a greater emphasis put on 'viewer choice,' such as it is. . . . Netflix, Hulu, Amazon, and the rest are deeply invested in these structures (each interface may look similar, but works according to distinct inner logics) and in creating the ideal consumer flow, intended to keep us watching for as long as possible." He also notes: "The roots of these practices, though, lie further back than the arrival of streaming."

Netflix's binge model for shaping viewing protocols in relation to the wider media ecosystem focuses on generations of users familiar with clicks, likes, and shares. But it is clear that binging in the streaming age is transforming how people must watch, and people should be aware of these changes and their consequences (Pitre, 2019). Netflix had a great deal to do with the phrase "binge-watching," referring to the habit of consumers consecutively watching multiple episodes of a television show, including drama, rather than watching them based on a regular weekly schedule. Netflix even coined a variation on the term: "binge racer" (Netflix, 2017). A binge racer is a viewer who aims to finish watching a full season of a show within twenty-four hours of its release. In a press release, Netflix (2017) proudly stated that the company had changed the way the world engages with stories—viewers watch when, where, and how they want, at whatever pace—and in so doing has given rise to a new kind of fan, the binge racer. According to Netflix, 8.4 million members have chosen to binge-race, and the only thing faster than their rate of watching is the rate at which this behavior continues to grow. Between 2013 and 2016, the number of people who finished a series on its launch day increased by more than twenty times.

As the rise of binge-watching in the OTT platform industry grows, binge-reading has become a regular means of enjoying webtoons over the past several years. As Netflix has taken advantage of binge-watching to capitalize on people's watching time, Korean digital platforms (including Naver and Kakao) have used the binge-reading model to monetize people's leisure time.

In the early 2000s, webtoons developed their identities as forms of snack culture indulged in during a short period of time. However, binge-reading has shifted its identity from snack culture toward a more serious and lengthy binge culture. While these two forms of consumption differ, the corporate motivations behind their exploitation are similar: namely, the capitalization of fans and the monopolization of their free time. Binge-reading has been highly commercialized, as digital platforms have adopted new forms of monetization strategies. The commercialization of digital culture is fundamental to webtoon platforms' financial strategies. This commercialization is characterized by people's shifting consumption habits—from initial free consumption in conjunction with snack culture to the purchase of webtoons in tandem with binge-reading—and how webtoon platforms exploit the temporal dynamics of webtoon culture. The popularity of webtoons indicates a need for media and cultural studies scholars to consider the broader social, cultural, and political implications of impatience and the ways in which cultural industries "are exploiting and monetizing that impatience" (Evans, 2016, 577).

Most of all, people's free time—including their time on national holidays, which in the past was presumably spent mostly interacting with family members and friends—has been increasingly occupied by webtoon platforms for the platform owners' profit. Through the development of the binge-reading model, webtoon platforms have influenced how people spend their free time and money. Such influence is directly aligned with contemporary neoliberal capitalism. These platforms have continued to develop new forms of binge practices to capitalize on the trend toward binge-reading (Pramaggiore, 2015). As Evans (2016, 574) argues, "whilst, to a certain extent, freemium games operate in ways that reflect techniques used by older media forms and consumer goods, their design equally exploits characteristics of emerging digital culture. In particular, they highlight the dichotomy between digital culture as open access and increasingly commercial. The fact that these games require no immediate payment in order to play them echoes the philosophy of open access and its fundamental opposition to more capitalist approaches." Likewise, the convergence of webtoons, the appearance of an open-source philosophy, and time-based monetization strategies is becoming a foundational ethos of the webtoon market, and a similar convergence can be seen in casual games and OTT platforms (Evans, 2016, 578). As one of the new and largest digital cultures, webtoon culture has become a source from which contemporary capitalism can obtain considerable benefits. Regardless of the unique characteristics of webtoon use among global youth and young adults, webtoons are also profitable digital culture, which can be identified as a symbol of contemporary cultural capitalism.

Conclusion

This chapter has critically discussed digital culture in relation to webtoons, which have become a major unique form of global youth culture. Webtoons have greatly transformed the manhwa industry and, more generally, cultural industries and youth culture. I examined shifts in digital youth culture that have occurred in tandem with the rise of digital technologies, such as digital platforms and smartphones. The term *webtoon* is a neologism of *web* and *cartoon*, and webtoons are directly connected to digital technologies. Webtoons as part of web 2.0 represent participation, sharing, and connectiveness. They are directly connected to smartphones, as webtoons are the first and largest popular culture that many people use smartphones to enjoy.

On the one hand, webtoons have encouraged the spread of snack culture, and many people enjoy webtoons for a few minutes at a time whenever they access webtoon apps created by digital platforms. However, webtoon series often develop as very intricate and complicated epics over many years. Thus, ironically, while as episodes webtoons are indicative of snack culture, as finished or partly finished entities they are comparable to lengthy books and manhwa—which makes them one of the most significant forms in binge-reading culture. As a result, many big-screen cultural creators adopt webtoons into big-screen culture.

On the other hand, webtoon platforms have developed binge-reading culture through the freemium business model and by collecting similar genres and themes for readers to enjoy. Both forms of binge-reading have been driven by webtoon platforms, which have strategically created them to attract people to the webtoon world as a means of maximizing revenue. In particular, the freemium model has been used by webtoon platforms as a major monetization strategy based on encouraging binge-reading. Since famous webtoons are also released in a printed manhwa format with vertical layouts, people can enjoy entire webtoon series through binge-reading during holidays or on vacations. Unlike previous generations, Millennials and members of Generation Z can manage their consumption habits when they enjoy webtoons. With freemium models, they can choose to pay to continue reading webtoons rather than waiting for episodes to be released for free, and they can enjoy webtoons quickly during their limited spare time. Binge-reading in the webtoon sector has continued to grow, as many consumers are willing to pay fees to read episodes sooner. Binge-reading is a hybrid of digital technology and culture, and "it challenges the traditional power dynamics of unidirectional broadcast flows from producer through viewer" (Steiner, 2017, 147).

However, the freemium business model and the binge-reading model are mainly the outcomes of digital platforms' capitalization strategies.

These two business models have significantly shifted people's consumption habits. As young people in particular have decreasing ability to wait for new episodes, these platforms use youth's cultural consumption habits to monetize content. This has transformed the major characteristics of webtoons, from free objects of snack culture to a subject of the cultural economy. Webtoons have developed several forms of youth culture, and they greatly influence both their fans and webtoon platforms in the capitalist cultural economy of the twenty-first century.

CHAPTER 4

Transmedia Storytelling of Webtoons in Big-Screen Culture

As webtoons have rapidly become an enjoyable type of cultural content among audiences of various age groups, particularly teens and young adults, cultural creators such as television producers and film directors have begun to pay attention to webtoons as source materials for their own cultural productions. Webtoons have advanced their identity as snack culture, as I discussed in a previous chapter. However, some webtoons are multi-episode series and are able to portray quite a few of the significant sociocultural dimensions of Korean society. In the early twenty-first century, Korean cultural industries had suffered from a lack of new ideas, as exemplified by the adaptation of Japanese manga for movies and television dramas that frequently failed in the Korean cultural market. But in recent years Korean cultural creators in the film, television drama, and digital gaming industries have increasingly turned to webtoons to develop a new type of culture (Jin, D. Y., 2019a; Pyo, Jang, and Yoon, 2019;).[1]

Bringing webtoons to big-screen culture offers more creative opportunities to television producers and filmmakers because they can take advantage of the many original ideas presented in webtoons, as well as of their fan bases and familiar story lines. In addition, webtoons are distributed through digital platforms, which typically charge filmmakers and television producers much less for the rights to original stories than the producers of other sources, including novels, do (Song, Y. S., 2012). Webtoon stories are also usually well designed and structured and thus are comparatively easy to transform into movies and dramas.

This chapter examines the ways in which webtoons have become major resources for transmedia storytelling. I discuss the reasons why this tiny snack culture has increasingly been converted into big-screen culture in recent years. I analyze a few exemplary cases—including *Misaeng: Incomplete Life*, *Itaewon Class*, *Cheese in the Trap*, *Along with the Gods: The Two Worlds*, and *Along with the Gods: The Last 49 Days*, all of which have been transformed from popular webtoons into successful big-screen content—to determine why and how cultural creators modify or expand webtoons' original stories as they are turned into big-screen products. I then discuss whether webtoon-based transmedia storytelling, one of the crucial elements of contemporary entertainment industries, has altered the media ecosystem.

Webtoons as a Novel Standard for Transmedia Storytelling

Several aspects of webtoons explain their rise as original sources of transmedia storytelling: these included diversity in genre and theme, popularity among Korean youth, the advancement of broadcasting systems, and webtoon's optimization for smartphones. As Jenkins (2011) argues, "transmedia storytelling represents a process where integral elements of a fiction get dispersed systematically across multiple delivery channels for the purpose of creating a unified and coordinated entertainment experience." Webtoonists and webtoon platforms have used transmedia storytelling strategies to maximize profit while promoting new youth culture.

Most of all, the diversity of webtoons' genres appeals to big-screen cultural creators as well as webtoon fans with varying tastes. As I discussed in chapter 1, webtoons have used various genres and themes as Korean society has experienced significant sociocultural changes. After their initial stage—when they focused on romance—webtoons continuously diversified, and their genres now include BL, thriller, fantasy, science fiction, and mystery. Webtoons from romance and *il-sang* to thrillers now address sociocultural issues deeply embedded in people's daily lives. When television producers and film directors cannot find good scenarios from other cultural materials, webtoons naturally attract their attention (Song, C. R., 2014), due in large part to their diverse, bold, and interesting subjects and themes. Webtoons used as source materials for big-screen cultures have greatly transformed the major themes and genres of contemporary Korean television programs and films. Big-screen culture now includes zombie, adventure, BL, and other genres that it did not contain before, since Koreans have become able to access such genres in the form of webtoons and are interested in them.

Webtoon stories are typically subtler than earlier manhwa. Since the late 2000s, webtoonists have developed long stories that go well beyond single episodes consisting of a few cuts. Such longer stories need various structures, conflicts, harmonies, and distinctive themes. In some ways, webtoons still seem to be a cultural snack, as readers usually enjoy them periodically. This is because webtoonists publish their work in installments, unlike novels that one reads from start to finish after publication (Jin, D. Y., 2019a). The length of many webtoons in recent years has expanded enough for them to be considered epics, making them reliable sources for big-screen content.[2] In this regard, Zur (2016, 203) notes that the webtoon "is a storytelling mechanism that can capture complex reality and the psychological state of its characters without having to commit to one particular narrative voice. Even with minimal text, webtoons give us access to the inner state of a wide variety of characters through suggestive images."

Another primary reason for webtoons' popularity as a transmedia storytelling source is their fan base. As one of the latest cultural forms of Korean cultural industries, successful webtoons attract many readers, and they often become fans of particular webtoons and webtoonists. In the twenty-first century, some popular webtoons have had a few million views. Webtoon fans are not only active but also interactive. When they read webtoons, they often post their opinions, share episodes on social media, and recommend webtoons to new users. They express their tastes and requests through various mechanisms, including social media. In some cases (e.g., BL), such fan activities eventually persuaded webtoonists to develop new genres (Hwang, 2018). When television producers and film directors turn these webtoons into big-screen culture, they can attract these fans as big-screen audiences. Taking a recent example, in March 2021 when tvN started to air the television drama *Navillera: Like a Butterfly*—based on a webtoon of the same name—that portrayed a retired mail carrier achieving the lifelong dream of becoming a ballet dancer at the age of seventy, the show immediately attracted an audience of fans who enjoyed the webtoon version. The webtoon started in 2016, and it had more than eighty-eight million views as of March 2021 (No, J. W., 2021). Clearly one of the chief strengths of the drama was its webtoon fan base (fig. 4.1).

Interestingly, the increase of the number cases of so-called loser syndrome among Korean youth has increased the popularity of webtoons and, therefore, their transmediality. Many Korean youth are struggling and feel that they are becoming losers in society. Such young people often sympathize with weird and loser webtoon characters. Just as global fans have enthusiastically received songs by BTS since the late 2010s, partially due to their lyrics that contain social commentary on topics from Korea's backward educational system to social inequality and political corruption, global youth who experience ordeals similar to those of Korean youth tend to like Korean webtoons (Herman, 2018).[3]

However, in the Korean context the term *loser* is complex, and some subcategories can be identified. First, many Millennials and members of Generation Z have gone through various socioeconomic ordeals, such as low levels of employment, soaring housing prices, and fewer promotion opportunities in companies, as well as a lack of money—which collectively makes their lives very difficult. In the past ten years, many college graduates have not secured decent jobs, and they have had to live day-to-day as part-time workers for many years. The unemployment rate of Koreans in their twenties increased from 9.3 percent in 2013 to 10.5 percent in 2018, and in 2018 the comparable rates were 8.6 percent in the United States and 3.6 percent in Japan (Kim, I. W., 2019). Therefore, they often feel that they will not be able to marry or have a home of their own in the foreseeable future.[4] Many young people who feel like they are losers consume content with light humor and fun as snacks. Since webtoons are a new way for Millennials and members of Generation Z to consume comics, it is natural to see webtoonists touching on the loser syndrome that many young people deeply sympathize with. Webtoonists pay attention to such hardships and often include struggling characters in their webtoons.

One of the exemplary webtoons portraying the loser syndrome is Yoon Tae-ho's *Misaeng: Incomplete Life*. It was originally posted on Daum Webtoon between January 2012 and July 2013, and it achieved huge

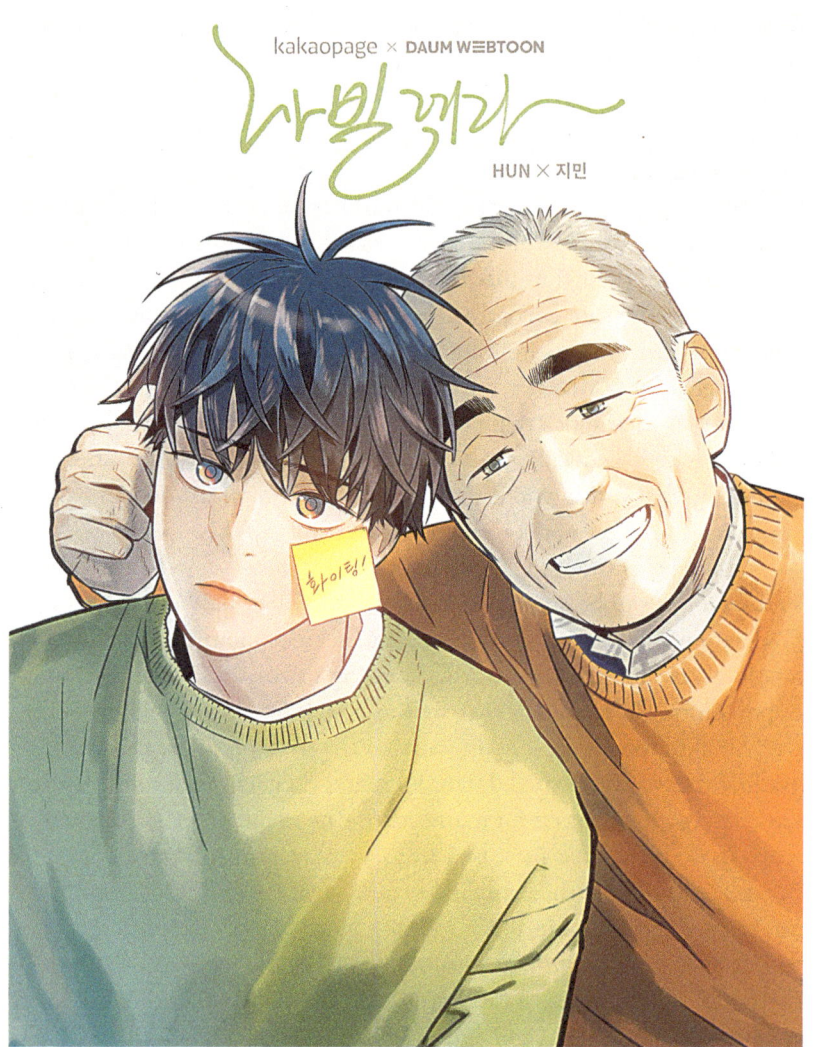

FIGURE 4.1 Art from the webtoon *Navillera: Like a Butterfly*. Source: ©Supercomix Studio Corp.

success. Yoon created *Misaeng: Part II* on KakaoPage, where it ran between November 2015 and May 2018, but he delayed completing the series while he worked on a newer webtoon, *Eorin* (posted in 2020). *Misaeng*'s success led it to be adapted into a number of cultural forms, including a television drama, film, and musical.

In *Misaeng: Incomplete Life*, Jang Geu-Rae (played by Im Si-Wan in the television drama), a passionate Go player since childhood, fails to become a professional Go player. After completing his military service, Jang is thrown into the workforce instead of being able to pursue his childhood dream. Through an acquaintance's recommendation, Jang begins to work for the trading company One International as an intern. The webtoon portrays the ways in which he manages to survive the life of an intern, which is not only difficult but also cruel: regular workers at companies often treat interns as their servants. When companies present gifts on national holidays to employees, for example, they give different presents to regular workers and temporary workers (including interns).

Misaeng: Incomplete Life focuses on a precarious intern and depicts his unpleasant office life. Many people in their twenties who hold part-time or temporary positions can sympathize with the protagonist and other office workers who are struggling with their salaryman lives. The webtoon portrays people who are very nervous about their futures, and therefore it appeals to many people who are either office workers or job seekers. Webtoons with such loser characters provide a temporary escape from harsh reality for youth who sympathize with their characters.

Second, this loser syndrome is also connected to so-called moron taste—that is, enjoying dumb but witty jokes. The webtoon written by Lee Mal-nyeon titled *Lee Mal-nyeon Series* is unrivaled in terms of being moron-like (Jin, D. Y., 2019a). In most cases, well-organized plots have an introduction, development, plot twist, and conclusion. However, Lee's webtoon has an introduction, development, plot twist, and moron taste. The final step could either result in disaster for the whole story or give it a unique charm (Sora's Webtoon World, 2012). For example, in the first panel of a four-cut webtoon, an old gentleman works at his home computer, but he is very sleepy. In the second cut, he decides to go to Star Bbucks (a coffee shop that is a knockoff of the American Starbucks), and says: "I am dying to sleep. I've got to have a coffee." In the following cut, he orders coffee, and a staff person says, "it's 4,300 won" (about $4). In the fourth and final cut, the webtoon shows him shivering: he has actually woken up from hearing this high price. He can't believe that the price of coffee is so high. This is a webtoon that was created more than ten years ago, when the price of a cup of coffee in the United States was around $2. Lee's sarcastic remarks frequently are based on trends among Korean youth or on the internet. Thus, in the mid-2000s, he "introduced a new type of content called '*byeong-mat*' (Korean for 'a taste of mind-numbing stupidity'), a short comedy webtoon that people could easily read through. This type of webtoon became very popular" (quoted in Do, D. W., 2015).[5]

According to the *Yonsei Annals*, a student newspaper at Yonsei University in Korea (Kwon, D. I., 2020), one of the major characteristics of the generation born in the 1990s is their love for *byeong-mat*—humor that is crude and dumb. *Byeong-mat* is everywhere in Korea, from redubbed movie clips to themed advertisements. The newspaper stated that this consumption seems likely to be connected to Korean youth's preference for authentic humor and use of YouTube. *Byeong-mat* YouTube channels contrast with the KBS (Korea Broadcasting System) comedy program *Gag Concert*, which is representative of old-school comedy. For more than two decades, *Gag Concert* had been one of the funniest and most popular comedy or gag shows in Korea, attracting over 30 percent of viewers at its peak. However, its viewership plummeted to 2 percent in 2020, and KBS terminated the program in June of that year (*DongA Ilbo*, 2020; Kwon, D. I., 2020). This decline in viewership was partially because nowadays young people, who are the primary audiences for this kind of gag program, prefer to watch various YouTube channels that are more sensitive to trends and have the extra perk of lax censorship. *Gag Concert* was staged and reused the same format and catchphrases for a few episodes. In contrast, popular *byeong-mat* YouTube channels such as *Wassup Man* and *Work Man* aim to be more genuine, are more receptive to viewers' suggestions, and change their formats (Kwon, D. I., 2020).

Lee Mal-nyeon has appeared on *My Little Television*, a personal internet broadcasting platform similar to AfreecaTV (a peer-to-peer technology-based video streaming service) and Twitch.tv (where hosts compete for real-time audience responses). Along with his untrained and fresh remarks, he has made webcomic shows featuring daily guests. Each time he appears, he sets new viewership records for the show (Park, J. H., 2016). Other webtoonists—including Gian84 (known for his webtoon *Fashion King* [*P'aesye-on Wang*], which was posted in 2011–2113 and adapted into a movie of the same name in 2014)—frequently appear on entertainment television programs. When *Men are Men (Ge-unomi Ge-unomida)*, a television drama on KBS2 that features the fictional webtoon production company Mytoon, started in July 2020, two famous webtoonists, Lee Mal-nyeon and Joo Ho-min (playing "writer Lee" and "writer Joo," respectively), appeared as Mytoon's fictional webtoonists. Both popular webtoons and webtoonists have huge fan bases, which is very attractive for big-screen cultural creators.

Last but not least, the loser syndrome is also present in *The History of Jji-Jil*. The closest English translation of this term *jji-jil* is "loser": it is primarily a derogatory term to indicate a person who is rude, obtuse, and insensitive, or *me-oje-ori* (which in turn can be translated as "a fool"). For example, the webtoon *The History of Jji-Jil* (a romance, written by Kim Pung and drawn by Shim Yoon-su) was published on Naver Webtoon between 2013 and 2017. In one of its typical silly moments, episode 26 shows how Minki, the male protagonist, is insensitive and crude (*jji-jil*). Minki wanted to apologize to his girlfriend, Sulha, after they had a big fight. In one panel, he even knelt down to show his sincere intention to apologize. When they eventually hugged each other in a following panel as a symbol of their restored unity, Minki abruptly said: "By the way Sulha, I am really, really sorry. It's my fault. However, you know that you made a mistake as well" (episode 26 of *The History of Jji-Jil*). Many webtoons portray this kind of unwelcome characteristic candidly, which appeals to many young readers. Some webtoons broadly depict losers from various perspectives, gaining attention from various cultural creators.

Webtoons also provide visual scripts, allowing other cultural creators to easily envision the story lines they could use in adaptations. Once the script for a film or television drama is written, the creators develop what is called continuity ("conti" for short) that refers to the script before shooting the film or drama. Webtoons are already visualized with manhwa-style texts and pictures, which makes it very easy for cultural creators to imagine how the content could be adapted (Chun, S. W., 2017). As Lee Jae Moon, *Misaeng*'s producer, stated, "webtoons are great resources for content producers because the original messages and episodes are already strong, and it is easy for us to add dramatics" (quoted in Lee, J. Y., 2015). In other words, webtoons' visual images and well-designed texts are intriguing, and these characteristics help many cultural creators easily transform them into movies and television dramas.

Meanwhile, the expansion of the broadcasting industry has helped the development of webtoon-based transmedia. Since the mid-1990s, Korea has developed new television channels, including cable and satellite channels, and as a result, the Korean broadcasting sector witnessed a surge of programs. For example, in 2011, the Korean government allowed new general programming cable channels, known as *jeogpyeon* (including JTBC, TV Chosun, Channel A, and MBN), to begin broadcasting. Major newspaper companies own all of these channels, and they air a variety of programs in a manner similar to that of the existing three terrestrial broadcasters: KBS, MBC (Munhwa Broadcasting Corporation), and SBS (Seoul Broadcasting System). Alongside some entertainment channels, that focus on dramas, including tvN and OCN, these new television channels have invested heavily in developing dramas and entertainment programs such as reality shows, and they often use webtoons as new sources for cultural production in place of other, once-reliable source material. Of course, the recent involvement of Netflix not only as a distributor but also as a producer of local-based cultural content, greatly influences webtoon-based transmedia storytelling, and many webtoon platforms now have to consider the potential release of webtoon-based cultural products on Netflix. The rapid shifts in the media ecology increase the expectation that broadcasters and digital platforms will collaborate to advance webtoon-based transmedia storytelling, developing a key aspect of the newly emerging media ecology and culture. In the Korean context, the recent growth of webtoon-based transmedia is "indicative of the highly adaptive and flexible nature of narrative and its intricate relationship to medium" (Park, H. S., 2021, 55). It has also been deeply connected to sociocultural, technological, structural, and economic elements that have greatly advanced this new form of transmedia storytelling.

Webtoons' Transmedia Storytelling in Television Dramas: Itaewon Class

Webtoon-based dramas are rampant. Whenever one browses Korean television channels, one finds dramas adapted from webtoons. The number of webtoon-based dramas has continued to grow since the early 2010s, and some of them—such as *Misaeng* (2014), *Scholar Who Walks the Night* (2015), *Cheese in the Trap* (2016), and *My ID Is Gangnam Beauty* (2018)—have been very popular. During the first half of 2020 alone, several webtoon-based television dramas aired, including *Memorist* on tvN, *Welcome* on KBS, *Itaewon Class* and *Mystic Pop-up Bar* on JTBC, and *Rugal* on OCN. And in the same period, seven out of twenty-four new television dramas on the three network channels (KBS, MBC, and SBS), JTBC, and tvN were webtoon-based series, reflecting the popularity of webtoons in the broadcasting industry (Kim, I. G., 2020). Also in 2020, Netflix aired a few Korean dramas based on webtoons, including *Sweet Home*. This demonstrates that broadcasters have turned their eyes to webtoons (table 4.1). As broadcasters mainly target Korean youth and young adults, they primarily focus on the genres that appeal to people in these age groups, including fantasy, romance, romantic comedy, mystery, and drama emphasizing social issues.

Among these recent dramas, *Itaewon Class* gained huge popularity as a drama webtoon and was eventually adapted into a television drama, which was also very successful. The webtoon *Itaewon Class* was created by Gwang Jin and posted on Daum Webtoon between December 2016 and July 2018. By the time it ended, it had received more than two hundred million views, one of the highest view counts at the time. It was then turned into a fee-based webtoon series. According to KakaoPage, it became one of Daum Webtoon's biggest successes (Park, J. W., 2020).

The television drama *Itaewon Class* (a series consisting of sixteen episodes) was aired on JTBC between January and March 2020. This webtoon adaptation was very successful, attracting 18 percent of viewers at its peak (fig. 4.2). *Itaewon Class* was expected to be a success as a drama because the original story had a strong following, meaning that many webtoon fans were expected to watch it. Given that it was aired on JTBC, one of four general programming cable channels, instead of one of the terrestrial broadcasting companies, it can be considered one of the most successful dramas in Korean broadcasting history. Interestingly, it was the first drama series produced by Showbox, a movie company that invested around $12.8 million in its production. Because the boundaries between cultural forms (for example, between films and television dramas) have been disappearing, Showbox decided to jump into the broadcasting sector by adding movie-like visual effects. Since Netflix (the most famous

Table 4-1 Selected Webtoon-Based Dramas Aired on Korean Television, 2014–2021

Year	Webtoon title	Webtoonist	Webtoon platform	Drama title	Broadcaster	Genre
2014	Misaeng: Incomplete Life	Yoon Tae-ho	Daum	Misaeng	tvN	Drama
	Dr. Frost	Lee Jong-Beom	Naver	Dr. Frost	OCN	Crime or thriller
2015	Scholar Who Walks in the Night	Jo Joo-Hee	KakaoPage	Scholar Who Walks in the Night	MBC	Historical or fantasy
	Hogu's Love	Yoo Hyun-Sook	Daum	Hogu's Love	tvN	Drama or comedy
	A Girl Who Sees Smells	Seo Soo-Kyung (Man Chwi)	Olleh market	A Girl Who Sees Smells	SBS	Crime or romance
2016	Cheese in the Trap	Soonkki	Naver	Cheese in the Trap	tvN	Romance or drama
	My Lawyer Mr. Jo	Kim Yang-soo (Hatzling)	Naver	My Lawyer Mr. Jo	KBS2	Drama
	Lucky Romance	Kim Dal-Nim	Naver	Lucky Romance	MBC	Romance
	The Gentlemen of Wolgyesu Tailor Shop	Lee Jong-Kyu	Daum	The Gentlemen of Wolgyesu Tailor Shop	KBS2	Drama
	Sweet Stranger and Me Urijib-e Saneun Namja	Yoo Hyun-Sook	Daum	Sweet Stranger and Me	KBS2	Romantic comedy
2017	Out of the World	Jo Geum-San	Daum	Save Me	OCN	Thriller
	Avengers Social Club	Sajatokki	Daum	Avengers Social Club	tvN	Drama
	Do It One More Time	Hong Seung-pyo (Miri)	Naver	Confession Couple	KBS2	Romantic comedy

Year	Title	Author	Platform	Korean Title	Network	Genre
2018	My ID Is Gangnam Beauty	Gi Maeng-Gi	Naver	My ID Is Gangnam Beauty	JTBC	Romantic comedy
	What Is Wrong with Secretary Kim	Kim Myung-Mi	Naver	What Is Wrong with Secretary Kim	tvN	Romantic comedy
	Clean with Passion for Now	Aengo	KakaoPage	Clean with Passion for Now	JTBC	Romantic comedy
2019	Item	Kim Jung-seok and Min Hyung	KakaoPage	Item	MBC	Mystery or fantasy
	Love Alarm Joahamyeon Ullineun	Chon Kye-young	Daum	Joahamyeon Ullineun	Netflix	Romance
	The Tale of Nokdu	Hye Jin-yang	Naver	The Tale of Nokdu	KBS2	Historical or romantic comedy
	Pegasus Market Ssamnida Cheollimamateu	Kim Gyu-sam	Naver	Pegasus Market Ssamnida Cheollimamateu	tvN	Drama
2020	Itaewon Class	Gwang Jin	Daum	Itaewon Class	JTBC	Drama
	Memorist	Jae Hoo	Daum	Memorist	tvN	Crime or mystery
	Mystic Pop-Up Bar Ssanggappocha	Bae Hye-soo	Daum	Mystic Pop-Up Bar Ssanggappocha	JTBC	Drama or fantasy
2021	Naviellera	Hun/Jinmin	Daum	Naviellera	tvN	Drama

Source: Compiled by author.

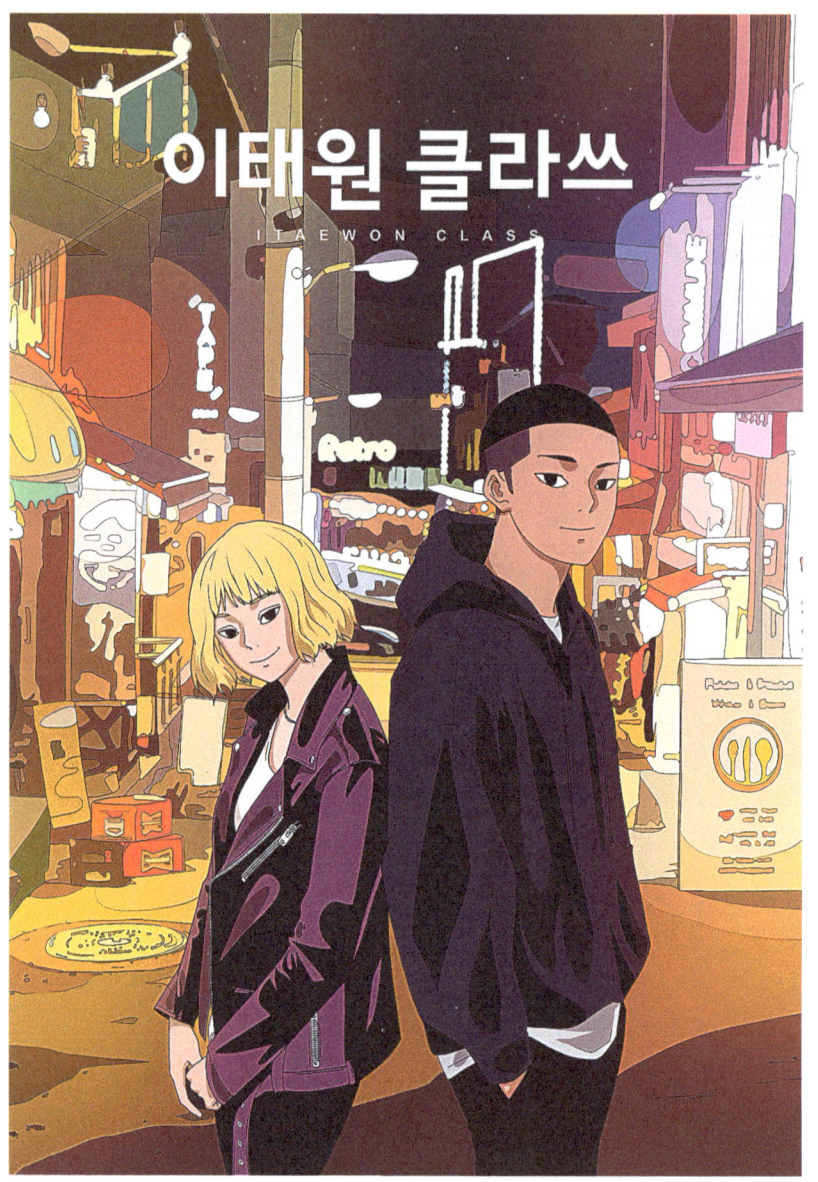

FIGURE 4.2 Art from the webtoon *Itaewon Class*. Source: Kakao Entertainment.

and largest OTT service platform) had purchased the global broadcasting rights to *Itaewon Class* by providing $8 million before production, *Itaewon Class* had already secured a global reach (Cho, Y. G., 2020). *Itaewon Class* clearly reflects the shifting media ecology surrounding webtoon-based transmedia storytelling, indicating that webtoons and webtoon-based transmediality have fundamentally changed the contemporary media environment.

One of the major themes in *Itaewon Class* is revenge, which is very common in various Korean cultural genres. However, it also clearly portrays people getting a second chance in life, as it develops a plot showing how young people who consider themselves losers are able to gradually achieve their dreams together. As I discussed above, the loser syndrome has been a distinctive characteristic of Korean youth culture. As Zur (2016, 201–202) points out, "the question of revenge and retribution remains a subject of keen interest among writers and filmmakers in South Korea today. . . . To an extent, philosophers agree that there is a compelling, intuitive feature to retributivism—the idea that perpetrators of a crime deserve to be punished equally, even if the punishment will produce no further good." However, *Itaewon Class* shrewdly mixes two seemingly unconnected themes: revenge and a second chance. More specifically, the central narrative revolves around Park Saeroyi (played in the drama series by actor Park Seo-joon), a kindhearted but introverted boy with few friends who dreams of becoming a police officer. In the first episode of the webtoon, Saeroyi and his father talk about friends in the car as they move to a new city:

Father: It's a pity to depart from friends.
Saeroyi: It's OK. I have no friends.
Father: In your new school, there is a student named Jang Geun Won who is the son of the CEO of Jangga. I hope you are in the same class.
Saeroyi: Should I get along well with him?
Father: If your chemistry fits well.
Saeroyi: I will get along well with him, given his status as the son of your company's CEO.

This short moment in the first episode succinctly sets up the overall plot of the webtoon, showing Park Saeroyi's personality, his close relationship with his father, and the upcoming conflicts with Jang Geun Won and Jangga.

In the first few episodes, Park Saeroyi's kindhearted nature has him save a classmate from being bullied by Jang Geun Won (played in the drama series by Ahn Bo-hyun) on the day he transfers to his new school after moving. As noted above, Jang's father is the CEO of Jangga, a food chain company where Park's father has worked for twenty years. Since Saeroyi punches Geun Won and refuses to apologize, he is eventually expelled, and his father is fired from Jangga. Geun Won's father, a financial supporter of the school, influenced Saeroyi's dismissal, which is a typical scene in Korean society. Adding to his misery, he becomes an orphan when his father is killed by Geun Won in a hit-and-run accident. Knowing that his father's death was Geun Won's fault, Saeroyi beats Geun Won up badly again. He then receives prison time for assaulting Geun Won, ruining his dream of becoming a police officer. Saeroyi swears revenge on Jangga by continuing his father's dream of starting a food business. Saeroyi's goal now is to open a pub and turn it into the biggest food company in Korea, while destroying Jangga. He eventually opens a restaurant in Itaewon, a neighborhood in Seoul known as a district for foreigner. Several interesting characters come to work with Saeroyi and eventually support his restaurant, including someone who spent time in prison with Saeroyi and a transgender woman chef (Jung, E. A., 2020).

As in the webtoon, in the drama the crew at the pub are all social outcasts with some twists. Saeroyi is a typical *heuksujeo* ("mud spoon" or "dirt spoon"), a term that refers to someone who struggles to make ends meet since he lacks rich and powerful parents with high connections.[6] The group includes Cho Yi-seo (played in the drama series by Kim Da-mi), an influencer and social blogger who is described as a sociopath by her classmates; Jang Geun-soo (Kim Dong-hee), the illegitimate second son of Jangga's CEO; Choi Seung-kwon (Ryoo Kyung-soo), another former convict; Ma Hyun-yi (Lee Joo-young), the transgender chef; and Tony Kim (Chris Lyon), an African-Korean foreigner who is searching for her father (a character not in the webtoon who was added to the drama to reflect the diverse nature of Itaewon).

Saeroyi's pub, DanBam, is home to all of these characters who have been cast aside by society because of social status, appearance, or sexuality. In Korea, former convicts face a lot of discrimination, and they often find it hard to get work after being released from prison. LGBTQ issues are not commonly discussed in conservative Korean society, and members of sexual minority groups and transgender individuals continue to be rendered invisible. However, LGBTQ representation is increasing somewhat with the popularity of the BL genre on certain webtoon platforms (discussed in chapter 1). *Itaewon Class* follows these loser outcasts as they receive a second chance at life (Soriano, 2020). The fact that Saeroyi manages to succeed gives many readers of the webtoon and viewers of the drama a sense of catharsis. Both versions of *Itaewon Class* have won praise for their realistic presentation of subjects such as prejudice against high school dropouts and discrimination against the LGBTQ community.

Webtoons often differ markedly from dramas based on them, due to the distinctive characteristics of the media. For example, the webtoon and drama versions of *Itaewon Class* have some significant differences. However, as the webtoonist wrote the drama's script, the two versions are closely synchronized compared to other webtoons turned into dramas—which allowed the drama to avoid serious criticism from followers of the original webtoon.

Today, in contrast to the situation a few years ago, webtoonists often gladly participate in the production of television dramas and films based on their webtoons. Not only are there increasing opportunities to develop their webtoons both as films and dramas and as cultural content for Netflix and YouTube, but the current media environment offers webtoonists a chance to participate so they can make sure that their ideas and creativity are preserved in big-screen culture (Han, S. B., 2020). Therefore, webtoon-based dramas these days are often very similar cultural to the original webtoons, which increases their likelihood of success.

As their transmedia storytelling continues, webtoons are thick with addictive plot twists. For example, *Itaewon Class* includes betrayal; murder; a cooking competition; the relationship between Saeroyi and his childhood crush, Oh Soo-ah (played in the drama series by Kwon Nara), who works as a top executive at Jangga; and a hypercompetent young upstart named Cho Yi-seo, who has vaguely sociopathic tendencies and works at DanBam. The story surprises and delights, while still offering a comforting sense that the good will remain good, while the bad will ultimately get their just deserts (Jung, E. A., 2020).

The television drama version of *Itaewon Class* made important changes to the plot of the original webtoon. In the first episode of the drama, Park's father and Oh Soo-ah, who lived in the same orphanage, had known each other for a long time before she met his son. In the webtoon, Oh Soo-ah first met Park Saeroyi and his father on the day they moved into a two-story house in a new city, next door to where she lived. The change in her background in the drama appears to be an attempt to explain her success-oriented personality: she is an orphan who becomes a career woman with high self-esteem. Park Saeroyi is quite shy and friendly, but in the webtoon he is probably attracted to her at first sight; in contrast, in the drama where he initially dislikes her. In the webtoon, after getting fired from Jangga due to his son's beating of Jang Geun Won at school, the older Park opens a fried chicken restaurant. In the drama, he opens a pub. The vehicle that Jang Geun Won used and eventually hit and killed Mr. Park was changed from a scooter in the webtoon to a car in the drama. Therefore, the decisive evidence that Jang caused the accident changed from a decal on the scooter to the car's license plate number.

In addition, in the webtoon the name of the pub that Park Saeroyi opens in Itaewon is Kkulbam, which means Honey Night. In the drama, the pub is Danbam, meaning Sweet Night. Nevertheless, the English neon sign for Danbam implies Honey Night in the drama, not matching the pub's name in Korean. Last but not least, the scene where Park Saeroyi and Cho Yi-seo first meet changes. In the webtoon, they encounter each other for the first time at the site of the scooter accident. In the drama, they first meet in the third episode when Cho Yi-seo is slapped by the borough chief's wife. This scene from the drama is certainly intended to portray Cho Yi-seo as a victim and/or loser (as a sociopath).

One of the most significant distinctions between webtoons and dramas is the original soundtrack (OST). When television producers turn webtoons into dramas, they always insert a few music tracks to appeal to audiences. OSTs are not strangers to Korean dramas, as many Korean drama fans enjoy not only dramas but also their music. Global Hallyu fans also enjoy many OSTs, as they generally like both Korean dramas and K-pop. For example, *Mr. Sunshine*, which was aired on tvN in 2018, had fifteen songs, and many of these were very popular as the drama became a huge hit. Likewise, *Itaewon Class* featured fifteen songs, including

"Start" (performed by Gaho), "Still Fighting It" (Lee Chan Sol), "Maybe" (Sondia), "Stone Block" (Ha Hyun Woo), "Our Souls at Night" (Sondia), and "Sweet Night" (V, a member of BTS). Producers insert these tracks into specific scenes to further immerse audiences in the drama.

As an example, in episode twelve, Park Saeroyi recruits investors to open chain stores around the country. However, the lead investor cheats him, and it turns out that this investor was working with Jangga's CEO, who wanted Saeroyi to fail. His success is hanging by a thread, and Oh Soo-ah asks him to forget his struggle to get revenge by saying, "How about you just stop your revenge on Jangga? Forget the whole thing and come to me. Let's be happy." Just then Cho Yi-seo calls Saeroyi to apologize, as it was her idea to expand the business. However, Saeroyi says on the phone: "I made my decision . . . the reason I was able to get back on my feet [after previous ordeals] was because I wanted to get revenge. Until I achieve that, I will never be happy." He is responding to Cho Yi-seo's apology and Oh Soo-ah's request simultaneously. At this moment, Kim Feel's song "Someday, the Boy" plays. The song begins "Time has since raised me and tells me to step into the world now," and it ends "Years from now. . . . Would he have gotten all that he had ever dreamed of?"

Whenever Saeroyi remembers his past and reassures himself about the importance of getting revenge, the song "Someday, the Boy" is heard. Similarly, when he overcomes a challenge and wants to convey that he is getting a second chance, Gaho's "Start" plays, smoothly matching the scenes. "Start" portrays excitement, positivity, and courage. The lyrics say in part: "New beginnings are always exciting. Like I can overcome everything. I want to keep going forward." They also say "I don't want to lose myself again," which perfectly matches the scenes' emotions. Just as *Itaewon Class* increased in popularity as evidenced by viewer ratings, Gaho's "Start" made it to number 1 on the Melon chart (the largest music-ranking system in Korea) in March 2020. The song has also been popular in many other countries, including China and Vietnam (Kim, S. Y., 2020).

Regardless of these differences, the two versions of *Itaewon Class* have many similarities, in particular in their use of original ideas and the personalities of the major characters. When the first episode of the drama version was aired, many webtoon fans were pleased to see a familiar plot, and they believed that the rate of synchronization would be 99 percent, or almost perfect. Big-screen culture creators may either expand or simply adapt original webtoons in their productions. In other words, a transmedia adaptation sometimes involves extensions to the original story to attract new audiences, and sometimes it minimizes changes so that the adaptation appeals to fans of the original webtoon. The former frequently occurs because big-screen productions have different priorities than webtoons, which are centered on mobility, small screens, and snack culture.

In the recent tradition of webtoon-based transmedia storytelling, one can easily find negative responses from webtoon fans who are not satisfied with such modifications or expansions of webtoons, and they express their concerns in various ways. For example, in the case of *Cheese in the Trap*—a romance or drama webtoon written by Soonkki between 2010 and 2017 that was turned into a television drama in 2016 and a movie in 2018—many fans originally did not like the female protagonist in the drama because they did not believe that she could properly represent the webtoon's character. The webtoon focuses on the lives and relationships of a group of university students, especially the difficult relationship between Hong Seol (the female protagonist) and Yoo Jung. Fans fiercely complained about the casting of Kim Go-eun as Hong Seol. Many questioned her chemistry with the popular actor Park Hae Jin, who was cast as Yoo Jung. When *Cheese in the Trap* was released as a movie, Kim Go-eun was not considered for the role by the director regardless of her acting skill (Hong, C., 2016).

Unlike *Cheese in the Trap*, *Itaewon Class* was successfully modified into a drama and approved by fans of the original webtoon. The modification of some parts of the original webtoon text in the transformation to big-screen culture was unavoidable, due to the different priorities, structures, and styles of the two cultural forms. Such modifications and expansions are welcomed by many audiences. However, webtoon-based transmedia storytelling has experienced both praise and criticism based on the level of adaptation or expansion. Regardless of differences in critical reception, however, it is not uncommon to see both webtoons and big-screen cultural content based on webtoons achieve huge commercial success, which drives the continued growth of webtoon-based transmedia storytelling in the Korean cultural industries.

Webtoons' Transmedia Storytelling in Films: Along with the Gods

In addition to successful adaptations of webtoons for television dramas, there have been numerous successful adaptations for films. Since the late 2000s, about sixty webtoons have been adapted by film directors, and the number of webtoon-based films continues to grow. From *A.P.T.* (2006) to *Killed My Wife* (2019) to *Space Sweepers* (2021), many filmmakers have used webtoons as original content sources.

While there are many webtoon genres, film adaptations have mainly focused on a few of the most popular, including drama, romance, action, thriller, and fantasy (table 4.2). There are some discrepancies between webtoons and films in classifying which genre a particular story belongs to. For example, the genre of the webtoon *The Chase* (*Ban-deu-si Jab-neun-da*) is identified as *il-sang*, whereas the 2017 movie version was categorized as a thriller by the Korean Film Council (2020), since the movie industry does not use the term *il-sang* as a major genre. Likewise, the genre of the webtoon version of *Student A* is classified as *hagwon*[7] or *il-sang*, but the 2018 movie version is categorized as drama. Similarly, the genre of the webtoon *Ba:Bo* (2008) is *sunjeong*, but the film is classified as a drama.

Along with the Gods: The Two Worlds (released in December 2017) and *Along with the Gods: The Last 49 Days* (August 2018), developed from Joo Ho-min's webtoon, have been the two most successful webtoon-based movies. The webtoon was published on Naver Webtoon between January 2010 and August 2012. It was designed in three parts: "The Underworld," "The Living World," and "The Gods' World." As a mix of melodrama, action, humor, and fantasy, it provides a modern twist to Korean folklore about the afterlife. It has been one of the most popular webtoons, in terms of viewers' reception: whenever Joo published new episodes, thousands of viewers expressed their opinions and feelings on Naver. Big-screen creators such as film directors and television producers can evaluate the popularity of a webtoon based on the number of fans it has, which are also potential fans of webtoons turned into cultural products (Jin, D. Y., 2019a).

Directed by Kim Yong-hwa, the two movies based on the webtoon were blockbusters, with a combined production cost of $40 million (the

Table 4.2 Selected Webtoon-Based Films Released in 2006–2021

Year	Webtoon title	Webtoonist	Webtoon platform	Movie title	Director	Genre
2006	A.P.T.	Kang Full	Daum	A.P.T.	An Byung-ki	Thriller or horror
2008	Ba:Bo	Kang Full	Daum	Ba:Bo	Kim Jung-kwon	Drama
	Sunjeong Manhwa	Kang Full	Daum	Hello, Schoolgirl	Ryu Jang-ha	Melodrama or romance
2010	Ikki	Yoon Tae-ho	Daum	Moss	Kang Woo-suk	Drama
	Geudaeleul Salanghabnida	Kang Full	Daum	Late Blossom	Choo Chang-min	Drama
2012	26 Years	Kang Full	Daum	26 Years	Cho Geun-hyun	Action
	The Neighbors	Kang Full	Daum	The Neighbors	Kim Hwi	Thriller
2013	The Fives	Jung Yeon-sik	Daum	The Fives	Jeong Yeon-shik	Thriller
	Secretly, Greatly	Hun	Daum	Secretly, Greatly	Jang Cheol-soo	Action
2014	Gat Funeral	Hong Gakga	Daum	Cat Funeral	Lee Jong-hun	Melodrama or romance
	Fashion King	Gian 84	Naver	Fashion King	Oh Ki-hwan	Comedy

Year	Webtoon Title	Webtoonist	Platform	Adapted Title	Director	Genre
2015	Timing	Kang Full	Daum	Timing	Min Kyung-jo and Park Tae-yeol	Animation
	Inside Men	Yoon Tae-ho	Hankyoreh Shinmun	Inside Men	Woo Min-ho	Crime
2017	Ban-deu-si Jab-neun-da	Daum Webtoon and 18 webtoonists	Daum	The Chase	Kim Hong-sun	Thriller
	Cheese In the Trap	Soonkki	Naver	Cheese In the Trap	Kim Je-jeong	Melodrama or romance
	Steel Rain	Yang Woo-suk	Daum	Steel Rain	Yang Woo-suk	Action
	Along with the Gods	Joo Ho-min	Naver	Along with the Gods: The Two Worlds	Kim Yong-hwa	Fantasy
2018	Student A	Hur6Pa6	Naver	Student A	Lee Kung-sub	Drama
	0.0MHz	GangZ.ak	Daum	0.0MHz	You Sun-Dong	Thriller or horror
	Along tith the Gods	Joo Ho-min	Naver	Along with the Gods: The Last 49 Days	Kim Yong-hwa	Fantasy
2019	Sidong	Cho Kum-san	Daum	Start-Up	Choi Jeong-yeol	Drama
	Haechijianha	Hun	Daum	Secret Zoo	Son Jae-gon	Comedy
	Long Live the King	Budnamusup	KakaoPage	Long Live the King	Kang Yunsung	Action
	Anaereul Jukyessda	Hinari	Daum	Killed My Wife	Kim Ha-la	Thriller
2021	Seungriho	Hongjacga	Daum	Space Sweepers	Jo Sung-hee	Science fiction or action

Source: Compiled by author.

two films were produced at the same time). This compares to an average production cost (including marketing costs) for domestic commercial movies of just $4.6 million in 2016 and $9.7 million in 2017 (Korean Film Council, 2019). Both films became huge box office hits. When the first movie was released, it immediately became an enormous sensation. More than 14.4 million people watched it at theaters, generating one of the highest total domestic box office revenues: $115.7 million. The second film attracted more than 12.2 million moviegoers and earned $102.6 million (Korea Film Council, 2020). The first film has topped box office revenues in several other Asian countries, becoming the highest-grossing Korean film in Taiwan and the second-highest-grossing one in Hong Kong (Park, J. H., 2018).

While these two movies are closely connected, their major themes are different. The story of *Along with the Gods: The Two Worlds* is about a dead man who is guided through his life's sins by grim reapers. In the afterlife, souls must pass seven trials in forty-nine days before they can be reincarnated. Ja-hong (played by Cha Tae-hyun) is escorted through the seven gates of hell by three guardians of death or grim reapers: Gang-rim (Ha Jung-woo), Hewonmak (Ju Ji-hoon), and Deok-choon (Kim Hyang-gi). Ja-hong is believed to be a paragon, accounting for the first honorable death in forty-nine days, and the three guardians believe that he will not only excel during the trials but also benefit their own afterlives in the long run. When Ja-hong was killed in the line of duty, he became a candidate for reincarnation (fig. 4.3).

There are a few differences between the webtoon and movie versions, although the basic premise remains the same. First, the nature of the major characters and relevant plots were greatly changed. In the webtoon Ja-hong is an average salaryman who died of work-related alcohol abuse, but in the film he is a heroic firefighter, which makes him a more respectable character. Second, in the webtoon, the dead are all assigned defense attorneys for their various trials in front of the underworld's gods. In the webtoon, the lawyer Jin Gi-han was one of the most popular characters, trying to help Ja-hong pass the seven trials. In the movie, however, Ja-hong is guided by three grim reapers, as the director removed the character Jin Gi-han. When the movie trailer was released, many webtoon fans complained because there was no Jin Gi-han in the movie version. Director Kim explained in a media interview, "I like Jin Gi-han, who is a very attractive

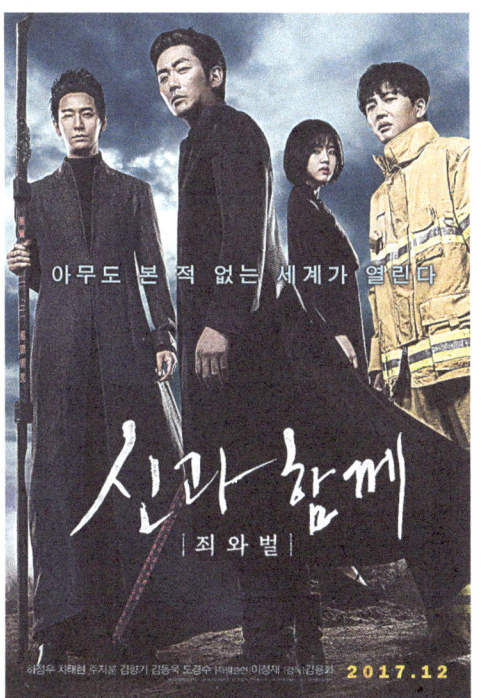 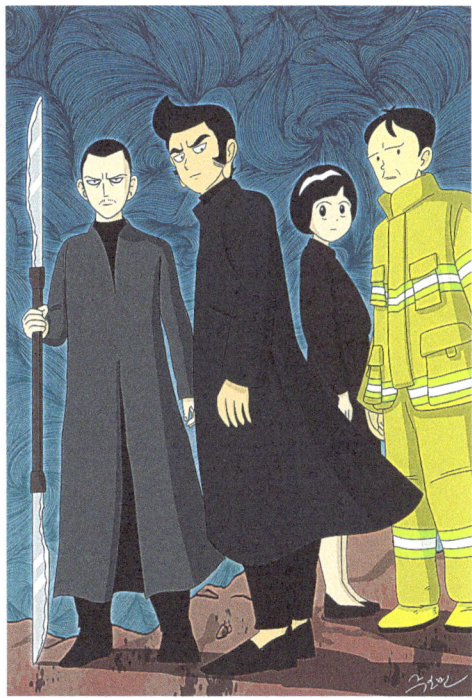

FIGURE 4.3   Movie and webtoon versions of *Along with the Gods*. (The webtoon-like image shown here is not from the webtoon itself but from the movie.) Source: Lotte Entertainment (movie version) and Naver Webtoon and Joo Ho-min (webtoon version).

character. I don't want to treat him lightly; however, when I have to explain that the underworld has a lawyer, it makes the plot more complicated than the elimination of the character. Within a period of two hours, it is not easy to include everything from the webtoon" (Cho, Y. K., 2018).

Third, the movie connects an unrelated subplot from the original story to the main plot of the movie by transforming a relationship among characters. A soldier who turns into an anger-filled lemur after dying as a result of an accident in the webtoon becomes in the film Ja-hong's younger brother, Su-hong (Kim Dong-wook), who unintentionally distracts Ja-hong from his trials in the underworld (Jin, M. J., 2017). Again, webtoon fans were not satisfied with these transformations, mainly because they worried about the loss of original tastes and themes. The transformations actually meant a shift in major themes, from justice in the webtoon to filial piety in the movie. When the director changed Ja-hong's occupation from an average salaryman to a righteous firefighter, he clearly wanted to make the movie as a maudlin tearjerker. Merely showing the sins committed by Ja-hong against his speech-impaired mother, who is portrayed as an angel with unconditional love for her son, is a powerful way to force tears out of the audience (Jin, M. J., 2017).

One such tear-inducing scene involves a flashback showing Ja-hong's plan to commit matricide to escape his struggles, but he was stopped by his brother, Su-hong, before he could kill his mother. The flashback reveals why Ja-hong desperately wants to see his mother again. During a dream that Ja-hong has, Ja-hong's and Su-hong's mother reveals that she never blamed either of them for their struggles, and Ja-hong attempts to embrace her but is unable to. This is one moment when audience members shed tears, as the director intended. Thus, the adaptation process implies the transformation of the original subject, theme, and genre to appeal to big-screen audiences. While these transformations are not always successful, big-screen creators always think about possible modifications to original sources to attract larger audiences.

The sequel, *Along with the Gods: The Last 49 Days*, does not exactly continue the saga. While part 1 dipped into the mythology of the death gods Gang-rim (Ha Jung-woo), Haewonmak (Ju Ji-hoon) and Deok-choon (Kim Hyang-gi), part 2 goes even further, combining the reapers' own quest for reincarnation with flashbacks to their past lives (Murray, 2018). In the sequel, the three reapers are about to gain new lives as promised by the king of Hades (the god of underworld) if they succeed in reincarnating one more person after forty-eight successful cases. However, things get complicated as Gang-rim seeks to give rebirth to Su-hong, who became a revengeful ghost after being killed in a military accident—which goes against the rules of the afterlife.

The king of Hades then gives the three reapers the task of fetching an old man—the grandfather of Dong Hyun, an elementary student—whom other reapers have repeatedly failed to bring in as he is guarded by the Seongju (house guardian) god in his home. The actor Ma Dong-seok plays a tender-hearted god who is strong enough to knock down multiple grim reapers in a single stroke but becomes helpless in front of humans. Haewonmak and Deok-choon come to visit the old man's house to carry out their mission and meet the Seongju god. They become curious about their past stories when the god claims that he knows the hidden past of the three grim reapers, who were human beings about a thousand years ago (Shim, S. A., 2018).

The film effortlessly weaves together the two main plots, each of which is set in both this world and the other, using a cross-cutting editing method. One plot revolves around Gang-rim as he tries to reincarnate Su-hong through multiple trials in the afterlife, and the other is centered on the Seongju god struggling to protect the old man, who is raising his orphaned grandson alone in a dilapidated hillside village facing urban redevelopment. Scenes from the past are seen in cross-cut flashbacks with the god as a narrator. The flashbacks provide important clues to understanding the whole two-part series, clarifying why the grim reapers had to wait a thousand years to be reincarnated and why Gang-rim, who is the defense lawyer at the trial, chose a troublesome man as possibly his last client (Shim, S. A., 2018).

There are many challenges and secrets along the way for each of the grim reapers to deal with. In tangling with the household god who protects the old man and his grandson, Haewonmak and Deok-choon recover lost memories from their lives in the tenth-century Goryeo Dynasty that realign their relationship to each other as well as to Gang-rim. Meanwhile, Gang-rim wrestles with his own demons, ancient fears, and hypocrisy, which the smart-mouthed former law student Su-hong is quick to point out. Whereas *The Two Worlds* had a destination it was clearly heading toward, *The Last 49 Days* seems more like a disconnected historical melodrama focusing on the grim reapers and their intertwined fates. At its core, "the first film was a simple, sentimental family drama about selflessness, morality and karma that unfolds in the here and now" (Kerr, 2018).

There are a variety of important differences between this second film and the webtoon version. First, in the webtoon "The Gods' World," which is the third part of the series, four gods protect a house: the Seongju god; Jowang (kitchen) god; Cheukshin (toilet) god; and Cheollyungshin (*shin* means God in Korean), who protects Jangdokdae, a terrace where *dok*, especially that containing *jang* (soy sauce), is stored in Korean mythology. However, in the movie, to simplify the plot, the Seongju god is the only one protecting the house. Second, in the webtoon, the grandfather dies before Dong Hyun graduates from elementary school. However, in the movie, with help from the Seongju god and the grim reapers, the grandfather lives to celebrate with his grandson, giving the story a happy ending. Third, in the webtoon, Dong Hyun's family is evacuated from their home due to an urban renewal plan. However, in the movie, the grandfather invests in a fund to keep his house from a loan shark and eventually protects the house. The first movie was criticized because of its tearjerker plot, and the second was criticized because it glamorized the dry and realistic webtoon story, converting it into an upbeat story with a happy ending to attract larger audiences.

Audiences generally understand that big-screen productions can't be the same as their sources, including webtoons. As Giovagnoli (2011) argues, in transmedia the original project's contents are available on different platforms without damaging or interfering with the original stories. Through transmedia storytelling, audiences feel that the original webtoons or novels and movies based on them have similar themes and subjects. However, once the original stories enter the transmedia storytelling process, it is inevitable that their content will be changed to appeal to different audiences. Franco (2015, 44–45) points out that "the transmedia practice contains both continuities and contrasts with the source text, with producers' perceptions of intended viewers' preferences." In this regard, Hills (2015) claims that modifying the original text is inevitable when developing it on another platform, due to narrative complexity. Webtoons such as *Itaewon Class* and *Along with the Gods* provide complicated epics, and cultural producers have to adjust the stories to accommodate different audiences, regardless of expected criticism by webtoon fans who are concerned about the distortion of original themes and subjects.

Webtoons' Transmediality as a Norm in the Cultural Industries

Many webtoons aptly portray various everyday realities that readers can easily identify with, and webtoons are easily adapted and transformed into other types of successful cultural content although they differ from other source materials, such as novels, manhwa, and animations. Webtoon-based transmedia have inevitably become a force in the culture industries and have greatly transformed cultural norms. The major emphases during the adaptation process are different for webtoons and other source materials due to a few distinctive characteristics of Korean society and cultural industries. Producing multiple texts through numerous media platforms adds value to a franchise, and fostering transmedia production is a response to transnationalization, both of which motivates audiences to collaborate on decoding various texts and images (Pamment, 2016; Pyo, Jang, and Yoon, 2019). This new trend shifts the structure of the contemporary webtoon ecosystem as well. Webtoons have greatly contributed to the growth of a new form of transmediality based on their unique characteristics, differentiating webtoon-based transmedia storytelling from previous types.

First and foremost, webtoons have begun to play a significant role in transmedia storytelling due in large part to their rich variety of fascinating stories, as well as their attractive visual images. The themes and genres of webtoons have rapidly evolved and diversified, drawing the attention of cultural creators who are thinking about using webtoons as sources for their cultural productions. In Korean cinema, for example, several movies released in recent years—such as *A Taxi Driver* (2017), *The Battleship Island* (2017), *I Can Speak* (2017), and *1987: When the Day Comes* (2017)—have emphasized the relationship between Korean films and a corrupt society (Jeong, M. A., 2017; Jin, D. Y., 2019b). However, filmmakers have had difficulties in finding source stories for such films, so they have turned their attention to webtoons—since webtoons often realistically depict various aspects of contemporary society or provide basic story lines that are generally not reflected in other materials.

Similarly, the movie *Along with the Gods* portrays serious sociocultural issues. The movie expanded on a story line surrounding an army accident that was not discussed in detail in the webtoon. Negative portrayals or press reports of accidents in the military are regularly suppressed by the Korean government. However, *Along with the Gods* detailed an incident involving Ja-hong, the main character, whose brother Su-hong had died during military service. During an investigation it was discovered that Lieutenant Park (played by Lee Joon Hyuk) had covered for Private Won Dong Yeon (Do Kyung Soo), who had accidentally shot Su-hong, and the two men had buried Su-hong, unknowingly while he was still alive, to hide his mistake. Rather than investigate the incident, the military simply reported Su-hong as missing in action. Such incidents are almost never properly investigated because the media cannot easily access information about the army. As a result, many Koreans believe that the army most likely regularly hides accidents like the one portrayed in *Along with the Gods*. This scene presents a potential truth that is rarely discussed in Korean society. The expansion in the movie of this story line from its version in the original webtoon showcases the potential validity of webtoons in cultural production.

Second, webtoon-based transmediality exhibits unique characteristics, in particular in relation to the modification process. Many webtoonists post their stories every week for years, which means that their webtoons must compelling both as short daily or weekly episodes and also as extended stories. In contrast, most films start a bit slowly and build gradually toward a climax. Thus, the dramatic structure of a big-screen product is often dissimilar to that of the original webtoon. Therefore, in some cases the adaptation of a webtoon to big-screen culture fails (Seo, B. G., 2015).

Dissimilarity is not unusual, and cultural creators have often skillfully modified original stories for their own cultural genres. As J. H. Park, Lee, and Lee (2019, 2184) point out, each cultural form "needs to be self-contained. This entails that a story introduced to different media—films, TV, video games, comics, and novels—provides viewers with different entry points into the story world in a way that each medium can be enjoyed separately." Here "central to transmedia storytelling is the expansion of the story world" (2191), and webtoon-based big-screen cultural products have achieved huge successes as they modify and expand, instead of sticking to, original stories. As Jenkins (2011) argues, "basically, an adaptation takes the same story from one medium and retells it in another. An extension seeks to add something to the existing story as it moves from one medium to another. . . . Any adaptation represents an interpretation of the work in question and not simply a reproduction, so all adaptions to some degree add to the range of meanings attached to a story." Webtoon-based transmediality is not always successful in the Korean cultural industries. However, cultural creators have focused more on potential than on risks in the modification of webtoons.

Third, webtoons' emphasis on cultural authenticity differentiates them from other sources that are available transmedially. As *Itaewon Class* and *Along with the Gods* clearly indicate, many webtoons represent Korean mentality and identity and are embedded in history and contemporary society. This is not always beneficial in transmedia storytelling, in particular in transnational cases. The cultural characteristics of Korean webtoons are sometimes so pervasive that it is hard for them to become popular in foreign markets beyond the Korean sphere. For example, *Misaeng* enjoyed nationwide success in 2014. But when the drama was exported to six countries, including China and the United States, its story of competition in the modern workplace and the scarcity of jobs did not resonate with foreign audiences as it did with Koreans. Some media critics have suggested that Korean webtoons have to create stories encompassing more universal topics, such as superheroes, fantasy, and fairy tales, which are frequently seen in Japanese anime used as sources for transmedia storytelling. However, cultural specificity in webtoons may be essential to their continued acclaim as both a unique cultural form and a source for transmedia storytelling within Korea (Doo, 2017). It is important to have cultural differentiation in adapted cultural products in order to appeal to foreign markets, and many webtoon platforms develop hybridity as a way to penetrate markets in other countries. However, it is clear that webtoon-based transmedia storytelling relies on inimitable stories that portray dynamic aspects of Korean society. Thus, it's necessary for both webtoonists and other cultural creators to acknowledge the significance of their work having local identities and authenticity.

Last but not least, television dramas and films filled with computer-generated imagery are being established as a new part of transmedia storytelling in the local cultural industry. *Along with the Gods: The Two Worlds* has as many as 2,300 shots with visual effects (Kim, S. H., 2017). As I mentioned above, $40 million was used on the production of the two *Along with the Gods* films, and about $15 million of that was used for computer-generated imagery (Lee, H. I., 2018). Given that Korean cinema has rapidly adopted the use of computer-generated special effects and that webtoons provide visual images, creators of big-screen culture can easily envision the transformation of webtoons into new cultural content with various special effects. As Scolari (2009, 589) points out, transmedia storytelling "not only affects the text but also includes transformations in the production and consumption processes," and producers "visualize new business opportunities for the media market as new generations of consumers develop the skills to deal with the flow of stories and become hunters of information from multiple sources." Due to their vivid visual images, webtoons are optimal sources for transmedia storytelling that emphasizes special effects.

In sum, webtoons have created new forms of such storytelling with diverse content to appeal to various tastes. Due to webtoons' rich visual images and texts, as well as their diverse themes and genres, cultural creators in the entertainment industries have attempted to transform webtoons into other cultural forms. Korean society has rapidly shifted since the late 1990s due to numerous political, economic, cultural, and technological transformations. This society is a treasure trove for webtoons, which "emerged in the context of the socio-cultural characteristics of Korea" (Jang, W. H., and Song, 2017, 179; see also Korea.com, 2016), and now webtoons act as primary sources for big-screen content. Webtoon-based transmedia storytelling has become the norm in the global cultural industries, and the adaptation process shifts major resources from Japanese manga, anime, and Korean webtoons to other cultural products while providing creative and converging ideas. Without a doubt, the adaptation and transmediation of webtoons in the cultural industries will increase.

Conclusion

This chapter has analyzed webtoon-based transmedia storytelling as a new cultural trend in the early twenty-first century. I discussed webtoons as a vehicle for transmedia storytelling in the Korean cultural industries and global cultural markets, including OTT services like Netflix. Based on the many young people who have become die-hard fans of well-made webtoons and webtoonists, the Korean webtoon sector and digital portals such as KakaoPage and Naver have developed unique strategies for using webtoons as primary sources for various cultural products, such as film, games, musicals, and television dramas.

As many webtoon stories are amusing and fresh and now sometimes even have sound and special effects as well as visual images, the adaptation of webtoons has been increasingly popular. As Stavroula (2014) points out, webtoons, which are at the convergence of digital technologies and digital content, have created new forms of stories. Cultural creators such as television producers and film directors are eager to commercialize and commodify webtoons through their transformation into big-screen cultural products (Nam, Y. J., 2020).

Undoubtedly, a few critical issues and even dangers arise in the current form of Korean transmedia storytelling, as has occurred with transmedia storytelling based on Japanese manga (for more on the media mix in Japan, see Steinberg, 2012). Problem areas in Korea include the commodification of webtoons and webtoonists, webtoons' loss of originality during the adaptation process, and the market dominance of a few mega portals (see chapter 2). The convergence of different media platforms ensures a closer relationship or even interdependency among different cultural sectors. However, "such a convergence of different media industries can undermine the autonomy of each different company, industry, or other social agents, resulting in the conscious avoidance of controversial issues" (Suzuki, 2019, 2208). Webtoons used to function as an outlet for diverse and even alternative voices, in contrast to mainstream media or large media corporations, which often hesitate to address certain controversial issues. However, as big television channels and film companies work to strategically modify content related to sensitive issues, webtoons turned into cultural content may lose their ability to depict or discuss delicate and controversial themes.

Meanwhile, current transmedia storytelling strategies led by digital platforms "tend to reduce or disregard narrativity by prioritizing characters, instead producing their characters as nonnarrative media forms (i.e., illustrations or designs) or commodities (i.e., character merchandise)" (Suzuki, 2019, 2209). Such an orientation in current transmedia storytelling can undercut or attenuate social critiques or political commentary that would have previously appeared in the narratives (not the characters) of webtoons (Suzuki, 2019).

Webtoon-based transmedia storytelling is not a fad: it will become a new norm in the global cultural scene. Webtoon-based big-screen cultural production will continue both nationally and globally, as long as webtoons continue to represent the shifting nature of our rapidly changing contemporary society. How to retain webtoons' originality in the adaptation process and avoid drastic commodification of original stories will be key issues in the further growth of webtoon-based Korean transmedia storytelling.

CHAPTER 5

Webtoons' Transnational Transmediality

Over the past two decades, Korean popular culture has become popular globally. A handful of cultural forms (including television dramas, films, and K-pop) continue to expand their global reach. As the success of the musical groups BTS and Blackpink, *Parasite* (which won four Oscars in 2020), and *Squid Game* (which was globally popular on Netflix in the fall 2021) prove, Korean popular culture is increasingly recognized by and attractive to many global audiences. The Korean Wave has continued to develop new cultural forms and digital culture, illustrating the continuous growth of Korean cultural content in the global scene.

Again, the webtoon sector is a relatively lesser-known industry, compared to other cultural sectors like K-pop, film, and dramas, given the influence of the Korean Wave in global cultural markets. However, as cultural content increasingly crosses national borders and is disseminated to diverse locations around the globe—primarily due to soaring rates of online transmissions (e.g., the use of social media and streaming services) as well as widespread international fan bases (Ju, 2019)—the global acceptance of webtoons has suddenly increased. While there are a variety of reasons for the increasing global attention to webtoons, one can argue that the adoption of Korean webtoons by the global cultural industries has been made possible partially, if not entirely, by the Korean Wave. Many foreign audiences already enjoy Korean cultural content, which lowers the barriers to accessing other local-based forms of popular or digital culture.

Unlike other cultural sectors such as television programs and films (which mainly export finished materials), webtoons are primarily digital content (which can be read on smartphones and apps in many parts of the world). Webtoon platforms, including Naver Webtoon, KakaoPage, and Daum Webtoon, have advanced their globalization strategies and developed smartphone apps for webtoon consumption. Webtoons have penetrated global cultural markets in both their original form and as sources for transmedia storytelling, and they have become a large part of Hallyu in the early twenty-first century.

This chapter investigates webtoons' global reach. I discuss the distinctive forms of webtoon Hallyu as a significant component of the New Korean Wave—the global penetration of Korean popular culture and digital technologies driven by K-pop, mobile gaming, and webtoon starting in the late 2000s. I also investigate webtoon-based transnational transmedia by mapping the ways in which webtoons become big-screen culture for global OTT service platforms as a new trend in the Korean Wave. Then, by discussing the tensions between hybridity and cultural specificity relevant to webtoons, I analyze the power relationships between local identities and glocalization strategies in global cultural markets. Through these discussions, I identify various major implications of the growth of webtoon Hallyu in contemporary cultural industries and provide insights on new norms in the Korean Wave.

Transnationalization of Webtoons

The transnationalization of popular culture and digital culture has grown continuously in recent years. Although a few Western countries have played major roles in cultural flows beyond their national boundaries due to their economic, technological, and cultural power, a handful of countries in the Global South have also increased their influence in the global cultural markets. Among these, Korea has substantially developed the transnationalization—a term referring to "a condition by which people, commodities, and ideas literally cross—transgress—national boundaries and are not identified with a single place of origin" (Watson, 2006, 11)—of local popular culture and digital technologies as cultural products such as television dramas, K-pop, and films. The Korean Wave is going global in a big way, and many of its fans in other countries enjoy various forms of Korean cultural content, including webtoons.

The Korean Wave arguably began in the mid-1990s, when Korean television programs and films became popular elsewhere in East Asia. While China, Japan, and Taiwan have continued to import and enjoy large quantities of Korean cultural products, the Korean Wave has continued to transform itself as a recognizable transnational force since the late 2000s (Kim, Y. A., 2013; Ju, 2019; Jin, D. Y., Yoon, and Min, 2021). Unlike during the early stage of Hallyu (when just a few cultural forms, such as television dramas and films, were major cultural drivers), in the new stage of Hallyu (known as the New Korean Wave [Jin, D. Y., 2016] or Hallyu 2.0 [Lee, S. J., and Nornes, 2015]) other forms of cultural content have advanced, including popular music (K-pop), webtoons, and digital games as well as digital technologies (e.g., smartphones).

While numerous factors drive transnationalization in popular culture, quite a few scholars (e.g., Iwabuchi, 2002; Kraidy, 2005; Lee, H. J., 2018) consider hybridity to be the major factor in the growth of transnationalization. The recent global reach of webtoons can be compared to the global circulation of Japanese manga or anime, which experienced the transnationalization process in global comics markets before Korean webtoons did. Thus, it's interesting to review the use of hybridity in the Japanese manga or anime industry so that we can compare it with the appropriation of hybridity in the Korean webtoon sector.

As H. J. Lee (2018, 366) points out, research on the transnational circulation and reception of Japanese manga or anime "has focused on the complex ways it is distributed and consumed, especially on how the hybridization of familiarity and difference is an essential aspect of its global appeal and reception." A handful of scholars (e.g., Iwabuchi, 2002; Bryce et al., 2010) argue that the global reach of Japanese manga or anime derives from their ability to mix universal story themes with other elements. These scholars especially highlight how Japanese culture develops nationless cultural content, known as "odorless culture" (Iwabuchi, 2002) and "no distinct culture, including an unnamed or unrecognizable setting" (Bryce et al., 2010), to increase a sense of familiarity and the potential to connect with global audiences. For Japanese cultural creators, the development of nationless anime or manga involves the "erasure of nationality or cultural specificity in the complex process of global distribution and reception [which] makes [Japanese popular culture] more attractive and acceptable for Western viewers by blurring the boundaries between what is foreign and local" (Lee, H. J., 2018, 366). Japanese cultural creators have depoliticized popular culture, including anime, and erased Japanese cultural identity to attract global audiences through the hybridization process.

However, as Pellitteri (2010, 120) points out, "certain Japanese features in the art and themes of anime and manga are inevitable.... [They are] Japanese in their appearance and themes, i.e., in all of those in which the names, landscapes, customs, and habits of the characters are evidently of Japanese origin." Despite the modifications made to Japanese works when they enter non-Japanese markets, the culturally specific elements (such as the clothing or behavior of characters, the setting, and the themes and messages of the narratives) incorporated into such works cannot be completely removed in the cross-cultural communication process, and these elements make the Japaneseness of the work obvious (Bryce et al., 2010; Pellitteri, 2010). Napier (2007) also demonstrates that a connection to Japan is an important part of the appeal of manga and anime for some consumers.

In the field of webtoons, as A. G. Shim and co-authors (2020, 844–845) aptly put it, globalization becomes an even more powerful force since webtoon content can deliver values and traditions embedded in Korea "through advanced technology, mature storytelling techniques and sophisticated visual styles." As I have discussed elsewhere (Jin, D. Y., 2016, 14–15), hybridization is strategically embedded in cultural politics because it not only aims for a mix of text, image, and sound to neutralize cultural products but is also related to cultural policy, the division of cultural labor, and the structure of power disparity. Hybridity implies power relations between Western and non-Western states, which results in the appropriation of global goods and services by local forces to create borderless cultural goods to attract global audiences. In this sense, hybridity can be thought of as the politicization of local culture. As a digital culture representing Hallyu, webtoons are especially culturally political because Korean popular culture portrays significant national mentalities and identities. Instead of disguising cultural identity or local specificity—that is, depoliticizing popular culture—Korean webtoons and the Korean

Wave in general have developed popular culture driven by local actors and containing local culture, which implies the politicization of culture. Therefore, the analysis of hybridity in the webtoon scene needs to pay careful attention not only to textual mixing but also to cultural politics. Several of the theoreticians mentioned above have mainly focused on the celebration of cultural mixture in hybridity discourse. However, the range of hybridity must be extended and discussed more broadly.

Webtoons as New Digital Hallyu in the Early Twenty-First Century

The visibility of the webtoon as part of the Hallyu phenomenon has rapidly increased in global cultural markets. The recent Hallyu trend is closely related to the development of digital technologies, and webtoons are an effective digital cultural product because of the convergence of digital technology and popular culture (Yecies et al., 2019; Jin, D. Y., Yoon, and Min, 2021). Webtoons have increased the number of global fans of Korean popular culture, as they target younger generations compared to traditional cultural products such as television programs and films. Until the late 2000s, global audiences needed to purchase CDs, cassette tapes, or DVDs or go to theaters or concerts to enjoy Korean cultural content. However, people can now enjoy music on various streaming platforms and access most webtoons on digital platforms and apps (Jin, D. Y., and Yoon, 2016).

The transnationalization of webtoons started in 2012, when Tapas Media, a webtoon syndicate, opened its Korean-style webtoon service platform in the United States. Originally, in tandem with Daum Kakao, the company recruited 1,200 designers and authors and translated fifty-two Korean webtoons for US users (Kang, T. J., 2014). Due to cultural differences between Korea and the United States, Tapas Media mainly published the most popular genre webtoons instead of *byung-mak*[1] and *il-sang* genre webtoons, since most Americans did not fully understand local-focused webtoon content (Hwang, J.H., 2010; Ministry of Science and ICT, 2017). Also in 2012, some cartoonists and webtoon companies established studios in the United States to attract foreign investment while expanding their markets. KOMACON, which supports and promotes Korean comics and animation, selected six emerging comic artists via a national competition and sent them to Los Angeles to work with US editors and creative teams. The agency further agreed to financially support appropriate collaborations between K-Studio and US companies, studios, or creators (K-Studio, 2012).

Ever since that time, webtoons have continued to grow in terms of the market share of Korean webtoons in global manhwa markets. As can be seen in table 5.1, Korea has increased its export of cultural products, including broadcasts, films, animation styles, music, and manhwa, since the late 2000s. K-pop and manhwa have led the New Korean Wave. Between 2010 and 2020, the export of K-pop increased by as much as 8.47 times, followed by manhwa (7.9 times), films (2.95 times), broadcasts (2.63 times), and animation (1.26 times). Exports of manhwa in 2020 earned $64.8 million, compared to $54.1 million for films, demonstrating that the manhwa industry has become one of Korea's major cultural industries and that currently manhwa is one of the most exported of Korean cultural forms (Ministry of Culture, Sports and Tourism, 2019 and 2020; Korea Creative Content Agency, 2019c and 2021; Won, 2020). It is not easy to determine the proportion of webtoons in global circulation in the manhwa sector. However, it is certain that webtoons are rapidly increasing their presence in global cultural markets, as they have been the most significant product in the manhwa sector in recent years.

The major regions to which products of the manhwa industry, including webtoons, have been exported have been diversified in recent years. When Korea exported $40.5 million worth of manhwa in 2018, the largest market was Europe (29.5 percent), followed by Japan (28.6 percent), Southeast Asia (20.4 percent), North America (13.1 percent), and China (6.1 percent). This contrasts with other Korean cultural industries, which mainly target the rest of East Asia and North America. Korean manhwa reach not only Asian markets but also North American and European markets. In fact, the manhwa industry is the only sector of Korean popular culture for which Europe is the largest market. Graphic novels are most popular in the European market, while people in Southeast Asia and Japan mainly enjoy webtoons. Japan, Indonesia, and Thailand each have huge webtoon fan bases (Ministry of Culture, Sports and Tourism, 2019 and 2020).

Table 5.1 Exports of Korean Cultural Products, 2010–2020, in Millions of Dollars

	2010	2011	2012	2013	2014	2015	2016	2017	2018	2019	2020
Broadcasts	184.7	222.4	233.8	309.4	336.0	320.0	411.2	362.0	478.4	474.3	486.9
Films	13.6	15.8	20.1	35.0	26.3	29.3	43.8	40.7	41.6	37.8	54.1
Animation	96.8	115.9	112.5	109.8	115.0	126.5	135.6	144.8	174.0	174.5	122.2
Music	81.3	196.1	235.1	277.3	335.0	381.0	442.5	512.5	564.2	756.0	688.9
Manhwa	8.2	17.2	17.1	20.9	25.0	29.3	32.4	35.2	40.5	46.0	64.8

Source: Ministry of Culture, Sports and Tourism (2014a, 2014b, 2019, and 2020); Korea Creative Content Agency (2019a and 2021).

Some foreign countries (including France, Japan, Vietnam, and Indonesia) have introduced the Korean webtoon model into their own comics industries, creating similar or new styles of webtoons. For example, as webtoons became more familiar and were received favorably in France, a new domestic comic company called Delitoon was started in 2009, influenced by the Korean webtoon sector. In the beginning, Delitoon's main product was scanned comic books rather than pure webtoons. However, the company has developed webtoon-style comics that it calls French webtoons. Since 2015, Delitoon has provided forty Korean webtoons and three webtoons produced by local creators (Kim, M. H., 2016; Jang, W. H., and Song, 2017). In Japan, since 2013 NHN Entertainment and Lezhin Comics have produced localized webtoons created by domestic webtoonists. Some of these webtoons that became popular have been reproduced as either books or animations and then exported to other countries. For instance, the webtoon *ReLife* was developed by the Japanese creator So Yayoi and reproduced as a television anime. *ReLife* is Japanese manga series in webtoon format, reflecting the influence of Korean webtoons on Japanese manga (Hong, J. M., 2017; Jang, W. H., and Song, 2017).

More importantly, it's crucial to acknowledge the significant role of webtoon platforms in the development of global cultural markets. The expansion of Korean webtoons' global reach began with its two major webtoon platforms, Naver and Daum (now Kakao). Naver started to upload webtoons in English and Chinese in July 2013. Daum Webtoon launched its global service in January 2014 through the US-based Tapas Media (Jang, W. H., and Song, 2017).

Naver, Kakao, and Lezhin Comics all started to develop globalization strategies in the early 2010s (Han, C. W., 2015), and they continue to diversify their transnationalization models. Popular webtoons are now being offered in local languages in many countries on the internet and mobile platforms. For example, Naver now provides webtoons in a variety of languages, including English, Chinese, Taiwanese, Thai, and Indonesian. It uploads Chinese-language webtoons through Line, its instant mobile messenger located in Japan.

Due to these platforms' efforts, Korean webtoons have rapidly penetrated foreign countries. As of December 2018, 2,198 Korean webtoons had been published in foreign countries (see table 5.2). By language, 645

Table 5.2 Webtoons in the Global Markets in December 2018, by Selected Platforms

Platform	Languages	Webtoons	Total
Line Webtoon	Chinese (simplified)	335	1,303
	Chinese (traditional)	329	
	English	263	
	Indonesian	192	
	Thai	184	
Lezhin Comics	English	219	533
	Japanese	314	
Toomics	Chinese (simplified)	49	184
	Chinese (traditional)	48	
	English	87	
Piccoma	Japanese	102	102
Tappytoon	English	76	76
Total		2,198	2,198

Source: Korea Creative Content Agency (2019b).

Korean webtoons were published in English (29.3 percent), 416 in Japanese (18.9 percent), 384 in simplified Chinese characters (mainly for readers in the People's Republic of China and Singapore; 17.4 percent), 377 in traditional Chinese characters (mainly for those in Taiwan, Hong Kong, and the Chinese diaspora; 17.1 percent), 192 in Indonesian (8.7 percent), and 184 in Thailand (8.4 percent) (Korea Creative Content Agency, 2019b).

In North America, Naver Webtoon's performance with Generation Z readers is already impressive. In the case of Line Webtoon, users under the age of twenty-four make up about 75 percent of total users. The Line Webtoon app ranked fourth among the iOS entertainment apps used by teenagers and people in their twenties. According to J. H. Park (2020), "Naver Webtoon has broadened the spectrum of new entertainment content and provided new opportunities to amateur artists worldwide," helping rapidly turn webtoons into a major portion of the Korean Wave. In the United States alone, the number of Line Webtoon's monthly active users surpassed ten million in November 2019, nearly doubling since 2014.

Line Webtoon recorded sixty million such users in the global market, who collectively brought the company about 600 billion won ($519 million) in content transactions in 2020 (Chung, J. W., 2020).

As Korean manhwa have increasingly become sources of original content for Hollywood movies, webtoonists have used localization strategies to target not only the webcomic market but also the movie and drama markets. In a study of Korean webtoons in the Chinese market, Yecies (2018, 123) points out that webtoons are "a key energizer of Korea's ever-expanding popular culture wave, and a significant content sector in the global online and mobile media/entertainment platform environment." Naver Webtoon and Daum Webtoon (KakaoPage) have clearly driven the growth of webtoon Hallyu in many parts of the globe.

The global successes of Korean webtoon platforms in Japan and the United States are especially meaningful because these two countries are the leaders of the global comics market. Korean platforms have dominated the webtoon market by moving paper comics to digital media and introducing scroll-based and mobile-optimized webtoons. There are a number of successful webtoons in the global markets. For example, Naver Webtoon's *True Beauty* (*sunjeong*, romance) by Yaongyi ranked second in terms of number of views on Line Webtoon in the United States in November 2019. Naver Webtoon's *Tower of God* (fantasy), which was released as a Korea-US-Japan joint anime on April 1, 2020, topped Reddit's weekly animation ranking. Since both the US and Japanese comics markets rely on traditional publishing, the Korean webtoon industry has had a chance to enter the digital comics market, and Korean webtoon platforms play a pivotal role in attracting members of the digital generations to the webtoon market (Park, M. J., 2020a). Marvel Comics produces comics mainly in the superhero genre, but Korean webtoons emphasize niche markets, such as romance and melodrama genres consumed as a form of snack culture (KOMACON, 2018a).

Japanese manga have been very popular among Japanese youth, and it might seem difficult for Korean webtoons to gain a significant audience in Japan. However, Korean webtoons have been relatively well received by digital netizens in Japan. For example, *Solo Leveling*, a Kakao-Page webtoon in the fantasy genre that was adapted from a Korean novel and is written by Chu Gong, is available on Piccoma. *Solo Leveling*, published in Japan since March 2019, has more than a million cumulative readers and was named the number one webtoon of 2019 on Piccoma (Park, M. J., 2020a). Piccoma has effectively developed structural hybridization strategies in that it recruits Japanese as well as Korean artists. About 70 percent of the webtoons that it publishes are created by Japanese artists, which provides local content for Japanese youth (KOMACON, 2018).

In Japan, webtoons—unlike Japanese manga, which in most cases are first marketed for a print audience and later promoted online on apps—"cater to digital device users from the get-go: Their format has already been optimized for personal computers and smartphones" (Osaki, 2019). Once webtoons spread on popular manga apps, Korean webtoons immediately attracted a Japanese youth following. Line Manga, launched by the messaging giant Line Corp. (a subsidiary of Naver, the Korean platform giant), boasted some twenty-three million users domestically in May 2019 and was the largest comic-reading app in Japan in terms of the number of users, providing access to a host of Japanese titles that had originally appeared in print. But driving the popularity of this mega app have been two Korean webtoons, *True Beauty* and *Lookism*—which collectively dominated the top two spots in the monthly subscriber ranking over a span of six months in 2019. Although some Japanese manga artists have considered shifting their format,[2] it is not an easy task since manga are designed to be read in physical print formats and therefore are not optimized for use on smartphones. Indeed, many manga are hard to read digitally because their letters are too small for smartphones (Osaki, 2019).[3] Mobile games in the United States, such as *The God of High School* (2011–present; action), *Tower of God* (2010–present; action and dark fantasy), and *Noblesse* (*Nobeulleseu*, 2007–2009; action and mystery) are also based on Korean webtoons.

Webtoons have been able to penetrate both the Global South and the Global North partially due to Hallyu's solid popularity. Therefore, webtoonists and webtoons are indebted to broader Hallyu cultural content. The webtoon has great potential as digital content in the global comics markets, and the number of webtoon viewers in the world is increasing quickly. Due to the recent penetration of Hallyu in the Global North, many North Americans and Europeans are familiar with K-pop and Korean cinema, which makes webtoons increasingly appealing to people in those regions.

Webtoons' Transnational Transmediality in the Global Cultural Sphere

Webtoons have increased their global presence as cultural products, and they play a key role in constructing transnational transmedia storytelling. Webtoon-based transnational transmedia are still in their infancy, but this IP-driven global penetration has rapidly increased. Webtoons are not only selling cultural content as weekly or finished products, but they are also providing original sources for global cultural creators, including OTT service platforms. The collaboration between the Korean cultural industries and Netflix (as well as other global OTT platforms) has driven the creation of a new form of Hallyu, since Netflix circulates Korean cultural content to global audiences simultaneously on a large scale (Kim, M. R, 2020). Netflix acknowledges that many people around the world enjoy Korean popular culture. In the United States, Korean dramas are watched predominantly through streaming sites such as Netflix and YouTube (Ju, 2019), and recently webtoons have provided new source materials to Netflix.

Netflix has developed IP-driven transmedia storytelling based on webtoons. *Kingdom* is the first program that Netflix funded and produced through local cultural creators. Based on the webtoon production company YLAB's webtoon series *Land of the Gods,* which was published in 2014 by Kim Eun-hee in her debut as a webtoon series writer and drawn by Yang Kyung Il, *Kingdom* and its original webtoon uniquely combine the social structure and politics of the Joseon Dynasty and the modern concept of zombies. The story was inspired by the *Annals of the Joseon Dynasty*, a record of Korean state affairs from 1413 to 1865. The *Annals* described tens of thousands of people who died of a mysterious illness, and Kim decided to reinvent the plague as a zombie virus (MacDonald, 2020). The story revolves around a Joseon Dynasty crown prince's investigation of an unknown epidemic that threatens the entire country. When Kim first conceived the story behind *Kingdom*, she did not see it as a television script. Instead, she conveyed the story in the 2015 webcomic *Burning Hell Shinui Nara* (*Land of the Gods*). When Netflix established its Korean subsidiary company in June 2019, one of its first major projects was *Kingdom* after staff members in the Seoul office visited Kim and inquired about its potential as a live action drama (Lee, M. A., 2019).[4] *Kingdom* became Netflix's first original Korean television series, with the first six-episode season airing in 2019 and the second in March 2020 (MacDonald, 2020).

At the start of *Kingdom*, the king has collapsed, and rumors of his death are spreading. The rumors are only half true: although the king did die, he returned as one of the undead—transformed into a monster. To protect their own power, the queen (played by Kim Hye-jun) and her father, Chief State Councilor Cho Hak-Ju (Ryu Seung-ryong), lock the king in his royal chambers and refuse to let anyone see him. That includes his son, the crown prince (Ju Ji-hoon). The prince is sent on a mission to discover the cause of a deadly plague spreading across the country. The prince's suspicions about the cause of the plague make him an even greater threat to those who would keep him from the throne. Not only do those in power want to kill him, but in their efforts to consolidate power, they ignore the hordes of zombies roaming the countryside. *Kingdom* follows the prince as he tries to unveil the evil scheme and save the people, who are being tormented by the strange plague (Jin, M. J., 2019).

Interestingly, unlike most other webtoons turned into big-screen culture, there is not a lot of commonality between the webtoon and the Netflix series. However, *Kingdom* has managed to attract hundreds of thousands of global viewers. When creating the zombies in her webtoon and drama, Kim Eun-hee saw a parallel between hungry people driven to desperation and the ravenous undead. As gruesome as the zombies seem, the plague is not the real villain in this drama: instead, the villains are those motivated by greed and the lust for power. At a press conference held in Seoul in January 2019, Kim said: "That period in history was grim, and people were treated unfairly by those with authority through taxes they had to pay. I wanted to depict that hungry and ragged period through the zombies" (quoted in Jin, M. J., 2019). In season 2 of *Kingdom*, the numbers of zombies grow, and they begin to upset the stratified Joseon society (MacDonald, 2020). Interestingly, the plot of *Kingdom* is comparable to contemporary society's crisis due to COVID-19, which began in late 2019. While people were encouraged to stay at home to prevent further spread of the virus, many tuned into various popular media depicting pandemic-like situations, including *Kingdom,* as Kain wrote in a March 2020 *Forbes* article:

It was actually kind of strange watching this show as fears surrounding COVID-19 . . . began to mount. Hearing news stories of the new virus spreading from China to Korea to Italy and then to . . . [ellipsis points in the original] everywhere, while watching a show about the start of a zombie pandemic was almost surreal. . . . [W]atching the very excellent *Kingdom* on Netflix is really an experience right now. Without spoiling the details, you see the start of the zombie pandemic and the desperate fight to prevent its spread, sort of like the beginning of *Fear the Walking Dead* but much, much better. In a weird way, it will make you glad that COVID-19 is just a bad virus and not the start of a zombie apocalypse. Not yet at least. Silver linings and all that (Kain, 2020).

When season 2 of *Kingdom* began to air in March 2020, it was the top-ranked show on Netflix in many countries—including Singapore, the Philippines, Thailand, Hong Kong, and Korea (Ryoo, 2020). Netflix released a ninety-two-minute special episode, titled *Kingdom: Ashin of the North*, in 2021 and is expected to release a third season of the drama. *Kingdom*'s success reflects how webtoons as an IP engine have greatly developed transnational transmedia, becoming one of the main parts of the Korean Wave. Netflix's adoption of a Korean webtoon to create *Kingdom* represents the expansion of an original story to fit with a new platform's unique features. In this light, transmedia storytelling conducted by Netflix includes not only plot but also characters and visual images. Netflix emphasized the necessity of expanding the original plot and visual images to develop cultural content that was adapted from the original story and expanded to emphasize visual attributes (Steinberg, 2012; Scolari, 2017).

Netflix has continued to develop webtoon-based transnational cultural adaptations, and as a result, the form of Hallyu in the entertainment sector has changed greatly. In the first half of 2020, Netflix announced that it would produce a new Netflix original series titled *All of Us Are Dead* and written by Chun Sung-il (Kang, M. J., 2020). *All of Us Are Dead* features a group of high school students who are faced with an extreme crisis when they become trapped in their school, while a zombie virus spreads like wildfire. It is based on a famous webtoon *Now at Our School* (*Jigeum Woori Hakkyoneun*), written by Joo Dong-Geun, which has been well-received in Indonesia, Thailand, and Taiwan as well as in Korea. Following in the footsteps of Netflix's popular *Kingdom*, *All of Us*

Are Dead became another exciting Korean zombie genre series, which was released in early 2022. *All of Us Are Dead* was made by Film Monster by JTB Studio and held the top position for several weeks in terms of the number of viewers upon its release on Netflix in January–February 2022 (Yonhap News, 2022).

Waller (2020) writes that "webtoons are proving to be fertile sources of intellectual property for Netflix to adapt into original series."

Webtoon-based transnational IP exporting has been larger than originally expected, as global cultural creators adapt Korean webtoons and transform them into digital games and animations. An exemplary case is *Tower of God*, which was written by SIU starting in 2010. The webtoon, which ran for three seasons and has hundreds of episodes, has had 4.5 billion views worldwide (Orsini, 2020). It is a "dark fantasy action series [that] centers on the journey of a young boy [named Twenty-Fifth Bam] as he battles his way through the mysterious Tower, building friendships, discovering the rules that govern this tower, and facing unimaginable terrors, as he strives to find the only friend he's ever known" (Crunchyroll, 2020a):

> Determined to be reunited with his friend, Bam also enters the tower. This tower is filled with magical energy Shinsu, as well as a variety of different species and people [*sic*] groups. The tower also has a strict caste system and hierarchy, with progression among its ranks determined by strength and intelligence. These groups include Regulars, who are the normal everyday citizens of the tower, the high powered Rankers, who govern the average class, and the 10 Great Families, who are led by King Jahad and rules [*sic*] all of the tower. King Jahad is effectively immortal, having struck a deal with the people of the tower long ago. Irregulars, including Bam, operate outside of these rules, however, and thus pose the threat of actually killing Jahad. Along the way, Bam forms a team to make his way to the top of the tower and find Rachel. . . . Featuring a somewhat complex battle system, as well as intense fights to go along with hit, one of the most obvious causes for *Tower of God*'s popularity is its action. Its art style and status as a webtoon further highlight the stylization of these fights, so fans are likely looking forward to seeing it get a full animated adaptation. (Donohoo, 2020)

In 2013, it was turned into a mobile game on Google Play. Not long after its original release, the *Tower of God* mobile role-playing game already had over a hundred million players. In addition, the original *Tower of God* received an official English translation by Line Webtoon in 2014, and it was adapted for mobile gaming in 2016.

Most significantly, *Tower of God* was released as an anime in April 2020 and was simulcast in Korea, Japan, and the United States (Donohoo, 2020). Although the numbers of anime based on non-Japanese sources have gradually increased, it is still very rare to witness the adaptation of Korean webtoons into Japanese anime. However, as many Japanese as well as other global audiences have enjoyed Korean popular culture and digital technologies since the early 2000s, it is not unusual for global Hallyu fans to enjoy webtoons, which consequently drives Japanese anime makers to pick up properties like *Tower of God* and turn them into anime programs (Donohoo, 2020).

The animated work's Japanese title is *Kami no Tō* (Tower of God). Telecom Animation Film (*Lupin the Third: Part 5*, *We Rent Tsukumogami*, and *Orange*) produced the anime, while Sola Entertainment managed the production of the series. Crunchyroll—an American distributor, publisher, and licensing company focusing on streaming anime and manga—streamed the series when it premiered in the spring of 2020. The website for the anime said that the series would have a simultaneous release in Japan, Korea, and the United States due to the webtoon's popularity, and Crunchyroll (2020b) introduced it on its website as follows:

> Synopsis:
> Reach the top, and everything will be yours.
> At the top of the tower exists everything in this world, and all of it can be yours.
> You can become a god.
> This is the story of the beginning and the end of Rachel, the girl who climbed the tower so she could see the stars, and Bam, the boy who needed nothing but her.

Crunchyroll and Webtoon Production are also producing a new anime based on Jeho Son and Kwangsu Lee's *Noblesse* (in the genres of action and comedy), while Production I.G, Inc. is animating the work (Hodgkins, 2020).

Meanwhile, in 2018, the Lan Kwai Fong Group in Hong Kong signed a collaboration agreement with Korea Telecom and through this collaboration has developed new films and television dramas from webtoons managed and owned by KTOON (a national website for cartoons that is provided by KT) under Korea Telecom. The Lan Kwai Fong Group plans to target the greater China and US markets by producing big-screen materials based on five famous webtoons, including *Andromate* and *Iron Girl* (Lan Kwai Fong Group, 2018).

Webtoon-based transnational transmedia have added a new form of cultural flow to the Korean Wave, as IP has become one of the most significant components of globalization. Digital platforms (both national platforms such as Naver and Kakao and global platforms such as Netflix) have played a key role in the transnationalization of local popular culture, meaning that platformization has become part and parcel of the Korean Wave and global cultural industries. According to Lynn (2016, 13), "while some of the more operatic claims about the uniqueness or the innovative nature of webtoons in Korea should be taken with a grain of salt, the medium has grown with a rapidity that few, if any, predicted."

National and global digital platforms also play a major role in the process of transnational cultural distribution. As a result, contemporary transnationalization can be said to be controlled by a handful of mega digital platforms. As Li (2020, 236) points out, "the paradigm of storytelling is often considered the center of transmedia strategies, for the production and consumption of narratives are believed to be the forces that drive transmedia synergy." In this setting, every unit or fragment in a transmedia system—such as a comic, animation, toy, or sticker—is consumed by fans as a part of the narrative, but the fundamental driving force behind this transmedia consumption is not the various small narratives but the grand narrative or worldview that unites them all. Along with the rise of digital platforms in the recent decade, however, the focus has begun to shift from content to platform (Li, 2020, 236).

What is interesting is that transmedia storytelling in the realm of webtoons is notably different from OSMU (one-source multi-use) because of webtoons' emphasis on the worldview. Fans consume a great number of small narrative fragments across many different media—manga, anime, films, and games—to gain access to the grand narrative (Steinberg, 2012, 179). For example, in the midst of proliferating variations and fragments, character design based on any previous cultural content such as novels and anime is centrally controlled by the producer and studio, which maintains a certain level of consistency (Steinberg, 2012; Li, 2020, 233–234).

Outside of Japan, the print comic world uses the term *universe* (*segyekwan* in Korean) instead of *worldview* (see Kang, E. W., 2018; Jang, M.J., 2019). *Universe* here describes the ways in which stories unfold and backgrounds are established, as can be seen in the Marvel Universe—where the stories in various comics and other media published by Marvel Comics take place. For example, Iron Man appears not only in his own movies but also in other movies that exist in the Marvel Universe. Characters in novels and movies also use universes to view the world (Kang, E. W., 2018). Korean webtoon platforms including KakaoPage and webtoon production companies such as YLAB develop their own universes to expand transmedia storytelling—meaning that they expand original stories through IP to create other cultural products such as films, television dramas, and games (Kim, H. J., 2020). KakaoPage has prioritized the construction of an IP universe similar to the Marvel Universe, indicating that this webtoon platform plans to develop stories that unite all the small narratives based on IP and expand the life cycle of various IP-based webtoon materials (Kim, H. W., 2021).

One of the latest examples of an IP universe is *Space Sweepers*, the title of a webtoon published in 2020 and a film released on Netflix in February 2021. *Space Sweepers* is Korea's first blockbuster movie set in space. Before the film's release, the distribution company Merry Christmas and KakaoPage formed a partnership to expand the film's IP through various story formats. According to KakaoPage, "'Space Sweepers' is setting a precedent of investing into its IP from the very beginning of developing the film script. . . . It's not merely a video format of a webtoon or vice versa. We plan to build our own 'IP Universe' through this property" (quoted in Lee, J. L., 2020).

In this regard, Steinberg (2017a) points out that the rise of mediating platforms effectively merges content with platforms, which increases transmedia convergence of another kind. For Korean cultural industries, "the rise of [the] IP system marks a transitioning and converging point between content and platform. Although the terminological root of IP in intellectual property links it to the centrality of content, the fact that it is platform providers, instead of content industries, who raised the concept and proposed the model of IP complicates the situation by aligning the genealogical and operational origin of IP with the techno-economic logics of platforms" (Li, 2020, 237).

Webtoons have emphasized not only media convergence but also IP-based transnational transmedia, although they also export print manhwa that originated from webtoons. Thus, the transnationalization of webtoons has been quite different from that of other forms of cultural content.

Transnational Participatory Culture and Fan Translations

Webtoons have provided great platforms for participatory culture through fan translations, which constitute one of the major transnational activities in this cultural sector. Unlike other cultural forms, webtoons clearly merge text and images. Due to this unique characteristic, original texts need to carefully translated into various different languages, and thus the translation has become a major component of the transnationalization of webtoons. Although webtoon platforms have provided translation services, in many cases a fan translation of webtoons existed before the official translation was introduced. This transnational participatory culture continues in spite of official translation services. Fan translation can be seen as a form of pop cosmopolitanism that enables global fans to learn the source text's culture and language, thus moving beyond their local context (Sung, S. G., 2018).

It is critical to explore webtoons' fan translations in comparison with official translations to examine the reasons behind the continuation of fan translation and its implications in transnational participatory culture. Webtoon fans can be differentiated from traditional comic fans. Comic books are popular culture artifacts, but they are different from other cultural objects because their fan culture has been "almost exclusively centered around a physical, possessable text" (Brown, 1997, 26, cited in Stevens and Bell, 2012, 74). As Stevens and Bell (2012, 755) point out, "comic books have historically served as the focal point of a social subgroup of those interested in comic book texts, demarcating consumers into readers, collectors (fans), and investors. Additionally, those who consume only ancillary products, such as comic book movies or television versions, without consuming the actual texts are not considered fanatics. In the past, in order to credibly call one a comic book fan, a person had to own comic books he or she had read." However, webtoon fans do not need to possess any physical books or goods, and they mostly following transmedia practices with webtoons on platforms—meaning that they enjoy webtoon-based big-screen culture and compare webtoons and big-screen cultural content.

Webtoons have almost entirely been created and published digitally on the web, making them easy to distribute globally through webtoon platforms. Their digital format, easy serialization, global audience, and dedicated fan bases "make them easily translatable to transmedia production" (Castillo, 2016). As the Korean Wave has shown, the translation of Korean cultural content has become part of global youth culture, and a major fan activity is translation. Like K-pop fans, webtoon fans have contributed to introducing popular Korean products to local audiences. For example, BTS gets its "message across to international audiences" partially due to "fan translators, who are an integral part of the K-pop fandom. . . . A lot of labor goes into making translations immediately accessible to an English-speaking fan base. While fan translations are largely unmonetized, the unpredictable nature of a group's content output can leave fans dedicating anywhere between a few minutes to 10 hours translating on a given day" (Kelley, 2017). Global webtoon fans translate webtoons and share them with other fans even before webtoon platforms officially provide webtoon services in global comics markets (Jang, W. H., and Song, 2017). Many webtoons have been translated into various languages by a few webtoon platforms. However, translations into other languages are often done through fans' participatory culture (Sung, S. G., 2018).

However, the translation process demonstrates some differences between fan translations and official translations, as fans' and digital platforms' approaches differ: the former generally want to preserve original meanings and expressions, while the latter want to hybridize webtoons linguistically. For example, *Lookism* (*Oemojisangjui*) is a webtoon written and illustrated by Park Tae-joon that began appearing on Naver Webtoon in November 2014. The story revolves around a high school student who can switch between two bodies—one fat and ugly, the other fit and handsome. Naver Webtoon officially started to translate the webtoon into a few languages, including English, in June 2017. In the English version, however, many characters' names were changed from Korean names to common English ones: from Hyung Suk Park to Daniel, Tae Sung Lee to Logan, Ha Neul Park to Zoe Park, Sung Yi Jin to Zack, and Mijin to Mira. In addition, the platform changed the monetary values in the webtoon from Korean won to American dollars.

Obviously, Naver was applying a hybridization strategy to attract English language users in the global marketplace. However, fans were not satisfied with these official translations and translated *Lookism* using the original names and context. Many webtoon fans feel that modifying the original Korean text diminishes their identity as fans as well as the webtoon's identity. Fans are especially concerned about onomatopoeia, the use of words that phonetically imitate what they describe. As Fulton, who translated Yoon Tae-ho's *Ikki* into English, points out,

> onomatopoeia is a constant challenge. Do we Romanize sound-words (ŭisŏng'ŏ) or use English equivalents? For example, to represent the sound of a motor vehicle, both the engine and the wheels on the road surface, Yoon uses boooong. We utilized that Romanization, prompting one of my students to ask why we hadn't used the English vroooom instead. Good question. A similar decision is involved in translating ŭit'aeŏ, Korean words that represent actions rather than sounds—for example hoek, which indicates a sudden movement. In this case we opted for Romanization, figuring that however one pronounced this word, the aspiration required by the initial h might prompt readers to think of similarly aspirated words such as whoosh or whirl. (2019, 2236)

There are other types of translations by webtoon platforms that combine official and fan translations. In other words, Korean webtoon platforms have attempted to go global by providing translations in multiple languages and cooperating with global comic book companies, which are typical glocalization strategies. One of the most famous translation sites is Webtoon Translate (2020), a crowd sourced translation service where fans can legally translate their favorite webtoons into various languages and share them with a global audience. The website clearly explains that it was created to serve as a venue where one's favorite webtoons can be introduced to a wider audience using other languages and to share content. Thus, the website does not allow translation with an intent different from that of the author. The website asks that any translation convey the intention and context of the original author. As of May 19, 2020, global fans had volunteered to translate ninety-four webtoons into many different languages on Webtoon Translate, including *Noblesse* (into thirty-two languages), *Tower of God* (thirty-two), *Wind Breaker* (thirty-two), and *Kubera* (thirty-one). More than 8,500 individuals and almost ninety teams have participated in translations. For example, in June 2020 Webtoon Translate stated, "*Save Me* is now available for translation." In its notice section, Webtoon Translate (2020) stated, "We have added a new webtoon to WEBTOON TRANSLATE. *SAVE ME* is now available for translation! . . . Due to regional policies, fan Translations for *SAVE ME* are not available for languages in which the official webtoon is released." Many of the translators use a webtoon character as their avatar and translate their favorite webtoons with no monetary reward. Fans can participate in any way they want: translating, proofreading, or editing font formats. However, while team translation is open only to certain groups.

Global fans of Korean webtoons participate in online activities to consume webtoons together, learn about webtoon cultures together, and absorb information about other cultures. Translation is one of the most significant forms of participatory culture for global webtoon fans (Sung, S. G., 2018). Global webtoon fans emphasize the importance of original texts and tastes that portray local identities, instead of losing cultural authenticity through translation processes managed by webtoon platforms. At the same time, fan translation has been organized and appropriated by digital platforms, furthering the platformization of webtoons. In other words, fan translation clearly reveals a conflict between fandom culture and the business model of webtoon platforms that use fans as free labor.

As I discussed above, many fans volunteer to translate webtoons because they want to preserve the works' original meanings and ideas. Such fans feel a sense of community through participation. In this regard, Mansson and Myers (2011) argue that fans as affective users enjoy sharing their work on social media platforms and thus work with excitement. Hardt and Negri (2004, 110–111) argue that affective labor "produces or manipulates affects such as a feeling of ease, well-being, satisfaction, excitement, or passion." For these authors, online activities (including fan translation) are a form of affection. Hallyu fan labor, including K-pop translations, is mostly characterized by unpaid affective labor "through often prosumer activities of fans" (Sun, 2020, 391).

However, it is critical to understand that fan participation in social media activities is a form of exploitation initiated, either explicitly or implicitly, by digital platforms. Fans are not compensated for their time and energy: in other words, they are providing free labor (Fuchs, 2010; Andrejevic, 2011; Jin, D. Y., 2015b). Fans as webtoon translators are commodified. There are certainly some positive aspects of affective labor. However, as Terranova (2000, 33) argues, "simultaneously voluntarily given and unwaged, enjoyed and exploited, free labor on the Net includes the activity of building Web sites, modifying software packages, reading and participating in mailing lists, and building virtual spaces on MUDs (multi-user dungeons—a multiplayer real-time virtual world game)." Fan labor has turned webtoons into sites of "passionate co-creation, intense contestation," but "ruthless capitalization" (Tai and Hu, 2018, 2372). Terranova (2000, 37) argues that "free labor is the moment where the knowledgeable consumption of culture is translated into excess productive activities that are pleasantly embraced and at the same time often shamelessly exploited." The voluntary involvement of affective labor in webtoon translation has turned into a commodification process, meaning that fan translation is commodified by webtoon platforms.

Fandom culture cannot be merely passive and exploited by digital platforms. However, the free use of fan labor by webtoon platforms is culturally incorrect. The conflict between fandom culture in which fan labor "draws out the multiple fan identities that encompass layered levels of creative engagements in the affective economy" of webtoons (Sun, 2020, 403) and capitalist webtoon platforms' strategical use of fan labor to extend their webtoons' popularity and profits in the global cultural sphere continues to grow. Fans deserve to receive credits in cultural production and consumption, and webtoon platforms must provide necessary supports such as tools, space, and financial subsidies to fans so that fandom culture can flourish.

Hybridity versus Cultural Identity in the Webtoon Sphere

Two different but related theoretical perspectives on the webtoon transnationalization process needs to be discussed: the authenticity and the glocalization of webtoons. As the success of several Hallyu products (including films, television programs, and K-pop) proves, cultural industries and producers need to develop globalization strategies to attract foreign audiences. Through the hybridization of Korean and other cultures, local cultural content may be able to penetrate global cultural markets. However, as I briefly discussed above, one of the primary characteristics of the rise of webtoons and webtoon-based transmedia is cultural authenticity that reflects local mentalities and identities. Although we cannot deny the necessity of cultural hybridization, we should also emphasize the significant role of local identity, given that webtoons' unique worldviews are the major reason for their growth as source materials for transnational transmedia.

To begin with, unlike other cultural forms that emphasize the hybridization of local Korean culture and global culture, webtoons emphasize not hybridity but the Korean identity embedded in the various stories that webtoonists create. This does not mean that webtoons do not use hybridity. Since Korean webtoons are consumed transnationally, webtoon companies continue to develop localization strategies in foreign countries by cultivating local groups to create new types of webtoons. This is a clear example of transnational consumption and the re-creation of glocal culture (Jang, W. H., and Song, 2017). Webtoon platforms have continued to use hybridity as one of their major globalization strategies. For example, in Japan, Kakao changed the title of *Itaewon Class* to *Roppongi Class*, as Roppongi in Tokyo is a district famous for its clubs and nightlife—comparable to Itaewon in Seoul. Yecies (2018, 135) argues that the success of webtoons in China has been achieved since "'de-Koreanizing' webtoons has become a key strategy, primarily achieved by adapting and transforming original Korean elements into Chinese cultural content."

In this regard, Jinsoo Lee (the CEO of KakaoPage) stated in an interview with a popular newspaper that "the major trend in the manhwa sector is fantasy. As the famous Japanese manga *Dragon Ball* does not show its nationality, KakaoPage's *Solo Leveling* (*Na Honjaman Lebel-eop*) does not have nationality. We clearly pursue the localization strategy" (Park, M. J., 2020a). However, the level of hybridity in webtoons is relatively limited because webtoons' major strength is their unique stories, which are embedded in historical or contemporary Korean society.

In fact, in global webtoon markets, Korean webtoons have become popular not because of the elimination of their Koreanness, but because of their emphasis on local identity. For example, when the webtoon-based Netflix *Kingdom* was aired, many people were immediately attracted to it due to its representation of Koreanness, and they immediately liked the *gat* (a traditional hat of the Joseon Dynasty). The hats were worn by noblemen (known as *yangban*) and scholars (*seonbi*). When the University of British Columbia community center in Vancouver, Canada, hosted a festival to honor the lunar new year in February 2020, one of the hats was exhibited and was very popular among Canadians who had watched *Kingdom* on Netflix.

Another exemplary case is Lezhin Comics's webtoon *The Lady and Her Butler*, which was influenced by the famous Korean fable *Agassiwa Ureongchonggak*. The webtoon, which portrays a man who did all kinds of housework and his romance with a woman, was very popular in the United States in 2018 (Lim, K. U., 2018). In the webtoon, when a broke and homeless man offers to keep house in exchange for temporary housing, Sooha agrees and finds that the man prepares everything well, providing homemade dinners, clean sheets, and freshly ironed clothes. Sooha eventually falls in love with him. Unlike American comics, which are commonly confined to action or thriller genres, Korean webtoons are popular because they include a variety of genres (including *il-sang*, gag, and romance) based on everyday chores. In Goodreads, an American social cataloging website, for example, one reviewer said, "This is actually an ongoing comic but I'm just going to rate it 5 stars because I binged all the available chapters and it's so adorable, I was squealing and laughing so much!!! I love it." Another reviewer stated:

> This manhwa should be held as the proper way to write a romance story. It's amazing and perfect in every single way possible. i think the reason this story works so well is because the characters are real, they think the way real people think, and the reason and motivation for their actions are both believable and understandable. you understand that Sooha doesn't want a man in her life, not because of some bad breakup or any other reason along the line of "all men are pigs" yada. she doesn't want to depend on a man because of what she saw in life, because of what life had done to her and her mother and how they both coped with it in very separate ways. it's something that can very well happen in real life, and it resonates.[5]

Likewise, the majority of foreigners like webtoons that show Korean identities instead of hybridizing the texts. Webtoon platforms and webtoonists need to acknowledge that retaining cultural authenticity is more important than losing it in a desire to reach global cultural markets.

Structurally, webtoon Hallyu have advanced different forms of global flows and hybridity. The webtoon industry has penetrated foreign cultural markets through the material exportation of finished webtoons (even as print manhwa, after the completion of a series), the advancement of digital platforms and apps, and the creation of transnational transmedia storytelling in tandem with global OTT platforms. It has also developed global participatory culture, as can be seen in the case of webtoon translation. After achieving huge success in Korea, both the manhwa industry and digital platform corporations (including Naver, Daum, and Kakao) have strategically penetrated the markets of other countries, both in Asia and the West. Webtoons are considered next-generation content that can appeal to overseas comic book readers and fans (Park, H. K., 2014).

Korea's market is small in comparison, and as a result of webtoons' increasing popularity with foreign readers, now seems to be the perfect time for Korean webtoon providers to go global. Webtoons have been able to develop an international presence in the Korean Wave tradition, as the major tools used to enjoy Korean Wave content are digital technologies, which develop digital Hallyu. Due to the ubiquitousness of digital platforms, mobile and networked modes of cultural consumption have become the default with regard to the transnational circulation of webtoons and therefore Hallyu. As Lamarre (2015, 96) points out, "this is surely because multimedia formations have become such an ordinary part of daily activity (in the form of working and communicating across platforms) and of consumption (every product now seems to entail multiple media versions)." In other words, the transmedial and transnational process of developing webtoons has been greatly supported by digital platforms. Digital technology is not only the vehicle used to deliver local content globally, but that technology also constitutes important content, as exemplified by the global penetration of Korean smartphone technology and its many apps (Jin, D. Y., Yoon, and Min, 2021). Webtoon platforms (either independent webtoon-focused portals or platforms owned by mega internet portals), have taken a leading role in the distribution of Korean webtoons, both nationally and globally.

The Korean webtoon sector, driven by digital platforms, has developed a new model of cultural production. The webtoon industry has not only added to existing Hallyu but has also transformed the Korean Wave trend in that it has emphasized digital Hallyu, the expansion of target regions to Europe and North America, and IP-based transmedia storytelling. The webtoon format is still not familiar to many global comic readers, but the Korean webtoon industry has increased its global reach through both webtoons and IP-based transmedia. In other words, webtoons have actualized a new form of cultural flow that is increasingly based on IP. Therefore, it is expected that IP-based Hallyu will become the next stage of the Korean Wave. The fundamental characteristic underlying this new stage are the unique stories being told through webtoons, which are sometimes hybridized but remain intact in many cases. Again, Korean webtoons focus on contemporary or historical uniqueness. Korean experiences resonate with global youth, who have similar ones in their own countries. The globalization of webtoons suggests a shift in the focus of cultural flows from hybridity to cultural identity.

Conclusion

This chapter has discussed and analyzed the ways in which webtoons have become one of the major cultural forms in the Korean Wave. Unlike other existing cultural forms such as television programs, films, K-pop, and digital games, webtoons have characteristics that are advanced and unique in the Korean Wave. The number of manhwa exports from Korea, including webtoons, is continuously growing at a rate comparable to the number of exports from the Korean film industry, and most of that growth is due to webtoons. While the popularity of print manhwa has decreased, webtoons have rapidly increased their global reach in the early twenty-first century.

Webtoons have developed unique forms of global reception, as they are exported in various ways to foreign markets. Since people enjoy webtoons on their mobile platforms, domestic webtoon platforms have improved their global platforms and app, and global users download webtoon apps created by these platforms to enjoy Korean webtoons. Global fans also translate Korean webtoons into other languages. In other words, many global webtoon fans enjoy Korean webtoons on their mobile gadgets, including smartphones, and further global participatory fandom culture.

Most of all, Korean webtoon platforms have also increased the use of transnational transmedia storytelling global media and cultural firms to produce webtoon-based big-screen content, such as television programs, films, digital games, and animation. In particular, several webtoon platforms have recently worked with Netflix, the largest OTT service platform in the world, to produce webtoon-based cultural content. Netflix now produces cultural content like *Kingdom* for global audiences. This clearly implies that the notion of foreign export has changed due to webtoons. Unlike other cultural industries that mainly export finished products and organize cultural activities (e.g., K-pop concerts), webtoons have combined various forms of global reach, from the export of finished content to the use of transmedia storytelling. As Japanese anime and manga have already demonstrated (Ohsawa, 2018), with characteristics such as transmedia storytelling, media convergence, attractive fantasy worlds, and fan activities—all of which are embedded in historical or contemporary Korean society—Korean webtoons have become available for global consumption.

There are some concerns about webtoons' global reach, mainly because of rampant piracy in several countries (Kim, B. S., 2018). Since many countries have not developed legal webtoon readerships, Korean webtoonists and webtoon platforms lose not only revenues but also creative opportunities. Digital piracy is the single most important factor impeding further development of the legitimate webtoon business as well as other major cultural sectors, including music and film. The dramatic changes ushered in by cutting-edge digital technologies have increased the magnitude and relevance of IP rights infringement. Given the significance of innovative designs in the realm of webtoons as a form of open source for platforms, IP has become important for designers and corporations because of the platforms' desire for massive profits. Korea needs to advance digital technologies to protect creativity from digital piracy, both nationally and globally, so that the country can increase not only its role as an exporter of cultural products but also its benefits from domestic-based platforms and IP rights.

CHAPTER 6

Sociocultural Perspectives on Webtoonists

Over the years, a number of webtoonists have become very successful, as they build a devoted fanbase and generate significant annual income. As I discussed in chapter 2, many Korean young people would like to work as a webtoonist and dream of becoming famous like Yoon Tae-ho (the author and artist of *Misaeng: Incomplete Life*). Some artists do achieve success and become famous webtoonists, but for the majority, becoming a famous webtoonist is not a realistic dream. Nonetheless, aspiring artists see popular webtoonists as role models and symbols of success. Accordingly, many webtoon fans, amateur webtoonists, and media scholars are interested in learning about successful webtoon artists' career progression and trajectory, training processes, and working conditions.

Most webtoonists fall into one of two groups. The first consists of artists who originally worked in manhwa, training as apprentices and then working as professional artists before switching to webtoons with the rapid growth of digital technologies and webtoon platforms. The other group is made up of young webtoonists who do not have any manhwa experience. From the beginning of their careers, these artists created and published their work directly on webtoon platforms, including Dojeon Manhwa on Naver Webtoon and Manhwa in World on Daum. Regardless of whether they came to webtoons from manhwa or were immersed in webtoons from the beginning of their career, webtoonists have been greatly influenced by a few prominent webtoon artists.

There has been no academic analysis of webtoonists, but only sporadic media reports. To investigate several important dimensions of the webtoon industry, this chapter mainly discusses Yoon Tae-ho, one of the most successful and influential webtoon artists during the past fifteen years. In June 2019, I organized an international conference called Asian Transmedia Storytelling in the Age of Digital Media, at the University of British Columbia, in Vancouver, and invited Yoon to be a keynote speaker and talk about his successful career and vision as a webtoonist. About a hundred students and twenty conference presenters came to listen to his speech in a jam-packed classroom on the downtown campus.

Yoon delivered his keynote speech titled "Korean Webtoons: History and Future Directions" during a two-hour slot for a lecture and questions and answers, and he discussed various compelling inside stories not easily heard about otherwise. During in-depth interviews before and after his keynote speech, he also shared his experiences, ideas, and visions related to the webtoon world—discussing with me, in particular, the status of webtoonists in the industry. His speech and these interviews can teach us much about the sociocultural workings of the webtoon industry from the perspective of a webtoonist, including job security, working conditions, and the ways in which youth can enter the webtoon world.

In this chapter, I first address Yoon's life as a manhwa artist and webtoonist, as well as his most popular and successful webtoons. Second, I document Yoon's keynote speech, but I have reorganized his talk into a few major subcategories to allow readers to clearly comprehend the important themes identified in his presentation. There are summaries the keynote speech, along with some brief interventions from me to clarify and contextualize Yoon's points. Keep in mind that these interventions serve to clarify only, and not disrupt nor reinterpret, Yoon's comments. Finally, I discuss Yoon's role as a leading webtoon artist based on my interview with him to give readers an engaging and interesting perspective on webtoonists. I expect that this unusual documentation of the major characteristics of one of the leading webtoonists will shed light on critical discussions about Korean webtoonists as a new cultural icon, as well on webtoonists' vision of digital culture (including transmedia storytelling)—which I hope will both further critical discourse surrounding cultural production in the digital era and also aspiring webtoonists with new perspectives on the industry.

Yoon Tae-ho's Manhwa and Webtoons

Born in 1969, Yoon has authored a number of webtoons, many of which—including *Moss* (*Ikki*, 2008–2009), *Misaeng: Incomplete Life* (2012–2013), and *Inside Men* (2010–present)—have garnered notable success (fig. 6.1). This has led to him becoming a role model for aspiring manhwa artists and webtoonists. Since his debut, Yoon's works in both traditional printed manhwa and webtoons have met with great acclaim from numerous fans. With the successive publication of webtoon works such as *Yahoo* (a reinterpretation of Korea's modern history; 1998), *Moss* (a gory thriller that opens with the death of the protagonist's father in a quiet village), and *Misaeng: Incomplete Life* (a touching portrayal of the life and struggles of an office worker), Yoon became one of the leading webtoonists in Korea, winning multiple awards and recognitions—including the president's award at the Korea Content Awards event in 2012 (Literature Translation

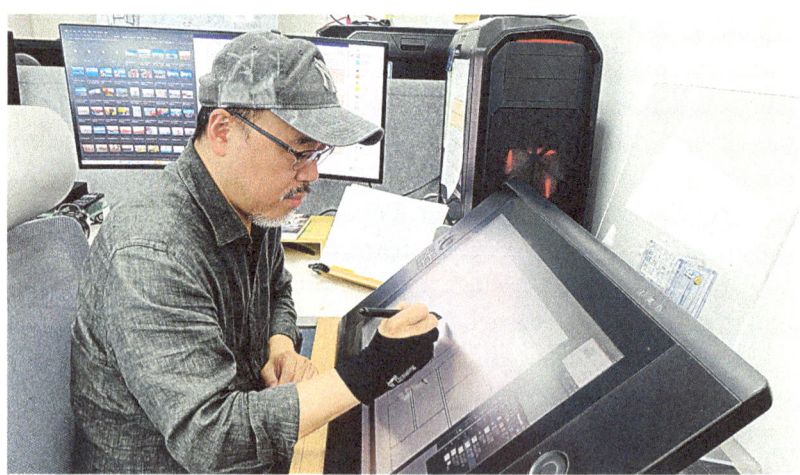

FIGURE 6.1 Yoon Tae-ho working on a new webtoon. Source: ©Supercomix Studio Corp.

Institute of Korea, 2014). In addition to his personal success, Yoon has mentored young webtoonists and regularly attempts to help new artists. For example, during a 2014 forum, he had this advice for young cartoonists: "Creating your own content is the best way to succeed as a cartoonist. I've always said to young cartoonists that they need to focus on making their own content, but they should be cautious about that. . . . If their illustrations and stories are good enough, they will eventually be adapted for a drama or film. If cartoonists succeed in drawing original content that touches everyone, that will be a real example of creativity" (quoted in Baek, B. Y., 2014b).

What is notable about Yoon's career is his experience in the manhwa industry apprentice system before he began working independently as a webtoonist. Since embarking on his webtoonist career, Yoon has established Nulook (a manhwa content management company that represents Kang Full and Joo Ho-min, among others) and has served as president of the Korean Cartoon Association. Interestingly, Yoon has also invested in Justoon, a new webtoon platform launched by Wisdom House in 2017, and is currently investigating blockchain as a means of reaching investors to develop a new financial resource system. Thus, Yoon has been a successful webtoonist, businessman, administrator, and visionary. Of course, not all his attempts have been successful. However, even his unsuccessful efforts have provided valuable lessons for other webtoonists and for webtoon platforms.

Yoon made his professional debut in 1993 with the serialization of *Emergency Landing* (*Pisang ch'angnyuk*) in the monthly magazine *Jump*. Before this, his work had been rejected eight times by publishers, which was not unusual.[1] Often, people are most proud of their first work, but Yoon thought his first published work was trash. During his interview with a popular newspaper in 2013 (Ki, S. M., 2013), Yoon said, "the story was terrible and the drawings were too showy." He noted that "the storyline was the key to success. 'I was a fool to think that I could learn to write a wonderful story just by reading others' works.' With that revelation, Yoon changed his style of self-training. In a bid to learn the ins and outs of writing a good manuscript, he copied out the script for 'Sandglass,' a popular Korean drama in the 1990s, word for word" (Ki, S. M., 2013). He has since written more than twenty major webtoons. Yoon's endless efforts to improve his craft are closely related to various sociocultural forces, such as extreme competitiveness and strong work ethics, which are deeply embedded in Korean society.

Yoon Tae-ho's Major Works as Manhwa Artist and Webtoonist

- 1993 *Emergency Landing* <비상착륙>
- 1996 *A Husband Living Alone* <혼자 자는 남편>
- 1996 *Yeonsiibyeolgok* <연씨별곡>
- 1997 *Chunhyangbyeolgok* <춘향별곡>
- 1998 *Yahoo* <야후>
- 1998 *Yeol-pung Hagwon* <열풍학원>
- 1999 *Strange Kids* <수상한 아이들>
- 2001 *A Rude Life* <발칙한 인생>
- 2001 *Romance* <로망스>
- 2006 *Siren* (story only) <싸이렌(스토리)>
- 2006 *Spirit God Bari Gongju* <영혼의 신, 바리공주>
- 2007 *Ikki* (*Moss* in English) <이끼>
- 2008 *You Are There* <당신은 거기 있었다>
- 2008 *Around the World* <주유천하>
- 2009 *Seti* <세티>
- 2010 *Leaders United* <리더스 유나이티드>
- 2011 *Inside Men* <내부자들>
- 2012 *Misaeng: Incomplete Life* <미생>
- 2013 *Operation Chromite* <인천상륙작전>
- 2014 *Pine* <파인>
- 2014 *Unknown Planning Office* <알 수 없는 기획실>
- 2015 *Misaeng Season 2* [unfinished] 2 <미생 시즌 2>
- 2017 *Origin* <오리진>
- 2020 *Eorin* <어린>[2]

Several of these webtoons have been adapted as big-screen content, including *Moss* (a movie released in 2010), *Misaeng* (a television drama and movie, 2014), and *Inside Men* (a movie, 2015). Many popular media and scholars call Yoon a pioneer or a leading figure in the Korean manhwa industry. H. K. Lee (2016) at *Korea Daily* considers him to be one of the most notable webtoonists and someone who has helped shape manhwa culture into what it is today, saying that he

> acted as a pioneer leading the transition from printed, black and white manhwa to webtoons. In his first hit online series, Yoon created an eerie world in his murder mystery webtoon *Moss*. The classic whodunit storyline, inspired by gothic literature about one man's journey to uncover the truth behind his father's death, became an internet sensation after its publication in 2008 to 2009. Yoon, known for reflecting the reality of Korean society in his work, garnered 1 billion hits on his twelfth webtoon *Misaeng* published on Daum from 2012 to 2013. Young Koreans resonated with the office politics depicted in the webtoon, commiserating with the main character's life as a corporate underling. . . . Yoon encourages aspiring webtoonists to continue developing original content, stating that it is the best way to succeed as a cartoonist.

Due to Yoon's efforts to bring new life into the Korean manhwa industry, Yi (2019, 55) recognized Yoon "as a K-*manhwa* regenerator in a new digital ecology."

Most of all, Yoon's webtoons have touched on numerous serious sociocultural issues (including injustice, corruption, and social instability), and he continues to portray socially and economically underrepresented people and their everyday ordeals. His role in the webtoon world has been influential, and his perspective on and vision of the rapidly growing Korean industry provides a unique look into it.

Based on Yoon's keynote speech and interviews, the next few sections discuss his career development and his perspectives on webtoons.

Becoming a Cartoonist in the Pre-Webtoon Era: A Keynote Speech

Until the early 2000s, manhwa in book form were based on manhwa published in various magazines. Cartoonists and manhwa publishers needed to attract manhwa readers who would want to buy manhwa books after reading manhwa magazines. Once people read parts of a manhwa in a magazine, they often bought manhwa books, including those containing all of the episodes. During this period, it was critical to become an individual disciple of a manhwa guru. Back then, to become a cartoonist, one had to be accepted into and pass a very strict training program with this kind of teacher–disciple system.

Thus, at the age of twenty-five, I started my career as a disciple of Hur Young Man, one of the most famous cartoonists at the time. Although I had not written any manhwa in magazines, Hur generously admitted me as his apprentice because he believed in my potential. Of course, I visited his office a few times [in my efforts] to become his disciple, which was not easy given that many young cartoonists were also competing for the position.[3]

Entering the apprentice system did not guarantee the trainees success; they had to complete a long, harsh, and tedious training process. Once young cartoonists earned a disciple position under manhwa gurus, they had to train for at least seven years before drawing manhwa characters' faces. In more detail, the trainees were able to paint only the hair of the main character for a year. During the next one-year period, they only drew nonhuman subjects, like trees and flowers. Then they had to spend five years drawing a character's body or some background materials. In other words, for a year, they painted white lines only, or black hairs, and then painted backgrounds of grass, cars, and buildings for many more years. Again, during this period, trainees were able to draw bodies excluding people's faces. Because characters (people's faces, of course) make up 70 percent of manhwa, disciples needed this long training process to be able to draw very delicate facial expressions—laughing, crying, and yelling.

People who strongly wished to become cartoonists sought to become disciples of famous cartoonists to watch their teacher's drawing and see how their teacher constructed story lines and characters. However, I left Hur's office instead of waiting for seven to ten years because I could not learn the ways in which he drew manhwa. Some disciples could not learn their teacher's works even after a ten-year training process, which placed the disciples in a dire situation.

Compared with the manhwa system, webtoonists are not required to endure this kind of established, tedious training process. Because some webtoonists attained their fame with no formal apprenticeship, many people who wanted to become print cartoonists immediately changed their minds and decided to become webtoonists. Instead of participating in a ten-year training program, some readers of others' webtoons a day earlier would become webtoonists in a day or two, as long as they had some talent and skill. Of course, this new way of becoming a webtoonist has some negative aspects. For example, webtoonists without training experience may not be able to deal with the most challenging situations, whereas well-trained disciples would understand the process and could overcome some difficulties relatively easily.

How to Become a Webtoonist in the Twenty-First Century

In the early 2000s, cartoonists who neither created print manhwa nor reached the disciple position began to post their drawings on their personal webpages. Some, including Kim Poong, became popular this way early in their career. In the print manhwa era, cartoonists needed skills; therefore, people who were trained by big names like Hur Young Man were typically selected to draw manhwa for magazines. However, along with the growth of the internet, some cartoonists who did not become disciples themselves, including Kim Poong, Kang Full, and Lee Malryeon, earned fame. Consequently, cartoonist hopefuls began to pay more attention to webtoons.

Of course, only a few webtoonists could achieve fame and earn significant money. I started to draw and post *Moss* [*Ikki*] [fig. 6.2], which made me the lead webtoonist on Mankick, one of the oldest webtoon sites, in January 2007. Some other early career webtoonists also posted their webtoons on Mankick. Of course, it was not a fairy tale. When I first started to publish *Moss*, nobody read it. Only three or four readers commented on each episode, and when I received nineteen comments—the highest thus far—they were mainly from my wife and acquaintances I had known for a while.

Back then, there were already several famous webtoonists. For example, Kang Full got about 1,500 comments on average per episode. I was depressed and thought of many issues. When Mankick closed for financial reasons, I restarted *Moss* by posting it on Daum, which became a turning

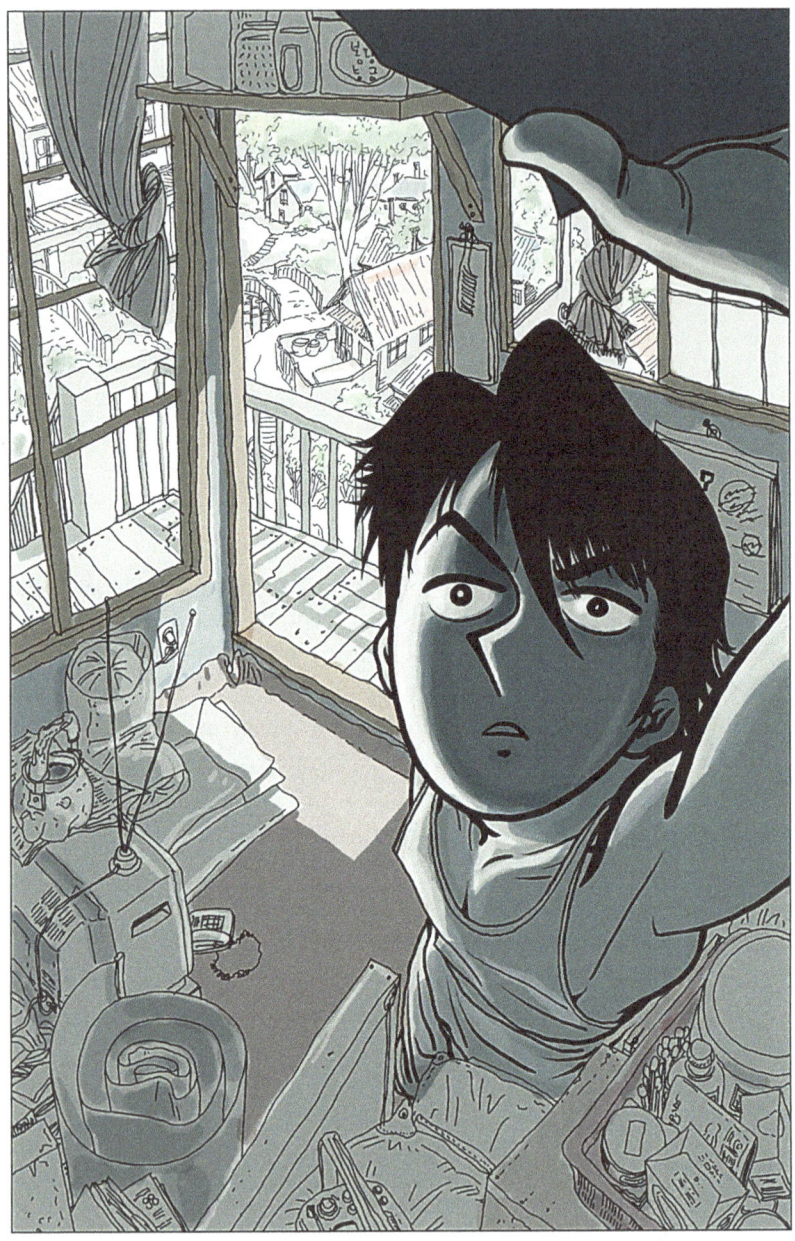

FIGURE 6.2 Art from Yoon Tae-ho's *Moss*. Source: ©Supercomix Studio Corp.

point in my webtoon career. Finally, many people began reading and enjoying the series, and eighteen movie companies approached me during the first three months after posting *Moss* on Daum. This certainly indicates that webtoons started getting many people's attention when webtoonists posted their work on a few major portals, including Daum and Naver.

Later, when I published *Misaeng*, many television producers and game developers approached me through diverse means. Some of them attempted to attract me by naming potential actors and actresses for a possible television version. Even a television producer at SBS—one of major Korean television networks—came to visit me with a writer. However, I decided to work with Kim Won Suk, a producer at the cable channel tvN. He and I talked a lot about the major characters, and I believe we shared some common ideas about the transmedia storytelling process. For example, unlike with other directors and producers, we did not mention anything about love lines between major male and female characters. This is the way that I transformed *Misaeng* into a television program.

Going back to the question of becoming a webtoonist in the new media environment, the process is still not easy. The barriers to becoming a webtoonist are becoming greater than before. Because many people want to be webtoonists, the incumbent webtoonists raise the bar themselves. In Korea, for example, there are about twenty manhwa departments in various universities, and each department produces forty to fifty undergraduate students every year. Before graduation, they come to Hongick University in Seoul to put a graduation exhibition together. During this exhibition period, people from webtoon platforms, including Naver and Daum, come and recruit talented future webtoonists. Many webtoonists who are college students want to work at Naver, Kakao, and Lezhin. However, they know they may not be able to because of the very stiff competition. Therefore, many who cannot attain a position with these major platforms start to create adult [or pornographic] webtoons to make money.

Transmedia Storytelling: Is It All about Money?

What I now want to emphasize is that webtoons are not free at all. On the contrary, they have never been free because of transmedia storytelling, although in the past webtoonists did not receive payments from webtoon portals. During the print manhwa era, if a manhwa was not popular, manhwa companies scrapped it to save space and paper. Manhwa companies used to discard all remaining manhwa two weeks after their initial sale. However, webtoons continue to get clicks as days go by, and some of them eventually draw the attention of big-screen producers.

More specifically, in the past many webtoonists published their webtoons with no monetary reward. However, "free" is not free at all because some webtoons ultimately bring money to their creators. For example, once webtoons are published on Daum, they remain there forever, meaning that they are "alive." Readers continue to click and write comments, one after another, following the webtoons' publication. Big-screen producers, such as film directors and television producers, also read these webtoons and begin to think about the possibility of transmedia work. Game developers and musical directors are also major fans and are creators who can transform webtoons into other cultural forms. Webtoons also become good candidates for producing characters and/or emoticons.

The nature of the contract also has substantially changed. When I started to publish my webtoons on Daum, there was one simple business contract for each specific webtoon. However, webtoonists in the late 2010s have a few more types of contracts, including a royalty contract. Webtoon platforms also try to secure intellectual property, sometimes for themselves and other times for the creators as well.

Previously, manhwa writers made money through the sale of manhwa books. In contrast, the commercialization of webtoons has been quite different. Unlike print manhwa, the webtoon's longevity on platforms—with its major features, such as unique story lines, vivid visual images, and diverse genres—may provide more opportunities than print manhwa [see Jin, D. Y., 2019a]. Luckily, Lezhin began paying fees to webtoonists, unlike during the early days of Daum and Naver. This has now become a new business model in the manhwa industry. As Lezhin began paying webtoonists up to 200 million won per month, Daum and Naver also began to pay webtoonists, although the payments were not sufficient. About forty platforms in total were in existence as of June 2018, including a few very successful platforms such as Daum, Naver, and Lezhin. I also began to receive fees for webtoon manuscripts that I created for a few platforms, including Daum. For *Misaeng*, I used to receive $100,000 per week during some peak periods.

There are also a handful of negatives with these webtoon platforms, although they certainly play a key role in expanding the webtoon market. The main one is that many platforms focus on adult/porno webtoons to attract more readers than other platforms. In other words, because of competition among these platforms, porno or semi-porno webtoons are rampant. This hurts quite a few webtoon companies and, eventually, webtoonists. The dream of many of the founders of these platforms is to [have them be] list[ed] on the stock market. However, the stock market does not allow the listing of platforms that focus on porno-type webtoons. This means that some platforms have difficulty securing external investment.

The Full Bloom of Transmedia Storytelling in the Digital Era

Transmedia storytelling based on webtoons has been thriving. However, webtoon-based storytelling did not produce profits in the early stages of this new form of adaptation. Webtoonist Kang Full's early webtoons that were turned into movies are good indicators. As several of Kang Full's works, such as *Love Story* (2003), *Ba:Bo* (2004), and *Apt* (2004) proved, many audiovisual creators started to pay attention to webtoons in the early 2000s. However, because these movies did not become commercial successes, audiovisual creators at that time were cautious about the role of webtoons as new resources for their movies and dramas.

Luckily, a movie version of my own webtoon *Moss* was made by the very famous movie director Kang Woo-suk. The movie *Moss* was very successful, attracting 340 million viewers. It was very good for the progress of webtoons and webtoon-based transmedia storytelling. Later, *Secretly, Greatly* [2013] became one of the highest grossing webtoon-based movies, attracting 780 million moviegoers. This greatly changed people's conception of the potential for webtoon-based transmedia storytelling.

Consequently, now many webtoonists plan to publish webtoon books while serializing their webtoons on platforms. Young people do not often buy books these days. Instead, they often pay money for what they read on their smartphones. However, adult readers who are accustomed to reading manhwa books still buy webtoon books. The book version of *Misaeng* sold eleven million copies in the first three weeks. The online version was a bit late, and people could not wait until the next episode came out. That is why webtoon books that include the final episode were popular.

As the result of this new business model, webtoonists develop cutting-edge techniques between each cut and each episode. Because a glimpse of the next episode is not shown on the smartphone version of the webtoon, readers who are curious about the next episodes have to buy webtoon books to see all the episodes at the same time. Of course, because some webtoonists are eager to maximize their income, webtoon quality cannot always be guaranteed.

Webtoons' Global Dream

Another major issue in the webtoon industry is globalization, given that the Korean domestic market is small and saturated. Webtoons are gaining popularity in many parts of the world. In particular, Korean webtoons are well known in East Asia, including Japan, China, and Taiwan. For example, *Misaeng* was exported to China, Taiwan, and Japan and sold 100,000 copies in Japan.

Webtoons have also been illegally copied in a number of Asian countries. *Alongside with the Gods: The Two Worlds*, written by Ju Ho-min, was illegally copied in some countries, for example. In China, many writers drew this webtoon, and they used the same story written by Ju. Compared with the Korean version, their characters were much cuter and prettier than those in the original webtoon.

However, for a few reasons Western countries have not yet embraced webtoons. Several factors are deterring the globalization of webtoons, mainly the lack of translation skills. Translation requires a lot of time and money. Translating a webtoon requires preserving the vivid and lively images. However, most translators are unable to develop a translation that appeals to Western readers. Naver has tried to penetrate the Western market by translating some of its webtoons into a few different languages, but it has lost a significant amount of money in doing so. Translation quality has been a big issue. Many webtoons use a great deal of slang, which is very important. However, illegal translations generally don't reflect these unique words that appeal to young people. Daum has spent about $10 million for translation, understanding the importance of quality translation. Webtoon platforms have branches in Japan and efforts are being made to absorb Japanese webtoonists into the Korean market so that they work together from the beginning.

Furthermore, webtoonists cannot receive the full benefits of globalization because of rampant piracy. When I went to a book fair in Frankfurt, Germany, a few years ago, people from Switzerland came to meet with me. I did not provide any material written in German, Italian, or French for Swiss people. However, because of illegal sites, they were already familiar with my webtoons, and they did not realize they were pirated. The violation of copyright laws has been quite problematic. Although Kang Full did not know anything about the Chinese manhwa market, we received news that his webtoons were pirated in China. In Korea, four million views per day proved the popularity of his webtoon. However, in China, it received forty million clicks daily. This suggests that one of the most significant potential markets for webtoonists has been ruined because of piracy. Illegal sites, both domestic and foreign, have hurt the Korean webtoon industry. Lezhin experienced a net loss of $14 million, largely because of these illegal sites. People who once to paid fees to Lezhin no longer do because they can enjoy the same webtoons on illegal webtoon platforms.

Because of the importance of the piracy issue, in April 2018, the Korean government announced a "joint countermeasure for overseas websites distributing pirated content." The government began developing technology to block illegal reproduction and distribution websites, such as The Night of the Rabbit, which distributed content, including webtoons, using servers in a foreign country. The Night of the Rabbit provided content for about 1,500 illegal copies of Korean webtoon series. Pirated content is shaking the foundation of the digital content industry [Yoon, Y. S., 2018]. According to the Korea Copyright Protection Agency, the amount of damage caused by the infringement of digital content copyrights increased from 1.07 trillion won in 2015 to 1.20 trillion won in 2017. A webtoon industry official said, "Pirate websites steal new series of webtoons that were carefully crafted by creators in two hours but private companies have limits to respond to them. . . . [I]t is urgent to come up with technical and political measures to block pirate sites that infringe on the copyrights with having servers in a foreign country and bypassing the domestic law" [Yoon, Y. S., 2018].

Interview With Yoon Tae-ho

This part of the chapter is based on my personal interviews with Yoon before and after his keynote speech. We met at a café for two hours to talk about his experience as a lead webtoonist and his vision for transmedia storytelling. Some parts overlap with his speech. After the speech, we briefly met again to check a few points. In this section, I attempt to avoid any duplications with the speech by emphasizing other major issues.

> **Jin:** You have published several interesting and popular webtoons. Other than webtoons, what is your favorite hobby? Are they [your hobbies] related to your work?
>
> **Yoon:** I like to travel because I need to have some unusual and unknown experiences. Therefore, my travel is not separate from my vision and/or plan of my next webtoon work. For example, after the end of one webtoon, I went to some places, including Greenland, the South Pole, and Alaska. I spend all my energy when I create webtoons, and after the season, I am exhausted. I need to have a rest. However, through these trips, I also learn some new things. The places I visit provide new ideas. My hobby and my work are closely related.[4]
>
> **Jin:** Why did you become a webtoonist?
>
> **Yoon:** Mainly because of the market milieu. I used to draw regular manhwa. However, the market has declined. Many creators believed that it was time to become a webtoonist because of the increasing role of digital technologies. In particular, when I became a webtoonist after drawing manhwa, I was in my late thirties, and new blood had already started to jump into the webtoon market. It was the last opportunity for me to change my focus and career.
>
> **Jin:** Which kind of media environment was the most important during your transition time from a cartoonist to a webtoonist?
>
> **Yoon:** Digital convergence between old and new media is a major issue. However, the role of the smartphone had actually started to increase

around 2014. Until then, people still used PCs to enjoy webtoons. Back then, there were only limited webtoon applications, which deterred the webtoon boom on smartphones. In recent years, many applications have appeared to attract webtoon readers. The proportion of mobile users has increased rapidly to become the majority of readers, and about 70 percent of webtoon readers now use their smartphones to access Daum and Naver. Once people started to use smartphones because of convenience and convergence, they also began to enjoy webtoons on their smartphone [see Jenkins, 2006].

Jin: Webtoonists these days consider themselves as becoming part of big-screen culture through transmedia storytelling. What do you think of it?

Yoon: It is inevitable. As transmedia transformation becomes popular, webtoonists also need to think about synergy, meaning we have to keep this phenomenon in mind when we create new webtoons. This is not an issue to be judged as either good or bad, because it is already out there. However, what we have to think about are the major characteristics of webtoons and movies. With movies, time flies automatically and forcefully. Once you start to watch a movie at a theater, you must watch it until the end. Webtoons are different because the readers have a choice: they can scroll down the page or choose not to. They just stop reading their favorite webtoons at certain points and come back later to finish them. This means that webtoonists must fulfill webtoon-like features instead of always considering big-screen elements. If webtoonists cannot meet webtoon-like characteristics, their works cannot become big-screen productions.

Jin: There are several webtoonists or companies that create webtoons for multiple purposes, which means that they immediately produce dramas or movies while publishing webtoons.

Yoon: A few webtoonists conduct that kind of system. However, none of them has achieved commercial successes. Webtoons and big-screen forms are different. Once webtoons are published, television producers and film directors can adapt them to develop big-screen culture. Webtoonists have great freedom and creativity to write and draw new materials. However, once they are ordered by film companies or broadcasters, their imagination may be limited and controlled. Creating cultural products with freedom and developing cultural products with limitations are much different. If webtoonists create cultural products based on contracts, their works turn into commodities and are not cultural products anymore.

Jin: Why don't you direct movies yourself?

Yoon: Film directors must have almighty power. I don't think I have that kind of director quality. Film directors have to work with music directors, stage directors, and cast and crew. Therefore, they must have the ability to control and inspire these crews and actors. As a webtoonist, I am able to control my own work, but I cannot effectively control other components and actors. I want to create webtoons that I enjoy first, instead of big-screen productions.

Jin: There are webtoons that have been adapted into television dramas and movies, such as *Misaeng* and *Inside Men*. Although not your work, *Along with the Gods: The Two Worlds* also attained huge success at theaters. However, in each case the plot and structure were modified. What do you think about it?

Yoon: Although we as webtoonists have the original rights, we cannot intervene in the big-screen production process once we sell the rights to movie companies and broadcasters. Just as they cannot intervene in our creative process, we do not control their process, which is important. In addition, we have to avoid the risk of unnecessary involvement in the process. The success or failure of movies and television dramas adapted from webtoons should be their makers' sole responsibility.

Jin: What is your most memorable work among your webtoons?

Yoon: It would be *Misaeng*, because I worked hard to create it. I never worked at any ordinary companies, and therefore, I did not know anything about salarymen's life. It was an impossible mission from the start. In order to gather some resources, I contacted a few big trading companies. However, they refused to open their doors. Therefore, I had to find someone else who was working at a mid-size trading company. They provided a lot of necessary information.

Jin: You just finished the first part of *Misaeng II*. What is the major difference between this new webtoon and the first one?

Yoon: The first one was about impeccable interns and salarymen. However, the new one is about the owner of small companies. As a salaryman, your life has been set by your company; as the owner of a small company, you have to decide everything. Most of all, in big companies, you are only a part of a big system, which means that your emotions and feelings are not important. In small companies, everybody knows everybody's life and feelings. Therefore, the life in small companies is emotional. Your personal character matters. In this particular webtoon, I plan to portray the detailed and complicated relationships between the owner and the employees.

Jin: Do you plan to develop it in a big-screen form?

Yoon: I will start to create Part 2 this coming winter. tvN will make it as a drama. Again, although I have the transmedia adaption of my work in mind, I try to focus on creativity.

Jin: Your most recent transmedia storytelling case is *Inside Men*, but you did not complete it. Do you plan to do so?

Yoon: When I created it, I wanted to become a webtoonist who continuously studied and learned from our society. For example, whenever I wrote about some social issue, like the Gangnam leftists,[5] I tried to understand it well by learning about it carefully and added some fiction to dramatize it. However, when I came to the end of this particular webtoon, there was a conflict between the webtoon's characters and my own character. I felt that I was more conservative than the webtoon's characters, and therefore, I could not finish it. I have no intention of completing the work because it was already made as a movie. Although the nonfiction parts were not completed, the movie director liked the fiction parts very much. It is politically very sensitive. However, there was no external pressure because only a limited number of people accessed this particular webtoon.

Jin: Like in *Misaeng* and *Inside Men*, you have continued to develop some serious social issues. Do you have any reasons for that?

Yoon: Manhwa is a kind of journal, which means that webtoons have no choice but to reflect sociocultural characteristics of the era they are written in. I personally grew up in Gwangju in the 1990s and witnessed some social movements. That experience became a basis of my own personal character to be reflected in webtoons.

Jin: As a webtoonist, you are very vocal about the welfare of artists. What is the major reason behind that?

Yoon: The milieu surrounding the manhwa industry has changed. Previously, a few big manhwa companies and manhwa gurus controlled manhwa artists. However, in the 2010s, webtoonists publish their creative works on various platforms, and these platforms must treat webtoonists fairly, with transparency. Webtoonists must be respected when contracting with these platforms. For example, they must have enough time to carefully check the contracts, and they have to use legal services with qualified lawyers.

Jin: What do you think about the contemporary webtoon industry?

Yoon: The webtoon industry has been growing exponentially. As of June 2018, about four thousand webtoonists are working to create and publish their works. There are about forty webtoon platforms for these webtoonists.

During 2009–2010, there were only two to three hundred webtoonists. It has greatly expanded to become one of the major cultural industries, and this will continue.

Jin: What is the most significant agenda item for the webtoon industry?

Yoon: The most significant homework for the webtoon world is to find foreign markets. The domestic market is saturated. Therefore, without exploring the global markets, the webtoon industry cannot expand further. Korean webtoonists are not the sole players. Japanese manga and Chinese comics are also targeting global markets. Therefore, how to compete with these cultural producers on the global stage is a big issue we have to think about.

Jin: Can you explain any particular strategies to make inroads into global markets?

Yoon: It is significant to develop webtoons reflecting universal ideas in order to penetrate global markets. The success of Marvel movies, such as *The Avengers* and *Iron Man*, depends on their portrayal of universal themes—including family issues, friendship, and individual sorrow—that appeal to the general public. Although they are hero movies, people don't go to theaters without experiencing commonalities they can sympathize with. Likewise, to appeal to global audiences, Korean webtoonists must depict themes and issues that everyone feels. In other words, webtoonists have to develop insights to attract global audiences. Although drawing ability is important, understanding our contemporary society is also very important.

Jin: What is your advice to emerging webtoonists?

Yoon: One of the most significant parts is sustainability. Creating webtoons involves a lot of emotional effort, and webtoonists need to control their emotions to continue their quality work. For example, many webtoonists are easily affected by people's comments on their works. Some young webtoonists are too eager to see their works succeed and do not control their pace. When people cheer, these webtoonists go far beyond their capacity to please the audiences, which hurts creativity and continuity.

Jin: What are the most important systematic supports you can develop as the president of the manhwa association?

Yoon: We need to see two different parts. The government must support artists by providing necessary legal and financial measures. In particular, early career webtoonists cannot make enough money during the intersession between the first part and the second part of the same webtoon. I hope that the government provides some insurance to them so that they are able to continue their creative works.

Jin: What is the most significant agenda item for the webtoon industry, as the owner of a webtoon firm?

Yoon: I want to emphasize the importance of blockchain as a new business model as I focus on blockchain technologies. The internet provided some opportunities through the use of openness and accessibility to everyone. However, through mergers and acquisitions only a few limited portals and mega giants control the internet-related markets. In the blockchain era, I believe that webtoon companies and artists can share benefits by eliminating intermediaries. Although a few mega giants may control the market, we have some hope for transparent and collaborative mutual benefits when the companies and the artists work together.

More specifically, I plan to use blockchain in the webtoon business in order to fund-raise for the development of new webtoonists and webtoons. For this, the most important part is to write a white paper appealing to investors. In particular, creating good profiles of webtoonists will be key, because these papers show who they are and what they can develop. I still think about details because the methods of an ICO [initial coin offering; a fund-raising mechanism in which new projects sell their underlying crypto tokens in exchange for bitcoins and ether]—can be carefully decided. For example, I plan to write a new webtoon titled *South Pole* and have to decide on the total amount of money I need. Because I have to visit the South Pole and stay there for a long period of time, I need to secure some investments. To do this, I'll explain the ways in which I will write the webtoon and divide the profits, including those from subsequent movies and/or television dramas, which are not easy to determine.

ICOs are a relatively new business model but are rapidly becoming a dominant venture-funding model. Because I believe that some webtoonists or companies are successfully able to use ICOs on blockchain, I am now working with lawyers. As was the case with the initial stage of the internet, many people are very interested in this new form of investment opportunity, and I have to seriously consider it for my works and company.

Conclusion

The webtoon has become one of the latest and most significant forms of digital culture, and Korean webtoons have become sources for transmedia storytelling, both nationally and globally. Along with the rapid penetration of smartphones into society, the manhwa industry has shifted its focus from magazine manhwa and manhwa books to webtoons. Yoon, as one of the pioneers of the webtoon field, has created many popular webtoons reflecting sociocultural conflicts in contemporary Korean society, which eventually were turned into big-screen cultural products. Partially due to his contributions in advancing webtoons and webtoon-based transmedia storytelling, many amateur webtoonists have sought to become another Yoon, while big-screen culture creators are attempting to make webtoon-based television programs and films. However, as Yoon emphasized, significant issues—including illegal piracy and a paucity of high-quality translators, as well as the growing number of adult genre webtoons—continue to hurt the webtoon world and the transnationalization of webtoons. What the webtoon industry must keep in mind, therefore, is avoiding excessive commodification and commercialism, while the Korean government and webtoon platforms need to provide reliable media milieus for the creation of high-quality webtoons.

CHAPTER 7

Webtoons' New Perspectives

In the early twenty-first century, Korea became not only the birthplace but also the hub of webtoons. The webtoon represents both the first cultural product and the first digital culture that Korea has created. Within two decades of the advent of webtoons in the Korean cultural sphere, webtoons have become a major cultural form. As a distinctive digital culture, webtoons have greatly appealed to many Koreans who seek a new type of culture. Influenced by Korean webtoons, other countries (including the United States, Japan, and China) have also recently developed webtoons. Webtoons as cultural content are perfectly suited for the digital era, as they have been digitally produced since the form's inception and are intended to be uploaded, disseminated, and consumed on digital platforms—in particular, using smartphone technology. The webtoon "follows the traits of television dramas and newspaper comic strips in that it is uploaded regularly (usually weekly), but interactions between authors and readers are much more spontaneous and direct in the online environment" (Pyo, Jang, and Yoon, 2019, 2162).

When Korean youth started to enjoy webtoons in the early 2000s, people considered webtoons to be a niche culture and assumed that they would be read by only a limited number of young people. However, webtoons have now entered the mainstream entertainment sector (Choi, J. W., 2020). People in their teens and twenties are the primary readers, but those in their upper twenties and thirties, who grew up in the early days of the form, and even some older people enjoy webtoons.

Since webtoons have significantly increased their readership, both nationally and globally, over the past two decades, the Korean government hopes that the webtoon industry will be the next major producer of high-quality content and has begun to use webtoons as a medium for transmedia storytelling (Kim, M. S., 2015; Ministry of Culture, Sports and Tourism, 2019). The Korean government did not develop substantial supporting mechanisms for the webtoon sector until very recently. However, as webtoons have demonstrated their position as treasure troves of content for the cultural and digital economy, the government has gradually increased its support for the webtoon industry. Given the increasing role of webtoons as IP engines, for example, the government has increased its financial subsidies to the webtoon sector, while developing controls to restrict illegal activities (Yecies et al., 2019; Ministry of Culture, Sports and Tourism, 2019).

Given the increasing popularity of webtoons, local cultural industries have begun paying attention to webtoons as both individual cultural content and source materials for transmedia storytelling. Many cultural creators in Korea have already developed webtoon-based cultural products. Quite a few global cultural firms and platforms, including Netflix, are interested in Korean webtoons as a new source of original adaptable content. Therefore, Korean webtoon platforms and webtoonists have greatly increased their IP-based penetration of foreign markets, as well as the number of their finished cultural products. For example, Netflix's original series *Kingdom* and Crunchyroll's anime *Tower of God* are based on Korean webtoons. *Space Sweepers* (a movie) and *Seungriho* (a webtoon; English title *Spaceship Victory*) were produced almost simultaneously during 2020, although due to COVID-19 the release of *Space Sweepers* was delayed to February 2021 and released via Netflix instead of in theaters, as originally planned. Webtoon-based transmedia storytelling has not only begun to overshadow the OSMU model of cultural creation, but it also drives the creation of alternative IP by creating transmedia universes, a process that has attracted the attention of cultural creators in various countries.

Globally, webtoons are certainly riding the Korean Wave. The manhwa industry was originally the smallest cultural sector in the Korean Wave. However, due to the global spread of webtoons, the manhwa industry has become comparable in size to the film industry through the exponential growth of foreign exports. Many global viewers can read Korean webtoons translated into their languages by either fans or webtoon platforms, as well as enjoying webtoon-based big-screen cultural content.

Webtoons have also provided diverse business models, methods of production and circulation, genres and themes, and webtoon artists. Webtoons have increased their role and visibility in the global cultural scene and led to the creation of new perspectives on the process of cultural production and platformization. Webtoons in Korea have introduced and developed a significant youth culture, which includes snack culture and binge-reading, and will experience further development as emphasis on AI and virtual reality as the industry grows.

Consequently, while seemingly representing only a small example of digital culture, webtoons have greatly transformed and influenced all types of cultural industries. As an emerging and increasingly important digital culture that has altered the Korean cultural sphere in general, webtoons have fundamentally shifted the business paradigm in various cultural industries. And since webtoons are continuing to rapidly expand their role in the global cultural scene, they are increasing their clout as a form of global youth culture in the digital culture sphere.

In this final chapter, I summarize a handful of major findings and expand discussions of a few focal points of digital culture—namely, platformization and transnationality in conjunction with transmedia storytelling—as some of the most significant characteristics defining contemporary Korean webtoons. Finally, I provide some concluding thoughts on the theoretical and practical implications of webtoons.

Webtoons as Digital Culture

Global youth consumption habits have rapidly changed, from family-oriented collective cultural consumption to individual cultural consumption on personal digital gadgets, including notebook computers, PCs, and smartphones. Access to these digital technologies allows youth to enjoy all kinds of popular culture individually. As the term *webtoon* illustrates, webtoons are a combination of digital technology and popular culture. Thus, they are both a new form of media convergence and an example of seamless cultural content that appeals to global youth and represents contemporary cultural activities. Unlike manhwa, popular in the form of printed books, webtoons can be read online. The personalization of cultural consumption has been intensified and expanded due to the growth of webtoon culture and digital platform technologies.

There are some other distinctive forms of digital culture on smartphones, including mobile gaming. However, webtoons are quite different from other smartphone-driven digital cultures. Webtoons may not be the first digital culture on smartphones, but they are the foremost cultural form that targets and is optimized for smartphones. The vertical layout of webtoons fits well on smartphones because people can simply scroll down on their phones to read webtoons with no restrictions on time or space. Verticality provides freedom to webtoon artists, as they can express their creativity with no specific barriers.

Compared to revolutionary webtoons, mobile gaming does not show any significant characteristics of media convergence. Mobile gamers are used to playing casual, simple games that people typically can enjoy anywhere, spending three to five minutes per game. Therefore, mobile gaming can be categorized as another form of snack culture. However, once people start a mobile game, they must finish it within a certain amount of time to move on to the next level. In contrast, people reading webtoons can return directly to the point where they stopped reading, if they have to set the webtoon aside temporarily. Webtoons thus are more flexible than mobile games. They are also less stressful since there is no competition. Webtoons symbolize individual digital culture that people can enjoy with flexibility and mobility.

As a snack-culture format, webtoons are capturing the attention of an increasing number of viewers. Webtoon fans enjoy this new form of digital culture mainly because of webtoons' cultural specificities. Webtoons represent the rapidly shifting contemporary Korean society. There are webtoons focusing on fantasy, and some webtoons emphasize a nationless worldview. However, the major themes and genres of webtoons focus on local culture embedded in historical or contemporary Korean society. In recent years Korea has experienced large-scale, roller-coaster-like changes, such as political, economic, and sociocultural shifts, and many Korean youth experience multiple adversities. They may have had difficulty in getting into a good university, getting through college in spite of a lack of money, finding a job after graduation, and finding a place to live because of soaring housing prices. Many college graduates in their early twenties have to work in part-time positions, which can make their life difficult. Some Korean youth feel that they are losers, and webtoons portray their hardships. By spending only a small amount of money, they can enjoy webtoons with characters with which they can easily sympathize.

Webtoons' emphasis on Korean youth's contemporary sociocultural experiences is one major reason for the sector's growth. Many webtoon artists have used their own experiences in creating their stories, and that often resonates well with readers. Therefore, unlike American comics and Japanese manga, which often focus on action heroes, the most popular webtoons are those dealing with sociocultural issues such as poverty, cyberbullying, suicide, youth unemployment, social injustice, and domestic violence (Jung, H. W., 2015), making webtoons one of the most important digital cultures for youth and young adults.

As noted above, webtoons have greatly influenced the development of binge-reading. Binge-watching and binge-reading are new trends among global youth. As Millennials and members of Generation Z have changed how they consume culture, webtoon platforms have taken advantage of the shifting media ecology, exemplified by Netflix's promotion of binge-watching. Millennials and members of Generation Z do not seem to want to wait for things and also want to consume cultural content when they have the time to do so. This means that readers often set aside some time to binge-watch and binge-read cultural content. From mobile gaming to OTT and webtoon platforms, digital platforms have not only advanced new business models but have also strengthened practices such as binge-watching, binge-playing, and binge-reading. Digital platforms monetize people's leisure time, impatience, and mobility, but webtoons are unique in monetizing people's binge-reading. Webtoons' major characteristics are closely related to people's role as audiences or consumers who use new forms of cultural consumption. Thus, webtoons have created a new digital and youth culture that Korean youth consume and global youth are beginning to enjoy.

Webtoons and Platformization

Webtoons have greatly advanced the platformization of cultural production, which has consequently transformed people's cultural activities. These changes are not minimal, but profound and diverse. Global digital platforms such as YouTube, Netflix, and Spotify initially acted as cultural distributors. However, they have developed their roles as producers and are deeply connected to people's cultural consumption, which has been shifting dramatically as consumers enjoy various cultural content on these platforms. As a new form of media convergence, webtoons add numerous ingredients to global youth culture. Webtoons are designed, published, and consumed on webtoon platforms, and people can enjoy webtoons immediately on their smartphones. This is the only digital culture in which the entire process of cultural production (including not just actual production but also distribution and consumption) can be synchronously actualized on digital platforms. Webtoons represent a new form of content created by "the mobile internet ecosystem" (Park, J. Y., 2019, 1). Webtoonists "started to draw bespoke, original content specifically for online consumption. . . . [A] new generation of webtoons, taking full advantage of the digital space, feature sound and visual effects" (Kim, M. S., 2015). Webtoon outlets and webtoon content have diversified with the use of various social media platforms and consumers' shifting cultural tastes. Korean webtoons and webtoon platforms have meaningfully transformed the global comic markets as well: "Webtoon content and platforms represent a unique content genre and distribution system developed in Korea. What users enjoy today is the result of years of optimization and transformation in areas such as platform services, content supply systems, story lines, and formats. Korea is indeed the global trendsetter in all aspects of webtoons" (Park, J. Y., 2019, 8).

In 2020, there were more than sixty webtoon platforms, either owned by mega digital platforms or operated as a form of webtoon-driven platform. However, KakaoPage (including Daum Webtoon) and Naver Webtoon have played leading roles in shaping webtoon culture. Several thousand webtoonists publish their webtoons on these platforms, and more than 140,000 people post as amateur artists on Challenge Manhwa (Dojeon Manhwa), a part of Naver Webtoon, to pursue their opportunities to become professional webtoonists (Lee, S. G., 2019). Many good webtoons are published every year that numerous fans enjoy, mainly thanks to the increasing role of webtoon platforms—in particular, the mega ones.

More importantly, the transformation of the cultural production of webtoons has paralleled the platformization of webtoons. In the early stage of webtoon development, digital platforms in the form of internet portals featured webtoons mainly in as a way to increase their traffic: Since many people visited their portals many times to read webtoons, they could claim that they were one of the largest or most popular portals. In that way, they were able to increase ad revenues. Major digital platforms eventually developed the freemium model, at least partially in tandem with the increase in consumers' binge-reading. Digital platforms have greatly transformed webtoons from niche cultural content used to promote the platforms' visibility to one of the major drivers of the platforms' development.

Naver and Kakao have platformized webtoons through corporate strategies, including new business models, structural transformations, transmediality IP engines, and the exploitation of artists and readers. While other global platforms have focused on particular business models—such as Facebook's use of advertising and Netflix's subscription model—webtoon platforms have diversified their business models to maximize their profits. As Li (2020, 237) points out, with the rise of various digital platforms in the last decade, the focus started to change "from content to platform."

Digital platforms as mediators have managed the entire process of cultural production. In particular, Naver and Kakao have strongly controlled the entire media ecology. US-based platforms such as Google, Facebook, and Twitter (ad-supported social media platforms) and Netflix (a subscription-based OTT service platform) have certainly also mediated the process of cultural production. However, Naver and Kakao have diversified their business models while advancing in-house production systems, and therefore their roles as mediators are larger and more diversified than those of the global corporate superpowers. As Nieborg and Helmond (2019, 203) point out, "the process of platformization has profound political economic and infrastructural implications." In securing new forms of dominance in the culture industries, Korean webtoon platforms have provided new perspectives on global cultural markets.

Of course, the platformization of webtoons has caused some serious issues, as digital platforms intensify the oligopolistic dominance of the webtoon market. Despite the transformative benefits of digital platforms for cultural production, it is crucial to understand that the emergence of the platforms has been "a new hegemonic constellation of 21st-century capitalism, and the neoliberal governance and exploitation of labor that concomitantly intensify" (Kim, J. H., and Yu, 2019, 1). Due to the platformization of webtoons, this new form of digital culture has rapidly become a symbol of contemporary capitalism.

Toward Transnational Transmedia Storytelling

Webtoons have transformed the notion of transmedia storytelling in various ways, and webtoons are playing a key role in Korean-originated transnational transmediality. Some webtoon platforms have diversified webtoons' moneymaking processes, with webtoonists and webtoon platforms working closely together from the planning stage onward to use webtoons in various cultural industries. Webtoons increasingly blur the distinction between cultural forms: webtoons are now part of manhwa, web novels, television programs, films, digital games, and musicals. These cultural sectors relate to webtoons based on the convergence of popular culture and digital technologies—in particular, digital platforms and transmediality. Therefore, they pay careful attention to webtoons. Moreover, participants in these cultural industries (e.g., film production companies) now themselves produce webtoons so they can use them immediately for their big-screen cultural productions.

Webtoons have greatly transformed the media ecology, as broadcasting, film, and game industries companies increasingly rely on webtoons. Webtoons have provided many fresh stories to cultural creators and industries. Webtoons' transmediality can clearly be seen in contemporary television programs and films. Whenever one changes television channels, one is likely to find a webtoon-based television drama. Although recent production has been delayed due to COVID-19, as of early 2021 at least five webtoon-based movies were in production. This illustrates that broadcasters and filmmakers in recent years have increasingly relied on webtoons for source material due to their original stories, visual images, and established fan bases. Webtoons have deeply influenced both media and cultural industries and media and cultural production.

Webtoons have also changed the culture of transmedia storytelling. In the cultural industries, the use of webtoon-based transmedia formats has become a new norm because such transmedia storytelling now goes beyond the traditional use of a single source. Given the recent growth of webtoon-based transmedia storytelling, digital platforms and webtoonists consider multiple production approaches from the beginning. When they publish a webtoon, they often simultaneously think about its adaption to films or television programs.

Most of all, webtoons have played a key role in transnational transmedia storytelling. Until the early 2000s, comics in Western countries and manga and anime in Japan were major source materials for big-screen culture. However, webtoons became major new sources for films, television dramas, games, and musicals first in Korea, and later in many other countries. In the US cultural market, Marvel Comics composes the largest portion of the market, followed by Japanese manga. However, they mainly focus on specific genres, such as superhero fiction. Producers constantly need new stories and often find them in Korean webtoons. Webtoons' timely advent, both nationally and globally, has provided new opportunities for global cultural creators to adapt them into big-screen content. This does not mean that webtoons are the largest source of material for global cultural creators, nor are they replacing US comics or Japanese manga or anime as source materials. Rather, webtoons have attracted the attention of some major global cultural producers (such as Netflix and Crunchyroll) that have continued to develop webtoon-based cultural content. Webtoons have increasingly gained popularity due to their diverse content. Webtoons span pretty much every genre, from romance to thrillers and from historical epics to crime stories. Due to webtoons' diverse themes and genres, which often are not commonly explored by Hollywood, major filmmakers are showing great interest in Korean webtoons (Choi, I. J., 2020).

Webtoons have also gradually transformed transnational cultural flows, both culturally and structurally. The webtoon industry has expanded the ways in which Korean cultural industries reach global audiences. These industries have penetrated the markets of other countries through finished cultural products, as can be seen in television programs and films or K-pop on YouTube. However, webtoons have used a new tool to attract global audiences. In addition, Korean digital platforms have established subsidiary companies in foreign countries. Since the mid-2010s Naver, Daum, and Kakao have established webtoon platforms abroad or invested in foreign webtoon platforms to extend their global reach. These overseas webtoon platforms create webtoons in two different ways: the introduction of translated Korean webtoons and the development of webtoons in foreign locations.

Thus, webtoons have contributed to the shift in the direction of culture exports from mainly top-down flows from Western to non-Western nations to a reverse flow from non-Western to Western nations. This new flow (see Thussu, 2006) was achieved because Korea was the first country to develop webtoons and webtoon platforms. Webtoons have evolved in global cultural markets differently from the way other cultural sectors evolved, as webtoons' overseas distribution involves the establishment of global webtoon outlets instead of using existing global platforms such as YouTube. Webtoon platforms in foreign countries have attempted to localize webtoons, recruiting local artists who emphasize local mentalities. Therefore, the platforms have developed structural hybridization. As Yecies (2018, 134) points out, "although parts of the world may have been slow to notice, a wide variety of Korean artists, agencies, policy makers, and vertically-integrated media companies have been developing this novel digital screen and convergent culture, and expanding the webtoon ecosystem."

For the most part, research on transmedia storytelling has focused on the relationship between story expansion and genre (see Bick 1996; Steinmüller 2003, cited in Beddows, 2012). Transmedia storytelling in the era of digital media has become "a norm in the cultural industries as it shifts the resources of cultural products while providing creative and converging ideas" (Jin, D. Y., 2019a, 2109). However, transmedia storytelling needs to be understood as a complex relationship between multiple factors, including the increasing role of webtoon consumers—not only readers, but also consumers of webtoon-based big-screen cultural content. The relationships among story modes, genres, and markets imply that cultural consumers are engaged by transmedia storytelling via processes that involve participation, design, and response (Beddows, 2012). Therefore, the formation of webtoon consumer culture greatly influences webtoons' cultural production.

Future Directions and New Perspectives

The webtoon as a new form of digital culture has influenced the entire process of cultural production—including the production, circulation, and consumption of cultural products—which is unprecedented. Webtoons are the next frontier in global cultural industries, and there is no doubt that they will continue to grow as a major constituent of Korean cultural industries and youth culture, as well as a part of the global cultural scene. As webtoons continue to evolve, their future as a form of digital culture is promising. However, there are several elements that webtoon platforms and webtoonists should consider to help foster the evolution of webtoons to the next level.

Most of all, I believe that webtoon platforms and webtoonists have to create webtoons based on local identities, instead of developing nationless cultural content. I am not arguing that webtoonists must be nationalistic. Rather, I emphasize that webtoons focusing on local mentalities (such as *Kingdom, Itaewon Class*, and *The Lady and Her Butler*) are often well received in global markets, as well as within Korea. In fact, the most significant requirement for local webtoons to become more popular in global cultural markets is their emphasis on local tastes. Webtoon artists do not need to downplay this major characteristic. Cultural identities and unique worldviews embedded in Korean society are often attractive to international readers and cultural creators. This should encourage webtoon platforms and webtoonists to publish webtoons that represent local specificities instead of mixing different cultures to appeal to global audiences. The saying "the more local, the more global" is a simple but powerful message for webtoon platforms and webtoonists, as well as for other cultural producers. Several cultural products in the realms of films, K-pop, and television dramas have also achieved global popularity through their use of Koreanness. For example, *Parasite*, a Korean movie directed by Bong Joon-ho, won several awards at the 2020 Oscars, partially due to its portrayal of local identities. Likewise, many global cultural consumers are eager to enjoy Korean webtoons and webtoon-based big-screen cultural content that includes Koreanness.

This does not mean that webtoonists and webtoon platforms should create only culturally specific webtoons. They can also develop more generally appealing content such as fantasy and BL webtoons that do not emphasize local identity but rather focus on global commonality for global youth. Authors in various popular media (Choi, I. J., 2020; Park, M. J., 2020a) have argued that the success of webtoons in global cultural markets has greatly relied on glocalization strategies, and the cultural industries do need to use such strategies. However, webtoonists can modify their original stories slightly to appeal to global audiences without losing Koreanness. The main issue is whether the content retains and develops cultural identities. Webtoonists and cultural creators more broadly must understand the significance of local mentalities, which are fundamental to the growth of webtoons, while also recognizing that global youth also enjoy some webtoons that portray worldviews with which they can sympathize. I believe that webtoons create a vibrant cultural sphere in which local mentalities can be shown, discussed, and respected within a hybrid culture, and that this vibrancy serves to drive the rise of the Korean webtoon world—both nationally and globally.

Webtoons and webtoon platforms also need to continue using diverse themes and genres, as some existing genres (including *il-sang*, *hagwon*, and *sunjeong*) are not only fun, but also quite engaging. Unlike other Korean cultural industries, webtoons have the flexibility to introduce genres such as BL and *il-sang*. Webtoonists also need to extend their scope, as recent webtoons include special effects through the use of virtual reality and AR. Unlike other cultural areas, the transmediality of webtoons pertains to webtoon fans who are not solely consuming webtoons but also enjoying webtoon-based big-screen content, meaning that digital media-driven production is required in the webtoon sector. Webtoon practices must develop the interconnectivity of webtoon themes and webtoon consumption relevant to transmediality. The webtoon industry needs to continuously develop new genres and digital technologies if it is to become one of the major cultural forms that appeal to global audiences.

Webtoonists also have to consider the balance between the creation of unique digital culture and the progress of the webtoon market. Webtoons create the world that a new culture resides in, and thus webtoonists have to think about what kind of world this should be. It is crucial for webtoon platforms and webtoonists to advance that world—not only as a venue for garnering profits, but also as a cultural sphere where people can enjoy unique and locally focused digital culture. Drawing on the work of Lazzarato (2004), Steinberg (2012, 183) points out, "contemporary capitalism is characterized not so much by the creation of products but by the creation of worlds." Furthermore, Lazarrato (2004, 94) argues the contemporary enterprise "creates not the subject (the merchandise) but the world where the subject exists. It creates not the subject (worker or consumer) but the world where the subject exists" (cited in Steinberg, 2012, 183). Capitalist valorization depends on the development of worlds (Steinberg, 2012, 183). Webtoons are relatively new, and webtoonists should emphasize the form's creation of a new world that can be developed as a cultural sphere, not as a financial one. Without understanding the importance of the logic of culture first, finance next, Korean webtoons will face tangible challenges from international competitors.

Overall, starting as a form of pure snack culture optimized for smartphones, webtoons have continued to diversify their cultural characteristics, from simple cartoon types of online manhwa to major sources for transnational transmedia storytelling. Webtoons are one of the most promising digital cultures, due to their distinctive characteristics that attract global youth and big-screen cultural creators. While the webtoon is not the only cultural phenomenon that originated in Korea, it is currently increasing its representation of the Korean cultural sphere in the global cultural markets. The webtoon is perceived as belonging to or stemming from Korea, but it is also increasingly experienced by global youth as their own culture of choice. Similar to Japanese manga, which is popular, both locally and internationally (Kacsuk, 2018, 16–17; see also Brienza, 2014), the webtoon has become a staple element of digital youth culture in Korea and shows significant promise of further expanding in other countries around the globe. The inroads made by a new media form—webtoons—may offer hope for the entire landscape of cultural industries. Designed specifically to be read on smartphones, webtoons are increasingly ubiquitous and appear to have a wide appeal, and their adaptation into television dramas and films has proven to be lucrative (Martin, 2018, 96). The webtoon is an archetype of what it means to have truly transnational circuits of cultural production. Webtoons' increasing roles in global cultural production and consumption furthers the possibility of forging affective ties among youth and young adults in a number of countries around the globe in relation to Korean culture and, as a possible extension, to Korea.

Notes

Introduction

1. In most cases, anyone born between 1981 and 1996 (people ages 26–41 in 2022) is considered a Millennial, and anyone born in 1997 or later, until the early 2010s, is part of Generation Z.

2. In contrast to hard power, which mainly refers to military power, soft power is "attractive power" used to "get outcomes that people want," and it relies primarily on the attractiveness of the culture of any country (Nye, 2004, 5–6).

3. The term *transmedia* was used for the first time by Kinder (1991). Kinder used the term *transmedia intertextuality* to define and discuss how narratives for children had moved into different forms of media and presented different levels of interaction. The prefix *trans* suggests the idea of passage, going further, changing from one condition to another, and exchanging. Since Kinder's definition, the word *transmedia* has normally been accompanied by the word *storytelling*, assuming a specific connotation on how narratives based on different channels and multiple languages are constructed (Ciastellardi and Di Rosario, 2015, 11).

1. Evolution of Webtoons in the Digital Platform Era

1. During a telephone interview I conducted on October 13, 2021, with the article's author, he explained that he had written the article based on a press release provided by AniBS. Back then, he said, "a few startups already used the term *webtoon*." Therefore, the term was certainly used at least earlier than the mid-1990s. In Ha Park, who is known as one of the best manhwa critics, also stated during a telephone interview with me on October 13, 2021, that "the term might be associated with the process of scanned manhwa as a digital form," a process that was first used in the mid-1990s. Although he did not identify the exact origin of the term *webtoon*, his blog on Naver claimed that

Kwang-su Thinking, discussed below in this chapter, was the first webtoon in Korea (Park, I. H., 2021).

2. Some argue that Korea's first webtoon is Han Hee-jak's *A Desert Island*, which was published in 1996 (Um, M. A., 2018). However, this was a scanned print manhwa that had already been published. In the mid-1990s, personal computers became popular, and some manhwa artists scanned their print manhwa and uploaded them to online home pages.

3. As has been well articulated (Cho, H. K., 2016), comics are a medium that entwines words and images. Their most fundamental elements are panels (or frames), gutters (the spaces between panels), speech balloons, and text boxes (or captions). For several decades, comics have maintained a certain look and format: boxes with images inside that are read left to right or right to left depending on the medium and language. However, webtoons are read top to bottom (Travers, 2017). One of the most significant differences that the vertical layout creates concerns the role of the gutter in webtoons. The gutters in conventional print comics are visually dull, usually narrow white spaces between panels. However, in webtoons, the gutter is used to create a diversified visual space to accompany the text. The gutter sometimes occupies more space than the panels and contributes to the narrative in various ways (Cho, H. K., 2016).

4. One of the major landmarks in the development of webtoons is their convergence with social media, including Facebook, Instagram, and Twitter. Due to the space restrictions on these media, some webtoons do not emphasize vertical layout or, therefore, vertical scrolling. The format of webtoons has changed, and the openness to change of webtoons has greatly contributed to the growth in their numbers (Park, G. S., 2018). While the vertical format has been one of the major characteristics of webtoons, it cannot be considered a requirement—meaning that the early forms of webtoons without vertical layouts also need be considered as webtoons as long as they have some of their other major features.

2. Platformization of Korean Webtoons

1. S. C. Kim and Lee (2019) also provide an analysis of the changes in the Korean webtoon industry through the use of platformization, focusing on economic aspects (market structure), politics (power relations), and infrastructure. They discuss the economic, political, and sociocultural implications of the significant shifts in the cultural production of webtoons, which have gained considerable attention as a major original story source in the cultural industry.

2. Naver also decided to invest approximately $321.6 million in beNX, a subsidiary of HYBE (previously known as Big Hit), the entertainment label that manages BTS, a seven-member boy idol group. BeNX will acquire Naver's V LIVE division. BeNX is the HYBE subsidiary that developed HYBE's popular direct-to-fan app platform, Weverse. Naver and HYBE will create a new global fan community platform that integrates the users, content, and services of Weverse and V LIVE. Meanwhile, Naver will cooperate with HYBE and beNX to continue its global leadership in fan community platforms (Stassen, 2021). Naver and KakaoPage are not only giants in the webtoon sector but also superpowers in the entire entertainment industry.

3. Due to the significance of the US market, Kakao acquired the firm Tapas Media in May 2021. Tapas, the first webtoon platform established in the United States, has a content library of some 80,000 webtoons. With the acquisition of Tapas, Kakao plans to compete with Naver Webtoon in the US webtoon market (Oh, D. S., 2021).

3. Webtoons' Digital Sphere

1. While the large portal sites Naver and Daum provided webtoons for free until 2014, in 2013 Lezhin Comics started to charge fees per episode. It's clear that KakaoPage and Naver learned from Lezhin Comics' fee-based webtoon business model (Park, E. J., 2016).
2. "Binging Webtoons," Reddit thread, https://www.reddit.com/r/webtoons/comments/axkh96/binging_webtoons/, accessed May 1, 2022.
3. "I Need a BL to Binge Read," Reddit thread, https://www.reddit.com/r/webtoons/comments/g5ochj/i_need_a_bl_to_binge_read/, accessed May 1, 2022.
4. Quora, https://www.quora.com/What-binge-worthy-webtoons-do-you-recommend, accessed May 1, 2022.

4. Transmedia Storytelling of Webtoons in Big-Screen Culture

1. In Japan, manga have been major source materials for big-screen culture during the past several decades. For example, *yōkai* (supernatural monsters in Japanese folklore) in Mizuki Shigeru's manga became hugely popular and were transformed into cultural products such as toys, movies, and games through transmedia expansion. However, due to a lack of new ideas and subjects, Japanese manga and even anime have lost momentum and are no longer the most significant sources for big-screen culture in Japan (Steinberg, 2017b; Lombardi, 2019; Suzuki, 2019).
2. The term *epic* here is based mainly on the length of stories. Some webtoons are comparable in length to novels or television series. In some cases, when all of the episodes are considered together, the length of a webtoon is equal to that of several books. Individually, several episodes still represent snack culture. However, it may take several hours or even days to finish reading the entire story. Thus, the connotation of *epic* in this book has nothing to do with the subjective quality of individual webtoons.
3. In many cases, K-pop songs "revolve around romance, partying and, on occasion, friendship and daily life. But tracks with underlying socio-economic and political meaning exist, and BTS is one act that regularly incorporates criticism of South Korean society into their music. Extremely popular in the U.S. regardless of linguistic and geographic barriers, many of BTS' fans, known collectively as 'ARMY,' or Adorable Representative MC of Youth, have said that the boy band's lyrics have inspired them. Littering a millennial-oriented message about societal woes throughout their discography, the group manages to frequently reference the struggles that young people go through and draw on their own experiences within South Korean youth culture" (Herman, 2018).
4. The jobless rate among Koreans ages 15–29 (including those with part-time work) hit 25.6 percent in July 2021, the highest since 2015 (Ku, E. S., 2020).

5. Although *byeong-mat* has gradually faded as more webtoon artists are turning to genre-based webtoons (Do, D. W., 2015), webtoons in this style continue to influence people's cultural activities, since many young people still like this type of content..

6. Greene (2019) writes: "A common English expression refers to the privileged few who are born 'with a silver spoon in their mouth.' South Koreans divide the world into *geumsujeo*, 'golden spoons,' and *heuksujeo*, 'dirt spoons.' This cutlery classification distinguishes the haves from the have-nots, giving a Korean twist to a universal sentiment. Like young people everywhere, many young Koreans fret that social mobility is declining. As with a number of other terms that were first used in contempt, some dirt spoons now embrace their label."

7. *Hagwons* are private schools that many Korean students attend outside regular school hours for extra study.

5. Webtoons' Transnational Transmediality

1. An internet slang term, implying something is in bad taste. Also used when a person witnesses something bizarre.

2. Several editors of Japanese manga publishers have moved to Piccoma and Line Manga in the past few years, and a variety of Japanese mangas have attempted to turn themselves into webtoons (Han, C. W., 2021).

3. While Japanese companies have also attempted to develop manga for American readers who use digital technologies, the formats are problematic due to the low quality of the translated product: "Translations were unreadable, as if they had been done by Google Translate or Babel Fish, and the choice of fonts was ugly, the naysayers contended. This was especially problematic given the high prices currently being charged. Moreover, reading manga on cell phones or computer screens, particularly at prices virtually identical to the cost of a print, may not be appealing to most readers" (Brienza, 2014, 389).

4. Action Square, a Korean company that develops games, announced in September 2020 that it was working on a new mobile game based on the Netflix series *Kingdom*, having signed a game development contract with the series production company (Im, 2020).

5. Goodreads, "Joli Mamon's Reviews, *The Lady and her Butler*," September 6, 2018. https://www.goodreads.com/review/show/2521317670.

6. Sociocultural Perspectives on Webtoonists

1. During our interviews, Yoon discussed these rejections and his path to becoming a manhwa artist as well as his switch to webtoons. These topics are discussed in later sections of this chapter.

2. The information about Yoon's works mainly came from Nulook Media (2020).

3. Yoon published his first manhwa, *Emergency Landing*, in 1993, five years after he became a disciple of Hur Young Man (SBS, 2019).

4. Yoon started to publish a webtoon titled *Eorin* (meaning *fish scale*) on Daum Webtoon and KakaoPage in March 2020, based on his adventures at the South Pole (Kim, H. A., 2020). *Eorin* was finished in March 2022.

5. The term *Gangnam leftists* "refers to people who live a rich life [in Gangnam, a neighborhood in Seoul] but have a proletarian mind. Originally it was used to make cynical remarks about the self-contradictory behavior of the so-called 386 generation [the generation of Koreans born in the 1960s who were very active politically and instrumental in the democracy movement of the 1980s]. However, it has more widespread use these days. . . . [I]t is a general term for people who have a leftist mindset but enjoy bountiful lives" (Yang, 2007).

References

Acuna, K. (2016). "Millions in Korea Are Obsessed with These Revolutionary Comics—Now They're Going Global." *Insider*, February 11. https://www.businessinsider.com/what-is-webtoons-2016-2.
Age of Webtoons (n.d.). http://phonetimes.co.kr/php/phone/news_print.asp?uid=274&code=knowledge.
Aggleton, J. (2019). "Defining Digital Comics: A British Library Perspective." *Journal of Graphic Novels and Comics* 10 (4): 393–409.
Aizu, I (2002). "A Comparative Study on Broadband in Asia: Development and Policy." In *Proceedings of the Asian Economic Integration—Current Status and Prospects*. Tokyo: The Research Institute of Economy, Trade and Industry (RIETI).
Aju News (2021). "Korean Content That US CNN Pays Attention to . . . 'Netflix Growth Engine.'" February 7. https://aju.news/en/korean-content-that-us-cnn-pays-attention-to-netflix-growth-engine.html.
Andrejevic, M. (2011). "Social Network Exploitation." In *A Networked Self: Identity, Community, and Culture on Social Network Sites*, edited by Z. Papacharissi, 82–101. London: Routledge.
Armstrong, J. K. (2014). "A Mostly Healthy Obsession: The Joy of Binge Reading." BBC, October 21. https://www.bbc.com/culture/article/20140317-the-joy-of-binge-reading.
Art Rocket (n.d.). "Tips for Creating Vertical Scrolling Webtoons." https://www.clipstudio.net/how-to-draw/archives/157055.

Bae, I. H. (2000). "The Heyday of the Internet Manhwa Webtoon." [In Korean.] *ETnews*, January 22. https://www.etnews.com/200001220015.
Bae, S. M. (2017). "Korea Starts Webtoons: We Should Export the System and Webtoons." [In Korean.] *Money Today*, August 21. https://news.v.daum.net/v/20170821062214678?f=p.
Baek, B. Y. (2014a). "Korea's 'Webtoon' Industry: Boom or Bust?" *Korea Times*, February 20. http://www.koreatimes.co.kr/www/news/culture/2014/02/203_151973.html.

Baek, B. Y. (2014b). "'Misaeng' Cartoonist Shares Advice for Success." *Korea Times*, December 7. http://www.koreatimes.co.kr/www/news/culture/2014/12/201_169462.html.

Baek, B. Y. (2014c). "Rise of 'Snack Culture.'" *Korea Times*, July 9. http://www.koreatimes.co.kr/www/art/2017/11/688_160731.html.

Baek, B. Y. (2017). "Award-Winning Cartoons Reflect Present Day Society." *Korea Times*, November 9. https://m.koreatimes.co.kr/pages/article.asp?newsIdx=239038.

Baker, D., and E. Schak (2019). "The Hunger Games: Transmedia, Gender and Possibility." *Continuum* 33 (2): 201–215.

Bang, H. K. (2018). *Kim Sung Hwan*. [In Korean.] Seoul: Communication Books.

Beddows, E. (2012). "Consuming Transmedia: How Audiences Engage with Narrative across Multiple Story Modes." PhD diss., Swinburne University of Technology.

Bick, I. (1996). "Boys in Space: Star Trek, Latency, and the Never-Ending Story." *Cinema Journal* 35 (2): 43–60.

Blake, M., and Y. Villareal (2019). "Are These End Times for Binge Culture?" *Los Angeles Times*, October 10. https://www.latimes.com/entertainment-arts/tv/story/2019-10-10/streaming-wars-binge-culture-netflix-model.

Bloter (2013). "Naver Reveals the Page Profit Share Program." [In Korean.] March 21. https://www.bloter.net/newsView/blt201303210002.

Brienza, C. (2014). "Did Manga Conquer America? Implications for the Cultural Policy of 'Cool Japan.'" *International Journal of Cultural Policy* 20 (4): 383–398.

Brown, J. A. (1997). "Comic Book Fandom and Cultural Capital." *Journal of Popular Culture* 30 (4): 13–32.

Bryce, M., C. Barber, J. Kelly, S. Kunwar, and A. Plumb (2010). "Manga and Anime: Fluidity and Hybridity in Global Imagery." *Electronic Journal of Contemporary Japanese Studies*, January 29. http://www.japanesestudies.org.uk/articles/2010/Bryce.html.

Bryne, W. (2019). What Is Digital Storytelling and What Has It Got to Do with Cultural Heritage?" *Europeana Pro*, August 6. https://pro.europeana.eu/post/what-is-digital-storytelling-and-what-has-it-got-to-do-with-cultural-heritage.

Burrowes, C. (2020). "Webtoons Are Poised to Become the Future of Anime." *CBR*, February 17. https://www.cbr.com/webtoons-future-of-anime/.

Castillo (2016). "Webtoons, the New Star of the Hallyu Wave." *Korea Daily*, October 3. http://www.koreadailyus.com/webtoons-the-new-star-of-the-hallyu-wave/.

Castro, D., J. Rigby, D. Cabral, and V. Nisi (2021). "The Binge-Watcher's Journey: Investigating Motivations, Contexts, and Affective States surrounding Netflix Viewing." *Convergence* 27 (1): 3–20.

Caves, R. (2000). *Creative Industries: Contracts between Art and Commerce*. Cambridge, MA: Harvard University Press.

Chae, H. S. (2018). *Webtoon's Medium Transformation*. [In Korean.] Seoul: Communication Books.

Chie, Y. (2013). "Manhwa in Korea: (Re-) Nationalizing Comics Culture." In *Manga's Cultural Crossroads*, edited by J. Berndt and B. Kummerling-Meibauer, 85–99. London: Routledge.

Cho, E. A. (2014). "Can Naver Webtoons Dominate the Global Cartoon Market?" [In Korean.] *Business Post*, August 14.

Cho, H. K. (2016). "The Webtoon: A New Form for Graphic Narrative." *Comics Journal*, July 18. http://www.tcj.com/the-webtoon-a-new-form-for-graphic-narrative/.

Cho, H. K. (2021). "The Platformization of Culture: Webtoon Platforms and Media Ecology in Korea and Beyond." *Journal of Asian Studies*, 80 (1): 1–21.

Cho, Y. G. (2020). "Showbox's First Challenge: Drama Itaewon Class Duck Happy Smile." [In Korean.] *Bell*, March 5. https://www.thebell.co.kr/free/Content/ArticleView.asp?key=202003031236480160104333&svccode=04.

Cho, Y. H. (2017). "Historicizing East Asian Pop Culture." In *Routledge Handbook of East Asian Popular Culture*, edited by K. Iwabuchi, E. Tsai, and C. Berry, 13–23. London: Routledge.

Cho, Y. K. (2018). "[Syndrome: Along with The Gods 2] Holds People Who Left." [In Korean.] *JoongAng Ilbo*, August 14. https://news.jtbc.joins.com/article/article.aspx?news_id=NB11680795.

Choi, I. J. (2020). "'I'm Not Envious of Bong Joon'-Ho: K-Webtoon Continues to be Praised Abroad." [In Korean.] *Chosun Ilbo*, April 9. https://news.chosun.com/site/data/html_dir/2020/04/09/2020040902077.html.

Choi, J. W. (2020). "K-Webtoons Become Mainstream, Go Global." *Korea Herald*, May 6. http://www.koreaherald.com/view.php?ud=20200506000728.

Choi, M. Y. (2020). "Naver Transforms Its Webtoon Business with a Focus on the U.S. Market." [In Korean.] *Hankyoreh Shinmun*, May 28. http://www.hani.co.kr/arti/PRINT/946894.html.

Chun, S. W. (2017). "From Webtoons, Movies, and Dramas Digging into Daily Life, to Postage Stamps." [In Korean.] *ETnews*, February 22. https://m.etnews.com/20170222000125.

Chung, A. Y. (2014a). "Generational Shift in Cartoon Industry." *Korea Times*, February 20. http://www.koreatimes.co.kr/www/news/culture/2014/02/386_151969.html.

Chung, A. Y. (2014b). "Snack Culture." *Korea Times*, February 2. http://www.koreatimes.co.kr/www/news/culture/2014/02/386_150813.html.

Chung, H. M. (1999). "Manhwa Internet Broadcaster, AniBS, Earns Popularity." [In Korean.] *JoongAng Ilbo*, June 22. https://news.joins.com/article/print/3792261.

Chung, J. W. (2020). "Naver's Global Webcomic Biz on Growth Track." *Yonhap News*, January 24. https://en.yna.co.kr/view/AEN20200123009000320.

Ciastellardi, M., and G. Di Rosario (2015). "Transmedia Literacy: A Premise." *International Journal of Transmedia Literacy* 1 (1): 7–16.

Crary, J. (2013). *24/7: Late Capitalism and the Ends of Sleep*. London: Verso.

Crunchyroll (2020a). "Crunchyroll Reveals First Slate of Crunchyroll Originals." February 25. https://www.crunchyroll.com/anime-news/2020/02/25/crunchyroll-reveals-first-slate-of-crunchyroll-originals.

Crunchyroll (2020b). "Tower of God Anime Debuts as Crunchyroll Original April 1." February 25. https://www.crunchyroll.com/anime-news/2020/02/25-1/tower-of-god-anime-debuts-as-crunchyroll-original-this-april.

Daliot-Bul, M., and N. Otmazgin (2017). *The Anime Boom in the United States: Lessons for Global Creative Industries*. Cambridge, MA: Harvard University Asia Center.

Daniels, L. (1998). *Superman: The Complete History: The Life and Times of the Man of Steel*. San Francisco, CA: Chronicle Books.
Daum Webtoon (2012). "Yoon Tae-ho's *Misaeng* Started." [In Korean.] January 17.
Daum Webtoon (2020). "About Us." [In Korean.] http://biz.webtoon.daum.net/about.
Dickensonian (2004). Editorial. 100 (464): 195–196.
Do, D. W. (2015). "Korean 'Webtoons' Turn to Technology, Genre-Based Stories." *Korea Times* November 2. http://www.koreatimes.co.kr/www/news/culture/2015/11/148_189995.html.
DongA Ilbo (2020). "'Gag Concert' Ends on June 26: Twenty-One Years of History, a Dissapointing 'Stop' after 1050 Episodes." [In Korean.] June 26. https://www.donga.com/news/Entertainment/article/all/20200626/101699796/1.
Donohoo, T. (2020). "What Is Tower of God? Get to Know the Korean Comic before the Anime." CBR.com, February 15. https://www.cbr.com/tower-of-god-get-korean-webtoon-explained/.
Doo, R. (2017). "Korean Webtoon Readership Growing, Themes Need Diversifying: Report." *Korea Herald*, February 5. http://kpopherald.koreaherald.com/view.php?ud=201702051802311809530_2.

Eisner, W. (2008). *Comics and Sequential Art: Principles and Practices from the Legendary Cartoonist*. New York: W. W. Norton.
Evans, E. (2016). "The Economics of Free: Freemium Games, Branding and the Impatience Economy." *Convergence* 22 (6): 563–580.

Fast, K., and H. Örnebring (2017). "Transmedia World-Building: The Shadow (1931–Present) and Transformers (1984–Present)." *International Journal of Cultural Studies* 25 (2): 636–652.
Foster-Simard, C.-A. (2011). "Henry James and the Joys of Binge Reading." *Millions*, March 17. https://themillions.com/2011/03/henry-james-and-the-joys-of-binge-reading.html.
Franco, C. P. (2015). "The Muddle Earth Journey: Brand Consistency and Cross-Media Intertextuality in Game Adaptation." In *Storytelling in the Media Convergence Age: Exploring Screen Narratives*, edited by R. Pearson and A. Smith, 40–53. Berlin: Springer.
Freeman, M. (2015). "Up, Up and Across: Superman, the Second World War and the Historical Development of Transmedia Storytelling." *Historical Journal of Film, Radio and Television* 35 (2): 215–239.
Freeman, M. (2017). *Historicising Transmedia Storytelling: Early Twentieth-Century Transmedia Story Worlds*. London: Routledge.
Freeman, M. (2018). "From Sequel to Quasi-Novelization: Splinter of the Mind's Eye and the 1970s Culture of Transmedia Contingency." In *STAR WARS and the History of Transmedia Storytelling*, edited by S. Guynes and D. Hassler-Forest, 61–72. Amsterdam: Amsterdam University Press.
Fuchs, C. (2010). "Labor in Informational Capitalism and on the Internet." *Information Society* 26 (3): 179–196.
Fulton, B. (2019). "East Asian Perspective in Transmedia Storytelling: The Multimedia Life of a Korean Graphic Novel: A Case Study of Yoon Taeho's *Ikki*." *International Journal of Communication* 13: 2231–2238.

Gillespie, T. (2010). "The Politics of Platforms." *New Media & Society* 12 (3): 347–364.

Gimenes, N. (2018). "What Is the Platformization? Learn How to Compete in the Age of Digital Platforms." Sensedia, October 24. https://sensedia.com/en/digital-business/what-is-the-platformization-learn-how-to-compete-in-the-age-of-digital-platforms/.

Giovagnoli, M. (2011). *Transmedia Storytelling: Imagery, Shapes and Techniques*. Pittsburgh, PA: ETC Press.

Greene, L. (2019). "Why It's Cool to Be a Dirt Spoon in Korea." *Economist*, March 4. https://www.1843magazine.com/upfront/brave-new-word/why-its-cool-to-be-a-dirt-spoon-in-korea.

Ha, J. M. (2016). "New Platforms and New Sources for New Korean Cinema ③: Webtoons." [In Korean.] *Hankyoreh*, March 20. http://www.hani.co.kr/arti/nglish_edition/e_entertainment/735818.html.

Han, C. W. (2013). *Manhwa's Cultural Politics and Industry*. [In Korean.] Seoul: Communication Books.

Han, C. W. (2015). "A Study on Industrial Development and Globalization Strategy for Webtoon Platform." *Korean Journal of Animation* 11 (3): 137–150.

Han, C. W. (2021). *Webtoon Business Dilemma*. [In Korean.] Seoul: Communication Books.

Han, S. B. (2020). "What's the Taste of the Drama 'Itaewon Class' Written by the Author of the Webtoon?" [In Korean.] *Hankook Ilbo*, February 14. https://www.hankookilbo.com/News/Read/202002121108033969.

Hancox, D. (2017). "From Subject to Collaborator: Transmedia Storytelling and Social Research." *Convergence* 23 (1): 49–60.

Hankyoreh Shinmun (2016). "When Do We Binge-Read Other Than on Holidays? Jump into Webtoons." [In Korean.] September 17. http://www.hani.co.kr/arti/culture/movie/761474.html.

Hardt, M., and A. Negri (2004). *Multitude: War and Democracy in the Age of Empire*. New York: Penguin.

Harvey, R. C. (1996). *The Art of the Comic Book*. Jackson: University Press of Mississippi.

Hay, J., and N. Couldry (2011). "Rethinking Convergence/Culture: An Introduction." *Cultural Studies* 25 (4): 473–486.

Helmond, A. (2015). "The Platformization of the Web: Making Web Data Platform Ready." *Social Media + Society* July–December: 1–11.

Herman, T. (2018). "BTS' Most Political Lyrics: A Guide to Their Social Commentary on South Korean Society." *Billboard*, February 23. https://www.billboard.com/articles/columns/k-town/8098832/bts-lyrics-social-commentary-political.

Hills, M. (2015). "Storytelling and Storykilling: Affirmational/Transformational Discourses of Television Narrative." In *Storytelling in the Media Convergence Age: Exploring Screen Narratives*, edited by R. Pearson and A. Smith, 151–173. Berlin: Springer.

Hodgkins, C. (2020). "Crunchyroll Unveils 7 'Crunchyroll Originals' Works Including Tower of God, Noblesse, God of High School." Anime News Network, February 25. https://www.animenewsnetwork.com/news/2020-02-25/crunchyroll-unveils-7-crunchyroll-originals-works-including-tower-of-god-noblesse-god-of-high-school/.156748.

Hong, C. (2016). "Kim Go Eun Puts Casting Issues to Rest with Excellent Acting in 'Cheese in the Trap.'" *Soompi*, January 16. https://www.soompi.com/article/810881wpp/kim-go-eun-puts-casting-issues-to-rest-with-excellent-acting-in-cheese-in-the-trap.

Hong, J. M. (2012). "K-Comics Leading the New Korean Wave: Talking about Cartoons from the 1950s and 1960s." [In Korean.] *Seoul Shinmum*, April 30. http://m.seoul.co.kr/news/newsView.php?id=20120430019003.

Hong, J. M. (2017). "Traveling abroad on a Popular Cartoon Platform: 'Webtoon Hallyu' Growing Stronger Through Localization." [In Korean.] *Seoul News Paper*, January 30. http://www.seoul.co.kr/news/newsView.php?id=20170131017002.

Hong, S. Y., and H. Y. Lee (2020). "Naver Headquarters Webtoon Operation in US to Accelerate Global Outreach." *Pulse*, May 29. https://pulsenews.co.kr/view.php?year=2020&no=551331.

Hwang, J. H. (2010). "Byung-mak Manhwa Emerges after Trash Drama." [In Korean.] *Media Today*, April 11. http://www.mediatoday.co.kr/news/articleView.html?idxno=87360.

Hwang, S. T. (2018). *Crowdsourcing Webtoon Storytelling*. [In Korean.] Seoul: Communication Books.

Im, Y. T. (2020). "Action Square, Netflix Original 'Kingdom'- Game Production." [In Korean.] *Maeil Economic Daily*, September 1. http://game.mk.co.kr/view.php?year=2020&no=898943.

Instagram. (2020). *Myeoneuragi*. https://www.instagram.com/min4rin/.

Iwabuchi, K. (2002). *Recentering Globalization: Popular Culture and Japanese Transnationalism*. Durham, NC: Duke University Press.

Jang, M. J. (2019). "Popular Music and the Establishment of *Segyekwan* (Universe)." [In Korean.] *Sisa Journal e*, May 24. http://www.sisajournal-e.com/news/articleView.html?idxno=200631.

Jang, S. Y. (2018). "Definition of Webtoons Based on the Pre-History of Webtoons." [In Korean.] In *Webtoons, How to Define Them?*, edited by KOMACON, 19–31. Bucheon, South Korea: KOMACON.

Jang, W. H., and J. E. Song (2017). "Webtoon as a New Korean Wave in the Process of Globalization." *Kritika Kultura* 29: 168–187.

Jenkins, H. (2006). *Convergence Culture: Where Old and New Media Collide*. New York: New York University Press.

Jenkins, H. (2007). "'We Had So Many Stories to Tell': The Heroes Comics as Transmedia Storytelling." Confessions of an Aca-Fan, December 3. http://henryjenkins.org/2007/12/we_had_so_many_stories_to_tell.html.

Jenkins, H. (2011). "Transmedia 202: Further Reflections." Confessions of an Aca-Fan, July 31. http://henryjenkins.org/2011/08/defining_transmedia_further_re.html.

Jenkins, H., S. Ford, and J. Green. (2013). *Spreadable Media: Creating Value and Meaning in a Networked Culture*. New York: New York University Press.

Jenner, M. (2018). *Netflix and the Re-Invention of Television*. London: Palgrave Macmillan.

Jeong, J. H. (2020). "Webtoons Go Viral? The Globalization Processes of Korean Digital Comics." *Korea Journal* 60 (1): 71–99.

References

Jeong, M. A. (2017). "The Relationship between Korean Movies and Society: Social Issues Succeed as the People Desire Justice." *Korean Cinema Today* 30: 60–63.

Jin, D. Y. (2015a). "Digital Convergence of Korea's Webtoons: Transmedia Storytelling." *Communication Research and Practice* 1 (3): 193–209.

Jin, D. Y. (2015b). *Digital Platforms, Imperialism, and Political Culture*. New York: Routledge.

Jin, D. Y. (2016). *New Korean Wave: Transnational Cultural Power in the Age of Social Media*. Urbana: University of Illinois Press.

Jin, D. Y. (2017a). "Anipang." In *The 100 Greatest Video Games*, edited by R. Mejia, J. Banks, and A. Adams, 9–10. Lanham, MD: Rowman and Littlefield.

Jin, D. Y. (2017b). *Smartland Korea: Mobile Communication, Culture and Society*. Ann Arbor: University of Michigan Press.

Jin, D. Y. (2019a). "Snack Culture's Dream of Big-Screen Culture: Korean Webtoons' Transmedia Storytelling." *International Journal of Communication* 13: 2094–2115.

Jin, D. Y. (2019b). *Transnational Korean Cinema: Cultural Politics, Film Genres, and Digital Technologies*. New Brunswick, NJ: Rutgers University Press.

Jin, D. Y. (2019c). "Korean Webtoonist Yoon Tae Ho: History, Webtoon Industry, and Transmedia Storytelling," *International Journal of Communication* 13, 2216–2230.

Jin, D. Y., ed. (2020). *Transmedia Storytelling in East Asia: The Age of Digital Media*. London: Routledge.

Jin, D. Y. (2021). *Artificial Intelligence in Cultural Production: Critical Perspectives on Digital Platforms*. London: Routledge.

Jin, D. Y., and K. Yoon (2016). "The Social Mediascape of Transnational Korean Pop Culture: *Hallyu 2.0* as Spreadable Media Practice." *New Media & Society* 18 (7): 1277–1292.

Jin, D. Y., K. Yoon, and W. J. Min (2021). *Transnational Hallyu: The Globalization of Korean Digital and Popular Culture*. Lanham, MD: Rowman and Littlefield.

Jin, M. J. (2017). "Epic Undertaking Fails to Impress: Fans of the 'Along with the Gods: The Two Worlds' Webtoon May Find the Film to Be Overly Sentimental." *Korea JoongAng Daily*, December 13. http://koreajoongangdaily.joins.com/news/article/article.aspx?aid=3042069.

Jin, M. J. (2019). "With Netflix, 'Kingdom' Looks to Be a Global Hit: Local Creators Hope the Zombie Thriller Creates More Opportunities." *Korea JoongAng Daily*, January 23. https://koreajoongangdaily.joins.com/news/article/article.aspx?aid=3058574.

Jin, M. S. (2020). "The Average Commute Time in Metro Seoul is 1 Hour and 27 Minutes." [In Korean.] *Hankyoreh Shinmun*, April 23. http://www.hani.co.kr/arti/economy/economy_general/941700.html.

Johns, J. (2011) "Korea Needs Predictable Regulatory Environment." *Korea Times*, May 15. https://koreatimes.co.kr/www/news/biz/2016/06/333_87003.html.

Joo, W. J., R. Denison, and H. Furukawa. (n.d.). "Manhwa Movies Project Report 1: Transmedia Japanese Franchising." Norwich, UK: University of East Anglia.

Ju, H. J. (2019). *Transnational Korean Television: Cultural Storytelling and Digital Audiences*. Lanham, MD: Lexington Books.

Jung, E. A. (2020). "*Itaewon Class*, a Korean Drama That Just Hits Different." *Vulture*, April 2. https://www.vulture.com/2020/04/itaewon-class-a-korean-drama-that-just-hits-different.html.

Jung, H. W. (2015). "South Korea's Webtoon Craze Making Global Waves." Agence France-Presse, November 24. https://finance.yahoo.com/news/s/south-korea-webtoon-craze-making-global-waves-041606407.html.

Jurgensen, J. (2012). "Binge Viewing: TV's Lost Weekends." *Wall Street Journal*, July 12.

Kacsuk, Z. (2018). "Re-Examining the 'What Is Manga' Problem: The Tension and Interrelationship between the 'Style' versus 'Made in Japan' Positions." In *Japanese Media Cultures in Japan and Abroad*, edited by M. Hernandez-Perez, 15–32. Basel, Switzerland: MDPI.

Kain, E. (2020). "Worried about a Global Pandemic? You Should Watch 'Kingdom' On Netflix." *Forbes*, March 12. https://www.forbes.com/sites/erikkain/2020/03/12/worried-about-coronavirus-you-should-watch-kingdom-on-netflix/#7e71114643bc.

Kakao (2019). *2019 Audit Report*. [In Korean.] Jeju, South Korea: Kakao.

Kakao (2020). *2020 Audit Report*. [In Korean.] Jeju, South Korea: Kakao.

Kang, E. W. (2018). *Spinoff*. [In Korean.] Seoul: Communication Books.

Kang, M. J. (2020). "Netflix Introduces New Original Series All of US Are Dead, Based on Popular Korean Webtoon." Press release, April 12. https://about.netflix.com/en/news/netflix-introduces-new-original-series-all-of-us-are-dead-based-on-popular-korean-webtoon

Kang, T. J. (2014). "South Korea's Webtoons: Going Global." *Financial Times*, July 28. https://www.ft.com/content/3b5a3b59-6aae-3c90-bf96-8ace895f32cf.

Kawano, K. (2019). "Boys' Love, the Genre That Liberates Japanese Women to Create a World of Their Own." *Savvy Tokyo*, January 17. https://savvytokyo.com/boys-love-the-genre-that-liberates-japanese-women-to-create-a-world-of-their-own/.

Keane, M., B. Yecies, and T. Flew, eds. (2018). *Willing Collaborators: Foreign Partners in Chinese Media*. Lanham, MD: Rowman and Littlefield.

Kelley, C. (2017) "Meet the BTS Fan Translators (Partially!) Responsible for the Globalization of K-pop." *Billboard*, December 21. https://www.billboard.com/articles/columns/k-town/8078464/bts-fan-translators-k-pop-interview.

Kerr, E. (2018). "'Along with the Gods: The Last 49 Days': Film Review." *Hollywood Reporter*, August 8. https://www.hollywoodreporter.com/review/along-gods-last-49-days-film-review-1133084.

Ki, S. M. (2013). "'Misaeng' Creator Makes Art from Company Malaise." *Korea JoongAng Daily*, February 18. https://koreajoongangdaily.joins.com/news/article/article.aspx?aid=2967318.

Kidd, D. (2018). *Pop Culture Freaks: Identity, Mass Media, and Society*. 2nd ed. London: Routledge.

Kim, B. S. (2018). "Search for Korean Webtoons in 200 Countries . . . Illegal Distribution Sites Are Also On the Rise." [In Korean.] *Chosun Ilbo*, February 16. https://biz.chosun.com/site/data/html_dir/2018/02/13/2018021301401.html.

Kim, H. A. (2020). "Writer Yoon Tae-ho Is Back with the New Webtoon *Eorin*—the South Pole." [In Korean.] *Edaily* March 14. https://www.edaily.co.kr/news/read?newsId=01728566625703320&mediaCodeNo=257&gtrack=sok.

Kim, H. J. (2020). "IP Universe Era—Korean Style Marvel Is Coming Soon." [In Korean.] *Seoul Economic Daily*, July 5. https://www.sedaily.com/News/NewsView/NewsPrint?Nid=1Z2XCOORN5.

Kim, H. W. (2019). "A Homosexual Drawing of Young Boy BL Explodes in Popularity Among Women in 1020 . . . Leading the Webtoon Market." [In Korean.] *Chosun Ilbo*, March 9. http://it.chosun.com/site/data/html_dir/2019/03/09/2019030900782.html.

Kim, H. W. (2021). "2021—The Webtoon Industry Focuses on the Expansion of Super IP and Globalization." [In Korean.] *IT Chosun*, January 1. http://it.chosun.com/site/data/html_dir/2021/01/01/2021010100297.html.

Kim, I. G. (2020). "Audio-Visual Hallyu Has Changed from the Supporting Role to the Leading Role—The World falls in Love with K-Webtoon." [In Korean.] *Munhwa Ilbo*, April 13. http://www.munhwa.com/news/view.html?no=2020041301032139179001.

Kim, I. W. (2019). "Among Major OECD Countries, Only Korea Shows the Spike in the Unemployment Rate." *HanKyung Economic Daily*, October 14.

Kim, J. H., and J. Yu (2019). "Platformizing Webtoons: The Impact on Creative and Digital Labor in South Korea." *Social Media + Society* (October–December): 1–11.

Kim, J. Y. (1998). "Multimedia Manhwa Becomes Popular." *ETnews*. March 28.

Kim, K. A. (2017). *Romance Web Novel*. [In Korean.] Seoul: Communication Books.

Kim, M. H. (2016). "Didier Borg, CEO of French Webtoon Company Delitoon, 'Korean Webtoons Are Attractive to Read.'" [In Korean.] *MK Times*, November 18. http://news.mk.co.kr/newsRead.php?no=803814&year=2016.

Kim, M. R. (2015). "A Case Study of Cross-Media Storytelling: Remediation of Webtoon Misaeng to Drama Series Misaeng." *Journal of the Korea Contents Association* 15 (8): 130–140.

Kim, M. R. (2020). "What Are the Most-Watched Dramas on Netflix in 2020?" [In Korean.] *Chosun Ilbo*, November 14. https://www.chosun.com/national/weekend/2020/11/14/UBLSJMI6SRG4RNQTOC7RHX3BH4/.

Kim, M. S. (2015). "'Webtoons' Become S Korea's Latest Cultural Phenomenon." *Aljazeera*, June 30. https://www.aljazeera.com/blogs/asia/2015/06/korea-latest-cultural-phenomenon-150630055653457.html.

Kim, S. C., and H. J. Lee (2019). "Platformization of the Webtoon Industry in Korea." *Culture and Society* 27 (3): 95–142.

Kim, S. G. (2016). "Web Novel Market 'Big Bang'—The Market Size Is Expected to Increase to 80 Billion Won This Year." [In Korean.] *Maeil Economic Daily*, December 7. https://www.mk.co.kr/news/culture/view/2016/12/848730/

Kim, S. H. (2017). "Korea VFX Today." *Korean Cinema Today* 30: 48–55.

Kim, S. J. (2019). "A Study on the Pattern Change of the Webtoon." *Cartoon and Animation Studies* 57: 311–340.

Kim, S. S. I., and Y. J. Lee (2022). "International Diversification Strategy of Webtoon Platforms: Focusing on Naver and Kakao Webtoon in Japan." *Manhwa Animation Research* 66: 589–628.

Kim, S. Y. (2020). "Ghao Tops, Due to the Popularity of 'Itaewon Class,' OSTs Continue to Rise on the Music Chart." [In Korean.] *Hankyung Economic Daily*, March 17. https://www.hankyung.com/entertainment/article/202003176471H.

Kim, Y. A., ed. (2013). *The Korean Wave: Korean Media Go Global*. London: Routledge.

Kim, Y. S. (2016). "Snacks Emerging as the New Entrée: How Snack Culture Permeates the Contemporary Era." *Yonsei Annals*, March 6. http://annals.yonsei.ac.kr/news/articleView.html?idxno=1607.

Kim, Y. W. (2018). "KakaoPage Acquires Indonesian Webtoon Operator." *Investor*, December 18. https://www.theinvestor.co.kr/view.php?ud=20181218000563.

Kinder, M. (1991). *Playing with Power in Movies, Television, and Videogames: From Muppet Babies to Teenage Mutant Ninja Turtles*. Berkeley: University of California Press.

KOMACON (2015). *The Blueprint of the Manhwa Transaction Environment Development*. [In Korean.] Bucheon, South Korea: KOMACON.

KOMACON (2018a). "2017 Manhwa Statistics Card News." [In Korean.] Press release, March 5. Bucheon, South Korea: KOMACON.

KOMACON (2018b). *Overseas Comics Market Research 2017*. [In Korean.] Bucheon, South Korea: KOMACON.

Koo, J. J. (2019). "The Critical Representation of Family in Changing Dailytoon—Focusing on Two Webtoon Series Danji and Myeoneuragi (The Daughter-in-Law)." *Journal of Korean Drama and Theatre* 65 (9): 71–98.

Korea Creative Content Agency (2013). "Now Enjoy Webtoons in a Smart Way: Webtoon Applications." [In Korean.] July 15. https://koreancontent.kr/1607.

Korea Creative Content Agency (2015). *Webtoon Industry Status Analysis*. [In Korean.] Naju, South Korea: KOCCA.

Korea Creative Content Agency (2016). *2015 Manhwa Content White Paper*. [In Korean.] Naju, South Korea: KOCCA.

Korea Creative Content Agency (2018). *The Basic Status of Webtoonists*. [In Korean.] Naju, South Korea: KOCCA

Korea Creative Content Agency (2019a). *2018 White Paper on Korean Cartoons*. [In Korean.] Naju, South Korea: KOCCA.

Korea Creative Content Agency (2019b). *2019 Analysis of Webtoon Industry Reality*. [In Korean.] Naju, South Korea: KOCCA.

Korea Creative Content Agency (2019c). *2019 Report of the First Half Content Industry Trend Analysis*. [In Korean.] Naju, South Korea: KOCCA.

Korea Creative Content Agency (2019d). *The Current Status of Webtoonists*. [In Korean.] Naju, South Korea: KOCCA.

Korea Creative Content Agency (2020a). *2019 Cartoon Industry White Paper*. [In Korean.] Naju, South Korea: KOCCA.

Korea Creative Content Agency (2020b). *2020 Analysis of Webtoon Industry Reality*. [In Korean.] Naju: South Korea: KOCCA.

Korea Creative Content Agency (2020c). *Contents Industry 2019 Outcome and 2020 Perspective*. [In Korean.] Naju, South Korean: KOCCA.

Korea Creative Content Agency (2021). *Trend Report of the 2020 Latter Half and Annual Content Industry*. [In Korean.] Naju, South Korea: KOCCA.

Korea Daily (2017). "7 Translated Korean Webtoon Recommendations to Binge Read." May 26. http://www.koreadailyus.com/7-translated-korean-webtoon-recommendations-to-binge-read/3/.

Korea Herald (2015). "Daum Kakao to Change Its Name to Kakao." September 1. http://www.koreaherald.com/view.php?ud=20150901000892.

Korea Times (2009). "100 Years of Korean Comics." June 2. http://www.koreatimes.co.kr/www/news/art/2009/06/135_46093.html.

Korea.com. (2016). "Webtoons as the New Trend for Korean Dramas and Films." January 8. http://www1.korea.com/bbs/board.php?bo_table=SHOW&wr_id=1501.
Korean Film Council (2019). *2018 Korean Film Industry Report*. Busan, Korea: KOFIC.
Korean Film Council (2020). "Box Office." Busan, Korea: KOFIC.
Kraidy, M. (2005). *Hybridity or the Cultural Logic of Globalization*. Philadelphia: Temple University Press.
K-Studio. (2012). "K-Studio Announces Launch Event for New Comic Art Studio in Los Angeles." 17 October. https://icv2.com/articles/comics/view/24166/k-studio-announces-launch-event
KT Economic Management Institute. (2015). *Webtoon Market Dreams of 1 Billion Market*. Seoul: KT Economic Management Institute.
Ku, E. S. (2020). "Youth's Unemployment Rate—The Highest Ever." [In Korean.] *HanKyung Economic Daily*, August 12. https://www.hankyung.com/economy/article/2020081206511.
Kwon, D. I. (2020). "Brace Yourselves, Here Comes 'the 90s.'" *Yonsei Annals*, April 4. http://annals.yonsei.ac.kr/news/articleView.html?idxno=2116.
Kwon, J. M. (2019). *Straight Korean Female Fans and Their Gay Fantasies*. Iowa City: University of Iowa Press.
Kwon, J. M. (2022). "The Commercialization and Popularization of Boys Love (BL) in South Korea." In *Queer Transfigurations: Boys Love Media in Asia*, edited by J. Walker, 80–91. Honolulu: University of Hawaii Press.
Kwon, J. Y. (2017). "Novelcomics Is Also Successful–Toward Global Mobile Content Platform." [In Korean.] *Aju Economy*, January 24. https://www.ajunews.com/view/20170123104822636.
Kwon, M. S. (2020). "K-Webtoon Catches Global Eye—Becomes the Leading Manhwa Export." [In Korean.] *MediaSR*, May 2. http://www.mediasr.co.kr/news/articleView.html?idxno=58583.
Kwon, O. S. (2014). "Korean Webtoons Go Global with LINE." *Headline*, July 6. https://medium.com/the-headline/korean-webtoons-go-global-with-line-b82f3920580e.

Lamarre, T. (2015). "Regional TV: Affective Media Geographies." *Asiascape* 2: 93–126.
Lan Kwai Fong Group (2018). "Lan Kwai Fong Group Partners with South Korea's Largest Telecom Company KT." PR Newswire, May 7. https://en.prnasia.com/releases/apac/lan-kwai-fong-group-partners-with-south-korea-s-largest-telecom-company-kt-209970.shtml.
Lazzarato, M. (2004). *Les revolutions du capitalisme*. Paris: Empecheurs de Penser en Rond.
Lee, D. W. (2012). "Marine Blues Turned into a Go-Stop Game." [In Korean.] *ZDNet*, June 12. http://www.zdnet.co.kr/news/news_view.asp?artice_id=20120612182001.
Lee, E. J. (2021). "Unfair Contracts for Webtoons and Web Novels are Rampant: Naver, Kakao Don't Care." [In Korean.] IT Chosun, April 14. http://it.chosun.com/site/data/html_dir/2021/04/13/2021041302449.html.
Lee, H. I. (2018). "The First $10M Film of 2018, *Along with the Gods*: Seven Reasons for its Success." [In Korean.] *Kyunghyang Shinmun*, January 3. http://news.khan.co.kr/kh_news/khan_art_view.html?art_id=201801031638001#csidxb222ded993fc36e9a9e9b33c7edc129.

Lee, H. J. (2018). "A 'Real' Fantasy: Hybridity, Korean Drama, and Pop Cosmopolitans." *Media, Culture & Society* 40 (3): 365–380.

Lee, H. K. (2016). "Manhwas, Webtoons, and the Storytelling behind It All." *Korea Daily*, October 3. http://www.koreadailyus.com/manhwas-webtoons-and-the-story telling-behind-it-all/.

Lee, J. L. (2020). "'Space Sweepers' Set for Webtoon Release ahead of Movie Premiere." *Korea JoongAng Daily*, May 25. https://koreajoongangdaily.joins.com/2020/05/25 /movies/Space-Sweepers-IP-webtoon/20200525180800170.html.

Lee, J. Y. (2015). "Webtoon-Based Drama and Films Will Boom in the New Year." [In Korean.] *DongA Ilbo*, January 5. http://news.donga.com/List/3/all/20150105 /68905908/4.

Lee, K. W. (2000). "Chollian, Manhwa Special Site Webtoon." *ETnews*, August 9.

Lee, M. (2008). "Will It Melt with Love in the Frozen Theater? Kang Full's Love Story Opens." [In Korean.] *Cine 21*, November 11. http://www.cine21.com/news/view/?mag _id=54086.

Lee, M. A. (2019). "Working-Level Staffs Are 'Captain': Creates Content Never Available Before in Korea." [In Korean.] *Economy Chosun*, July 15. http://economy.chosun .com/client/news/view.php?boardName=C00&t_num=13607364.

Lee, S. G. (2019). "Korean Silicon Valley, Pangyo: Of an Estimated 140,000 Webtoonists, Half Earn 1.6 Million Won per Month." [In Korean.] *JoongAng Ilbo*, May 12. https://news.joins.com/article/23464764.

Lee, S. J. (2016). *Kang Full: Manhwa Webtoon Artist Review*. [In Korean.] Seoul: Communication Books.

Lee, S. J., and A. M. Nornes, eds. (2015). *Hallyu 2.0: Korean Wave in the Age of Social Media*. Ann Arbor: University of Michigan Press.

Lee, S. M. (2017). *Current Status and Implication for Webtoon Market in the Americas*. Seoul: Korea Culture and Tourism Institute.

Lee, S. W. (2013). "Webtoons Are the New Stickers: Why Companies Should Keep Their Eyes on Asia's Latest Toon Trend." TNW, October 24. http://thenextweb .com/asia/2013/10/24/webtoons-new-stickers-companies-keep-eyes-asias-latest -toon-trend/.

Lee, S. Y. (2014). "South Korea's Daum, Kakao Shareholders Approve Merger." Reuters. August 27. https://www.reuters.com/article/us-kakao-daum-communicat/south-koreas -daum-kakao-shareholders-approve-merger-idUSKBN0GR11D20140827.

Lee, S. Y. (2016). "Snacking on the Online Snack Culture." October 6. http://www .theargus.org/news/articleView.html?idxno=1064.

Lee, Y. I., and H. J. Kim (2019). "Naver Webtoon Tops Global Online Comic Charts, Sales to Hit $502 Mn This Year." *Pulse*, September 24. https://pulsenews.co.kr/view .php?year=2019&no=760754.

Li, J. Y. (2020). "From Media Mix to Platformization: The Transmedia Strategy of 'IP' in *One Hundred Thousand Bad*." In *Transmedia Storytelling in East Asia: The Age of Digital Media*, edited by D. Y. Jin, 225–241. London: Routledge.

Lim, H. B. (2019). "2017 Today's Our Manhwa Award Serial Review: Danzi and. . . ." Webtoon Guide, November 6. https://www.webtoonguide.com/en/board/Review_en /11375.

Lim, H. W. (2018). "What Is the Business Model that Increased Kakao Page's Sales 100 Times?" [In Korean.] *Korea Economic Daily*, December 26. https://www.hankyung.com/it/article/2018122502591.

Lim, K. U. (2018). "Local Webtoon Defeats Avengers and Superman in the U.S." [In Korean.] *Chosun Ilbo*, April 26. https://biz.chosun.com/site/data/html_dir/2018/04/25/2018042503552.html.

Listly (2019). "How Much Is the Average Income of Webtoon Artist?" September 27. https://medium.com/issue-by-listly-io/how-much-is-the-average-income-of-webtoon-artist-35971b8bf4d3.

Literature Translation Institute of Korea (2014). *Introduction Material on Yoon Tae-ho*. Seoul: Digital Library of Korean Literature. https://library.ltikorea.or.kr/writer/200826.

Lombardi, L. (2019). "Shigeru Mizuki, The Legendary Manga Creator and Yokai Professor, Finally Gets His Due." *Wire*, January 7. https://www.syfy.com/syfy-wire/shigeru-mizuki-the-legendary-manga-creator-and-yokai-professor-finally-gets-his-due.

Lynn, H. G. (2016). "Korean Webtoons: Explaining Growth." *Research Center for Korean Studies Annual—Kyushu University* 16: 1–13.

MacDonald, J. (2020). "Writer Kim Eun-hee Shares Her Inspiration for the Historical Zombie Drama 'Kingdom.'" *Forbes*, March 12. https://www.forbes.com/sites/joanmacdonald/2020/03/12/writer-kim-eun-hee-shares-her-inspiration-for-the-historical-zombie-drama-kingdom/#5f3089dd71f1.

MacMillan, D., and P. Burrows (2009). "Inside the App Economy." *Business Week*, October 22. https://www.bloomberg.com/news/articles/2009-10-22/inside-the-app-economy.

Manovich, L. (2013). *Software Takes Command*. London: Bloomsbury.

Mansson, D., and S. Myers (2011). "An Initial Examination of College Students' Expressions of Affection through Facebook." *Southern Communication Journal* 76 (2): 155–168.

Marshall, C. (2016). "Korean Webtoons Entertain the World." Korea.net, March 3. http://www.korea.net/NewsFocus/Culture/view?articleId=133278.

Martin, D. (2018). "South Korean Animation Today: National Identity and the Appeal to Local Audiences." *Journal of Japanese and Korean Cinema* 10 (2): 92–97.

Matrix, S. (2014). "The Netflix Effect: Teens, Binge Watching, and On-Demand Digital Media Trends." *Jeunesse* 6 (1): 119–138.

Matsutani, M. (2009). "Manga: Heart of Pop Culture." *Japan Times*, May 26. https://www.japantimes.co.jp/news/2009/05/26/reference/manga-heart-of-pop-culture/.

McCloud, S. (1993). *Understanding Comics: The Invisible Art*. New York: Harper Perennial.

McKevitt, A. (2017). *Consuming Japan: Popular Culture and the Globalizing of 1980s America*. Chapel Hill: University of North Carolina Press.

Miller, N. (2007). "Manifesto for a New Age." *Wired*, March 1. https://www.wired.com/2007/03/snackminifesto/.

Miller, V. (2020). *Understanding Digital Culture*. London: Sage.

Ministry of Culture, Sports and Tourism (2014a). *2013 Content Industry: Final Statistics*. Seoul: Ministry of Culture, Sports and Tourism.

Ministry of Culture, Sports, and Tourism (2014b). "A Mid- to Long-Range Plan to Reach 1 Billion Won Sales in the Manhwa Industry." Press release, May 28.

Ministry of Culture, Sports and Tourism (2019). *2018 Contents Industry White Paper*. Seoul: Ministry of Culture, Sports and Tourism.

Ministry of Culture, Sports and Tourism (2020). *2019 Contents Industry Statistics Survey Report*. Seoul: Ministry of Culture, Sports and Tourism.

Ministry of Education (2020). *A Survey of Elementary and Secondary Education Students*. Seoul: Ministry of Education.

Ministry of Science and ICT (2017). *A Study of the Globalization Strategies of Webtoon Platforms*. Seoul: Ministry of Science and ICT.

Moura, H. (2011). "Sharing Bites on Global Screens: The Emergence of Snack Culture." In *Global Media Convergence and Cultural Transformation: Emerging Social Patterns and Characteristics*, edited by D. Y. Jin, 37–49. Hershey, PA: IGI Global.

MrBlue (2020). "Webtoon Genres." [In Korean.] April 25. https://www.mrblue.com/webtoon/genre/fantasy.

Murray, N. (2018). "Review: From Dinosaurs to Courtroom Drama, Overstuffed Korean Epic 'Along with the Gods: The Last 49 Days' Entertains." *Los Angeles Times* July 31. https://www.latimes.com/entertainment/movies/la-et-mn-along-with-the-gods-49-days-review-20180731-story.html.

Nam, D. Y. (2020). "Class Is Different in Content Strategy–Kakao Has a Plan." [In Korean.] *Tech M*, February 24. http://www.techm.kr/news/articleView.html?idxno=7816.

Nam, Y. J. (2020). "Korean Webtoon 'Wings' Easily Changes between Genres." [In Korean.] *Busan Ilbo*, May 10. http://www.busan.com/view/busan/view.php?code=20200510180909I3106.

Napier, S. (2007). *From Impressionism to Anime: Japan as Fantasy and Fan Cult in the Mind of the West*. New York: Palgrave Macmillan.

Naver (2014). "Webtoon 10th Anniversary." [In Korean.] http://campaign.naver.com/webtoon/.

Naver Webtoon (2018). "Company." https://webtoonscorp.com/en/.

Naver Webtoon (2019). *2019 Audit Report*. Seong-Nam, South Korea: Naver.

Naver Webtoon (2020a). *2020 Audit Report*. Seong-Nam, South Korea: Naver.

Naver Webtoon (2020b). "Binge Read by Themes." https://www.webtoons.com/en/collection/list.

Naver Webtoon (2020c). "Naver Makes the U.S. a Headquarters to Expand Webtoons' Global Growth." Press release, May 28.

Netflix (2017). "Ready, Set, Binge: More than 8 Million Viewers 'Binge Race' Their Favorite Series." Press release, October 17. https://about.netflix.com/en/news/ready-set-binge-more-than-8-million-viewers-binge-race-their-favorite-series.

Nieborg, D. B., and A. Helmond. (2019). "The Political Dconomy of Facebook's Platformization in the Mobile Ecosystem: Facebook Messenger as a Platform Instance." *Media, Culture & Society* 41 (2), 196–218.

Nieborg, D. B., and T. Poell. (2018). "The Platformization of Cultural Production: Theorizing the Contingent Cultural Commodity." *New Media & Society* 20 (11): 4275–4292.

No, J. W. (2021). "Webtoon Based on Drama 'Navillera' Released for Free on KakaoPage." [In Korean.] *Edaily*, March 22. https://www.edaily.co.kr/news/read?newsId =01712166628985944&mediaCodeNo=257.

Nulook Media (2020). "Yoon Tae-ho." [In Korean.] http://www.nulookmedia.co.kr /family/main.do.

Nye, J. S., Jr. (2004). *Soft Power: The Means to Success in World Politics*. New York: PublicAffairs.

Oh, D. S. (2021). "Kakao Acquires the First American Webtoon Company, Tatas; Will Compete against Naver in the U.S." [In Korean.] *Maeil Economic Daily*, April 11. https://www.mk.co.kr/news/it/view/2021/04/346556/.

Oh, D. S., and M. Choi (2020). "Naver Webtoon Takes Over Korean AI Startup V.DO." Pulse, January 15. https://pulsenews.co.kr/view.php?year=2020&no=49553.

Ohsawa, Y. (2018). "A Contemporary Version of Globalization: New Ways of Circulating and Consuming Japanese Anime and Manga in East Asia." *Josai International University Bulletin* 26 (6): 19–41.

Ok, H. Y. (2011). "New Media Practices in Korea." *International Journal of Communication* 5: 320–348.

O'Reilly, T. (2005). "What Is Web 2.0? Design Patterns and Business Models for the Next Generation of Software." September 30. https://mediaedu.typepad.com/info _society/files/web2.pdf.

Orsini, L. (2020). "'Tower of God' Puts Battle Anime Tropes to the Test." *Forbes*, April 1. https://www.forbes.com/sites/laurenorsini/2020/04/01/tower-of-god-puts-battle -anime-tropes-to-the-test/#16fe5ccd48f4.

Osaki, T. (2019). "South Korea's Booming 'Webtoons' Put Japan's Print Manga on Notice." *Japan Times*, May 5. https://www.japantimes.co.jp/news/2019/05/05/business /tech/south-koreas-booming-webtoons-put-japans-print-manga-notice/#.XOYZZ9 MzYIg.

Oxford Reference (2019). "Cultural Production." Oxford: Oxford University Press. https://www-oxfordreference-com.proxy.lib.sfu.ca/view/10.1093/oi/authority .20110803095652897.

Pamment, J. (2016). "Digital Diplomacy as Transmedia Engagement: Aligning Theories of Participation with International Advocacy Campaigns." *New Media & Society* 18 (9): 2046–2062.

Park, E. J. (2016). "With Success in Korea, Webtoons Look Abroad." *Korea JoongAng Daily*, January 4. https://koreajoongangdaily.joins.com/news/article/article.aspx?aid =3013509.

Park, G. S. (2018). *Webtoon: The Structure and Possibility of Webtoon Transmedia Storytelling*. [In Korean.] Seoul: Communication Books.

Park, H. K. (2014). "Daum Webtoon Goes Global." *Korea Herald*, December 17. http:// www.koreaherald.com/view.php?ud=20141217000431.

Park, H. S. (2021). *Understanding Hallyu: The Korean Wave through Literature, Webtoon, and Mukbang*. London: Routledge.

Park, I. H. (2006). "A Short History of Manhwa." Translated by Kim Nakho. *Media, Manhwa, and Everything Nice*, March 15. http://capcold.net/eng/blog/?p=11.

Park, I. H. (2021). "History of Korean Webtoons." [In Korean.] https://m.blog.naver.com/enterani/220542151355.

Park, I. J. (2020). "Naver Webtoon Riding High on the Korean Wave." *Korea JoongAng Daily*, February 27. https://koreajoongangdaily.joins.com/news/article/article.aspx?aid=3074326.

Park, J. (2020). "Webtoon Artists' Work—90 Percent of Revenues Are Taken out as Toll Fees." [In Korean.] *Hankyoreh Shinmun*, November 16. http://www.hani.co.kr/arti/PRINT/970061.html.

Park, J. H. (2016). "Webcomics Expanding Territory." *Korea Times*, August 18. https://www.koreatimes.co.kr/www/news/culture/2016/08/203_212225.html.

Park, J. H. (2018). "'Along with Gods' Looks to Be Another Blockbuster." *Korea Times*, July 25. https://www.koreatimes.co.kr/www/art/2019/11/689_252831.html.

Park, J. H. (2020). "Naver Webtoon Riding High on the Korean Wave." *Korea JoongAng Daily*, February 27. https://koreajoongangdaily.joins.com/news/article/article.aspx?aid=3074326.

Park, J. H., J. H. Lee, and Y. S. Lee (2019). "Do Webtoon-Based TV Dramas Represent Transmedia Storytelling? Industrial Factors Leading to Webtoon-Based TV Dramas." *International Journal of Communication* 13: 2179–2198.

Park, J. W. (2020). "'Itaewon Class' Success Reflects Thriving Webtoon Market." *Korea Times*, March 18. https://www.koreatimes.co.kr/www/art/2020/03/688_286372.html.

Park, J. Y. (2019). "Webtoons: The Next Frontier in Global Mobile Content." *Mirae Asset Industry Report*. Seoul: Mirae Asset.

Park, J. Y. (2020). "Media/Entertainment Rise of Webtoons Presents Opportunities in Content Providers." *Industry Report*. Seoul: Mirae Asset Daewoo Co.

Park, K. S. (2018). *Webtoon, Transmedia Storytelling's Structure and Possibility*. [In Korean.] Seoul: Communication Books.

Park, M. J. (2020a). "Webtoons, Big in Japan, Are Korea's Latest K-Export." *Korea JoongAng Daily*, April 20. https://koreajoongangdaily.joins.com/2020/04/20/industry/Webtoons-big-in-Japan-are-Koreas-latest-Kexport/3076275.html.

Park, M. J. (2020b). "Webtoons Make a Fortune in a Strong Manhwa Force Japan . . . Kakao Page Uses an Anipang Strategy." [In Korean.] *JoongAng Ilbo*, May 26. https://news.joins.com/article/23785476.

Park, S. H. (2018). *Webtoon Contents Platform*. [In Korean.] Seoul: Communication Books.

Park, S. K. (2013). "The Golden Days of Webtoon." *Postech Times*, March 20. http://times.postech.ac.kr/news/articleView.html?idxno=6814.

Pellitteri, M. (2010). *The Dragon and the Dazzle: Models, Strategies and Identities of Japanese Imagination: A European Perspective*. Latina, Italy: Tunué.

Perks, L. G. (2015). *Media Marathoning: Immersions in Morality*. Lanham, MD: Lexington Books.

Pitre, J. (2019). "A Critical Theory of Binge Watching." *Jstor Daily*, April 10. https://daily.jstor.org/critical-theory-binge-watching/.

Plunkett, L. (2016). "Early Anime Fans Were Tough Pioneers." *Kotaku*, November 22. https://cosplay.kotaku.com/early-anime-fans-were-tough-pioneers-1789281217.

Pramaggiore, M. (2015). "Privatization Is the New Black: Quality Television and the Re-Fashioning of the U.S. Prison Industrial Complex." In *The Routledge Companion to Global Popular Culture*, edited by T. Miller, 187–196. London: Routledge.

Pyo, J. Y., M. J. Jang, and T. J. Yoon (2019). "Dynamics between Agents in the New Webtoon Ecosystem in Korea: Responses to Waves of Transmedia and Transnationalism." *International Journal of Communication* 13: 2161–2178.

Quartz Weekly Obsession (2019). "Webtoons." May 29. https://qz.com/emails/quartz-obsession/1630197/.

Ram, A. (2016). "Asia to Be a Major Player in Transmedia Content." *DNA*, November 8. https://www.digitalnewsasia.com/personal-tech/asia-be-major-player-transmedia-content.

Ramirez, F. (2015). "Affect and Social Value in Freemium Games." In *Social, Casual and Mobile Games: The Changing Gaming Landscape*, edited by T. Leaver and M. Wilson, 117–132. New York: Bloomsbury Academic.

Rodriguez, A. (2019). "Netflix Execs Were Once Anxious about the Term 'Binge-Watching' So They Tried to Make 'Marathon' Viewing Happen Instead—But It Never Caught On." *Insider*, July 30. https://www.businessinsider.com/netflix-disliked-term-binge-preferred-alternatives-marathon-viewing-2019-7.

Ryoo, J. H. (2020). "Kingdom Itaewon Class—'Webtoon Realism' with Unique Worldview and Fresh Images Continues to Advance." [In Korean.] *JoongAng*, April 4. https://news.joins.com/article/23746941#none.

Salkowitz, R. (2018). "Stan Lee, Warren Ellis, Fabian Nicieza Highlight New Webtoon Series Launches This Fall." *Forbes*, August 30. https://www.forbes.com/sites/robsalkowitz/2018/08/30/stan-lee-warren-ellis-fabien-nicieza-highlight-new-webtoon-series-launches-this-fall/#5b85e6efa30a.

SBS (2019). "Webtoonist Yoon Tae-ho Met Hur Young Man during his Homeless Period." [In Korean.] May 2. http://sbsfune.sbs.co.kr/news/news_content.jsp?article_id=E10009480951.

Scolari, C. (2009). "Transmedia Storytelling: Implicit Consumers, Narrative Worlds, and Branding in Contemporary Media Production." *International Journal of Communication* 3: 586–606.

Scolari, C. (2014). "Transmedia Storytelling: New Ways of Communicating in the Digital Age." In *AC/E Digital Culture Annual Report*, 69–79. https://www.accioncultural.es/media/Default%20Files/activ/2014/Adj/Anuario_ACE_2014/EN/6Storytelling_CScolari.pdf.

Scolari, C. (2017). "Transmedia Storytelling as a Narrative Expansion: Interview with Carlos Scolari." In *Young and Creative: Digital Technologies Empowering Children in Everyday Life*, edited by L. Eleá, and L. Mikos, 125–129. Gothenburg, Sweden: Nordicom.

Seemiller, C., and M. Grace (2019). *Generation Z: A Century in the Making*. London: Routledge.

Seo, B. G. (2015). "What Is the Reason for the Growth of Webtoon-Based Dramas?" [In Korean.] *Herald Economic Daily*, November 24. http://news.heraldcorp.com/view.php?ud=20151124000235.

Seo, C. H. (2017). "Chosun Webtoon History That Can Be Read within 10 Minutes." [In Korean.] *Hangyereh Shinmun*, December 20. http://www.hani.co.kr/arti/special section/esc_section/824448.html#csidx387ee681d94001eb764f9f92ed99646.

Seo, E. Y. (2018). "The Meaning of Soonjeong Manhwa, Which Opens the Early Stage of Webtoon." [In Korean.] In *Webtoons, How to Define?*, edited by KOMACON, 39–51. Bucheon, South Korea: KOMACON.

Sharma, S. (2014). *In the Meantime: Temporality and Cultural Politics*. Durham, NC: Duke University Press.

Shim, A. G., B. Yecies, X. Ren, and D. Wang (2020). "Cultural Intermediation and the Basis of Trust among Webtoon and Webnovel Communities." *Information, Communication & Society* 23 (6): 833–848.

Shim, S. A. (2018, July 30). "(Movie Review) 'Along with the Gods 2': A Solidly Fun Sequel." Yonhap News Agency, July 30. https://en.yna.co.kr/view/AEN20180730005800315.

Shin, J. W. (2017). "KakaoPage to Apply the 'Wait Then free' Business Model on a Chinese Platform for the First Time." *Tech for Korea*, August 24. https://www.facebook.com/techforkorea/posts/to-chinese-consumers-of-tencent-dongman-wait-then-freestartup-koreanstartup-kaka/1929935517280890.

Slade-Silovic, O. (n.d.). "Horizontal VS. Vertical Videos: Which Video Format Should I Use?" COVIDEO. https://www.covideo.com/horizontal-vs-vertical-videos/.

Soh, J. (2008). "Soonjeong Stays True to Its Heart." *Korea Times*, December 4. http://www.koreatimes.co.kr/www/news/art/2008/12/135_35552.html.

Sohn, J. Y. (2014). "Korean Webtoons Going Global." *Korea Herald*, May 25. http://www.koreaherald.com/view.php?ud=20140525000452.

Sohn, J. Y. (2018). "Naver Webtoon Forms 'Studio N' for Webtoon-Based Film, Drama Production." *Korea Herald*, August 9. http://www.koreaherald.com/view.php?ud=20180809000611.

Sohn, S. I. (1999). *The History of Manhwa* (*Manhwa Tongsa*, volume 1). [In Korean.] Seoul: Sigongsa.

Song, B. G. (2018). "Am I the Main Character of the Webtoon? The Secret 40 Million People Saw Is 'Advanced Technology.'" [In Korean.] *Yonhap News*, January 15. https://www.yna.co.kr/view/AKR20180103003200887.

Song, C. R. (2014). "From a Movie Director to a Composer." [In Korean.] *Maeil Business Newspaper*, January 10. http://news.mk.co.kr/v7/newsPrint.php?year=2014&no=49947.

Song, J. E., K. B. Nahm, and W. H. Jang. (2014). "The Impact of Spread of Webtoon on the Development of Hallyu: The Case Study of Indonesia." *Journal of the Korea Entertainment Industry Association* 8 (2): 357–367.

Song, K. S. (2021). "Kakao M and Kakao Page Merged into Kakao Entertainment." *Korea JoongAng Daily*, March 4. https://koreajoongangdaily.joins.com/2021/03/04/business/industry/kakao/20210304191100343.html.

Song, T. H. (1999). "[Cyber] Netizens: (Cyber Culture) I See Comics in PC Rooms Now." [In Korean.] *Hankook Economic Daily*, November 8. https://www.hankyung.com/news/article/1999110804291.

Song, Y. S. (2012). "Webtoons' Current Status and Features and Webtoons-based OSMU Strategies." *Kocca Focus* 57 (August): 3–27.

Sora's Webtoon World (2012). "Here Comes 'Moron-Taste' Webtoon." December 18. https://podosora.wordpress.com.

Soriano, J. (2020). "Review: 'Itaewon Class' Is a Story about Second Chances and Reaching for Your Dreams." *Cinema Escapist* February 21. https://cinemaescapist.com/2020/02/review-itaewon-class/.

Stassen, M. (2021). "Naver to Invest over $320 M in Big Hit Subsidiary and Jointly Launch New Fan Platform." *Music Business Worldwide*, January 27. https://www.musicbusinessworldwide.com/naver-to-invest-321-6m-in-big-hit-subsidiary-benx-firms-to-create-new-global-fan-community-platform/.

Stavroula, K. (2014). *Transmedia Storytelling and the New Era of Media Convergence in Higher Education*. London: Palgrave.

Steinberg, M. (2012). *Anime's Media Mix: Franchising Toys and Characters in Japan*. Minneapolis: University of Minnesota Press.

Steinberg, M. (2017a). "Genesis of the Platform Concept: iMode and Platform Theory in Japan." *Asiascape* 4 (3): 184–208.

Steinberg, M. (2017b). "Media Mix Mobilization: Social Mobilization and Yo-Kai Watch." *Animation* 12 (3): 244–258.

Steinberg, M. (2020). "LINE as Super App: Platformization in East Asia." *Social Media + Society*, April–June: 1–10.

Steiner, E. (2017). "Binge-Watching in Practice: The Rituals, Motives, and Feelings of Streaming Video Viewers." In *The Age of Netflix: Critical Essays on Streaming Media, Digital Delivery, and Instant Access*, edited by C. Barker and M. Wiatrowski, 141–161. Jefferson, NC: McFarland.

Steiner, E., and K. Xu. (2018). "Binge-Watching Motivates Change: Uses and Gratifications of Streaming Video Viewers Challenge Traditional TV Research." *Convergence* 26 (1): 82–101.

Steinmüller, K (2003). "The Uses and Abuses of Science Fiction." *Interdisciplinary Science Reviews* 28 (3): 175–178.

Stelter, B. (2013). "Same Time, Same Channel? TV Woos Kids Who Can't Wait." *New York Times*, November 11. https://www.nytimes.com/2013/11/11/business/media/same-time-same-channel-tv-woos-kids-who-cant-wait.html.

Stevens, J., and C. Bell (2012). "Do Fans Own Digital Comic Books? Examining the Copyright and Intellectual Property Attitudes of Comic Book Fans." *International Journal of Communication* 6: 751–776.

Stone, C. (2022). "How Unhealthy Is Binge Watching? Press Pause, and Read On." *Reader's Digest*, March 7. https://www.rd.com/list/binge-watching-unhealthy.

Sun, M. (2020). "K-Pop Fan Labor and an Alternative Creative Industry: A Case Study of GOT7 Chinese Fans." *Global Media and China* 5 (4) 389–406.

Sung, S. G. (2018). "Implications of Webtoon Fan Translation vis-a-vis Official Translation." *Journal of East-West Comparative Literature* 46 (12): 173–197.

Suzuki, C. J. (2019). "*Yōkai* Monsters at Large: Mizuki Shigeru's Manga, Transmedia Practices, and (Lack of) Cultural Politics." *International Journal of Communication* 13: 2199–2215.

Tai, Z., and F. Hu (2018). "Play between Love and Labor: The Practice of Gold Farming in China." *New Media & Society* 20 (7): 2370–2390.

Terranova, T. (2000). "Free Labor: Producing Culture for the Digital Economy." *Social Text* 18 (2): 33–58.

Thussu, D. (2006). *International Communication: Continuity and Change.* London: Hodder Arnold.

Top, B. (2018). "Naver Webtoon Establishes Webtoon IP Bridge Company." *Venture Square World,* August 14. https://www.venturesquare.net/world/naver-webtoon-establishes-webtoon-ip-bridge-company/.

Travers, B. (2017). "Webtoons—How South Korea Is Creating the Future of Comics." *Medium,* July 2. https://medium.com/@benoittravers/webtoons-how-south-korea-is-creating-the-future-of-comics-e039c2994fcd.

Turner, G. (2021). "Television Studies, We Need to Talk about 'Binge-Viewing.'" *Television & New Media* 22 (3): 228–240.

Um, M. A. (2018). *Manga in Japan, and Webtoon in Korea.* 10 August. Seoul: KOFICE.

V, A. (2020). "How to Start Reading Webtoons (And 10 Series to Check Out)." *Medium,* February 26. https://medium.com/@aravaldez217/how-to-start-reading-webtoons-and-10-series-to-check-out-5f2d07388043.

Valtysson, B. (2010). "Access Culture: Web 2.0 and Cultural Participation." *International Journal of Cultural Policy* 16 (2): 200–214.

Van Dijck, J. (2013). *The Culture of Connectivity: A Critical History of Social Media.* New York: Oxford University Press.

Van Dijck, J., T. Poell, and M. de Wall (2018). *The Platform Society: Public Values in a Connective World.* New York: Oxford University Press.

Vincent, B. (2020). "From *Snotgirl* to *Giant Days,* Jump into These Binge-Worthy Graphic Novels and Webtoons." *MTV News,* April 22 http://www.mtv.com/news/3163571/graphic-novels-read-right-now/.

Vlessing, E. (2021). "Wattpad Storytelling App Sold for $600 Million to South Korean Firm Naver." *Hollywood Reporter,* January 19. https://www.hollywoodreporter.com/news/south-koreas-naver-buys-wattpad-storytelling-app-for-600-million.

Wajcman, J. (2015). *Pressed for Time.* Chicago: University of Chicago Press.

Waller, E. (2020). "Netflix Adapts Another Korean Webtoon." C21MEDIA, April 13. https://www.c21media.net/netflix-adapts-another-korean-webtoon/.

Watson, J., ed. (2006). *Golden Arches East: McDonald's in East Asia.* Stanford, CA: Stanford University Press.

Watson, J. (2006). "Introduction: Transnationalism, Localization, and Fast Foods in East Asia." In Watson, *Golden Arches East: McDonald's in East Asia,* 1–38.

Webtoon Translate (2020). *"Save Me* Is Now Available for Translation!" https://translate.webtoons.com/.

Wee, W. (2013). "Line Enters E-Book Business with Line Manga." *TechinAsia,* April 9. https://www.techinasia.com/line-enters-ebook-business-line-manga.

Weekly DongA (2017). "Red Days One after Another: American Dramas, Webtoons, Books for Binge Practicing." [In Korean.] October 3. https://weekly.donga.com/3/search/11/1077935/1.

Whitten, S. (2019). "Disney Bought Marvel for $4 billion in 2009, a Decade Later It's Made More Than $18 Billion at the Global Box Office." CNBC, July 21. https://www

.cnbc.com/2019/07/21/disney-has-made-more-than-18-billion-from-marvel-films-since-2012.html.

Wohn, D. Y. (2014). "Spending Real Money: Purchasing Patterns of Virtual Goods in an Online Social Game." In *Proceedings of the SIGCHI Conference on Human Factors in Computing Systems*, 3359–3368. New York: ACM. https://dl.acm.org/doi/10.1145/2556288.2557074.

Won, T. Y. (2020). "Webtoon, from Free Manhwa to the Major Force of the New Korean Wave." [In Korean.] *Sisa Journal*, April 2. http://www.sisajournal-e.com/news/articleView.html?idxno=216454.

Yang, S. H. (2007). "Gangnam Leftists." *Korea JoongAng Daily*, November 23. http://koreajoongangdaily.joins.com/news/article/article.aspx?aid=2883114.

Yecies, B. (2018). "Dreaming of Webtoons in China and the Next Korean Wave." In *Willing Collaborators: Foreign Partners in Chinese Media*, edited by M. Keane, B. Yecies, and T. Flew, 123–138. Lanham, MD: Rowman and Littlefield.

Yecies, B., and A. G. Shim (2021). *South Korea's Webtooniverse and the Digital Comic Revolution*. Lanham, MD: Rowman and Littlefield.

Yecies, B., A. Shim, J. Yang, and P. Y. Zhong (2020). "Global Transcreators and the Extension of the Korean Webtoon IP-Engine." *Media, Culture & Society* 42 (1): 40–57.

Yi, W. J. (2019). "Resisting the Spell of Oblivion: A Conversation with Taeho Yoon." *Verge* 5 (2): 55–75.

Yilmaz, R., and F. M. Cigerci (2019). "A Brief History of Storytelling: From Primitive Dance to Digital Narration." In *Handbook of Research on Transmedia Storytelling and Narrative Strategies*, edited by R. Yilman, M. Erdem, and F. Resulogu, 1–14. Hershey, PA: IGI Global.

Yonhap News (2009). "Seventh Encore Performance of the Play 'Kwangsoo Thinking.'" [In Korean.] March 3. http://news.nate.com/view/20090303n12996.

Yonhap News (2017). "62 Percent of Mobile Webtoon And Web Novel Users Are in Their Teens and Twenties." [In Korean.] February 21. https://www.yna.co.kr/view/AKR20170221026800017.

Yonhap News (2022). "'All of Us Are Dead' Tops Netflix Weekly Viewership Chart for 3rd Week." February 16. https://en.yna.co.kr/view/AEN20220216002800315#:~:text=Netflix%20said%20%22All%20of%20Us,4%22%20with%20619%20million%20hours.

Yoon, K. (2003). "Retraditionalizing the Mobile: Young People's Sociality and Mobile Phone Use in Seoul, South Korea." *European Journal of Cultural Studies* 6 (3): 327–343.

Yoon, K. H. (2014). "Korean Webtoon through Statistics: The New Way of Korean Manhwa over the Last 13 Years." [In Korean.] *Manhwa Zine*. https://m.blog.naver.com/PostView.naver?isHttpsRedirect=true&blogId=sisacartoon&logNo=220058038110.

Yoon, K. H., K. H. Jung, I. S. Choi, and H. S. Choi (2015). "Features of Korean Webtoons through the Statistical Analysis." *Cartoon and Animation Studies* 38: 177–194.

Yoon, S. H., S. Y. Kwon, and K. P. Lee (2015). "Understanding User's Behavior for Developing Webtoon Rating System Based on Laugh Reaction Sensing through Smartphone." CHI EA '15: Proceedings of the 33rd Annual ACM Conference Extended

Abstracts on Human Factors in Computing Systems, 2031–2036. https://dl.acm.org/doi/10.1145/2702613.2732920.

Yoon, S. W. (2016). "Kakao Separates Webtoon Business as Independent Subsidiary." *Korea Times*, September 4. http://www.koreatimes.co.kr/www/tech/2020/02/133_213283.html.

Yoon, Y. S. (2018). "Korean Gov't to Develop the Tech for Illegal Content Distribution Blacking." *BusinessKorea*, April 9. http://www.businesskorea.co.kr/news/articleView.html?idxno=21528.

Yoon, Y. W. (2001). "A Study of the Development of Sunjong Manhwa by Hwang Mina, Kim Kyerin, and Choi In-sun." MA thesis, University of British Columbia.

YPulse (2019). "The 20 Top Shows Gen Z & Millennials Are Binge Watching Now." October 17. https://www.ypulse.com/article/2019/10/17/the-20-top-shows-gen-z-millennials-are-binge-watching-now/.

Yun, J. H. (2019). "What Is Webtoon?" *Medium*, August 30. https://medium.com/mrcomics/what-is-webtoon-4926929b20d8.

Zur, D. (2016). "Modern Korean Literature and Cultural Identity in a Pre- and Post-Colonial Digital Age." In *Routledge Handbook of Korean Culture and Society*, edited by Y. N. Kim, 193–205. London: Routledge.

Index

Page numbers for figures are in italics.

A Man Like You, 42
affective labor, 153, 154
AfreecaTV, 106
AI (artificial intelligence), 67, 183; AI start-ups, 67; AI-supported cultural production, 67; AI-supported webtoons, 67
Alien Baseball Team, 88
All of Us Are Dead, 145, 146
Along with the Gods, 101, 119, 122, *123, 124,* 126–29
Always Human, 92
Amazon (company), 89, 95; Amazon Video, 90
Android (operating system), 34, 66, 68
Andromate, 148
animation, 7, 14, 17, 24, 32–33, 38, 42, 64, 126, 137, 139, 141, 146, 148, 159
anime, 2, 4–6, 16, 42, 86, 130, 134–35, 139, 147–48, 189, 197; American anime, 6; anime programs, 147; Japanese anime, 2, 16, 18, 45, 86, 129, 147, 159; Korea-US-Japan joint anime, 141
Apple (company), 40; iPhone, 40. *See also* iOS
apprenticeship, 25, 160, 166; apprentice system in the webtoon industry, 163, 166

apps (smartphone applications), 3, 5, 6, 14, 15, 37, 65–68, 98, 133, 136, 140, 157; manga apps, 142; webtoon apps, 37, 158
April Flowers, 91
APT, 119, 171
AR (augmented reality), 42
Awl, 91

Ba:Bo, 38, 39, 119, 171
big-screen content, 60, 71, 72, 101–2, 130, 159, 164, 175, 189, 192
big-screen culture, 3, 7, 8, 14, 17, 19, 28, 70–72, 85, 98, 100–102, 115, 118, 128–29, 133, 144, 151, 180, 189, 197
big-screen producer, 50, 170; big screen production, 16, 118, 126, 175–76
binge-consumption, 78, 87, 95
binge-reading, 5, 6, 8–10, 14, 18, 19, 60, 78–80, 85–98, 183, 185, 187
BL (boys' love), 28, 42, 43, 47, 92, 93, 101–2, 192; BL content, 43, 47; BL genre, 42, 115
blockchain, 163, 179
BomToon, 26, 42
Brass & Sass, 91
BTS (singing group), 103, 117, 132, 151, 196, 197

Burning Hell Shinui Nara (Land of the Gods), 143
byeong-mat, 106, 198n5

Canvas (Naver Webtoon service), 55, 66
capitalism, 52, 97, 188, 193
capitalization, 10, 11, 49, 96, 98, 154
cartoonist, 4, 20, 23, 25, 32, 35, 70, 77, 136, 163, 165–67, 174
CBR (Comic Book Resources), 2
Challenge Manhwa (Dojeon Manhwa), 55, 160, 186
Chase, The, 119
Cheese in the Trap, 6, 91, 92, 101, 109, 118
China, 3, 15, 25, 64, 117, 129, 134, 137, 139–40, 148, 155, 172–73, 181; Chinese characters, 140; Chinese comics, 178; Chinese cultural content, 155; Chinese diaspora, 140; Chinese manhwa market, 173; Chinese market, 64, 141; Chinese readers, 64
Chollian (PC communication service), 30, 33, 46; Cholian Webtoon, 33
circulation, 4, 9, 10, 11, 16, 49, 51–52, 183, 191; cultural circulation, 10; global circulation, 4, 11, 137; transnational circulation, 134, 157
CJ E&M (company), 72
comedy, 28, 91, 106, 147
Comics Today (internet portal), 36
commercialization, 47, 54, 64, 65, 70, 96, 170
connectivity, 73, 192; connectiveness, 98
convergence, 1, 11–12, 15, 40, 44, 51, 80–81, 86, 97, 130–31, 136, 175, 188, 196; digital convergence, 9, 174; media convergence, 6, 9, 12–13, 15–16, 76, 80, 95, 150, 159, 183–84, 186; technological convergence, 21; transmedia convergence, 149
COVID-19, 85, 91, 144–45, 182, 188
creator, 20, 34–35, 44, 55–56, 66, 73, 75, 81, 107, 129, 137, 139, 170–71, 173–74; big-screen creator, 39, 41–43, 119, 124; big-screen culture creator, 118, 180, 193; content creator, 53; cultural creator, xiii, 3, 6–7, 12, 14–17, 38, 50, 52, 67, 98, 100–101, 107, 127–30, 134–35, 143, 146, 182, 188–89, 191–92; manhwa creator, 24; media creator, 13; webtoon creator, 32
Crunchyroll (company), 147, 182, 189
cultural activity, 5, 48, 78, 80, 83, 159, 183, 185, 198
cultural authenticity, 128, 153, 155, 157
cultural consumption, 9, 11, 37–38, 40, 77, 85–88, 94–95, 99, 157, 183–86
cultural content, xii, 1, 3, 5–8, 15, 17, 21, 38, 40, 43, 45, 47–49, 51, 65, 68, 71–73, 76–78, 81, 83–85, 90, 94, 100, 108, 115, 118, 126, 129, 131–32, 134, 136, 142–43, 145, 148, 151, 155, 159, 181–83, 185–87, 189, 190–91
cultural economy, 68, 99
cultural identity, 135, 136, 158, 192
cultural industry, xii, 1, 5, 10–14, 16–18, 24, 40, 48–50, 59, 61–62, 64, 67–70, 73, 81, 85, 97, 100, 102, 118, 127–130, 132–33, 137, 148–49, 154, 159, 178, 182–83, 188–89, 190–93, 196
cultural market, 1, 2, 42, 45, 47, 49–51, 76–77, 100, 130, 132–33, 136–37, 139, 155, 157, 189–91, 193
cultural product, 1, 6, 16–18, 46, 49–50, 69, 76, 108, 119, 129–31, 133–34, 136–37, 143, 149, 159, 175, 180–82, 189–91, 197
cultural production, 3, 9, 11, 12, 17, 34, 39, 49, 51–52, 59, 67–69, 71, 75–77, 84, 100, 108, 127–28, 154, 157, 161, 183, 185–88, 190–91, 193
cultural studies, xi, 10–11, 97

Daum, 3, 4, 26, 27, 35, 39, 47–52, 55, 60–61, 63, 65, 67, 70, 77, 81, 139, 157, 160, 167, 169–70, 173, 175, 190, 197
Daum Kakao, 26, 136
Daum Webtoon, 18, 26, 27, 35, 40, 48–49, 54, 64, 70, 76, 103, 109, 133, 139, 141, 186, 198
Days of Hana, 92
Delitoon (company), 139

digital comic, 4, 6, 31, 35, 66, 141
digital culture, 2, 6, 9–12, 19, 47–48, 52–53, 60, 80, 89, 95–97, 133, 135, 161, 181, 183–84, 186, 188, 191, 192
digital game, xii, 3, 6, 7, 10, 61–62, 134, 146, 158–59, 188
digital media, 9–10, 13–15, 141, 190, 192
digital native, 37, 46, 84; digital native youth, 5
digital platforms, xi, 1, 3–4, 6, 9, 13–15, 17–18, 21–22, 45, 48–52, 56–63, 67, 68, 69, 71, 73, 75–77, 79–85, 88–90, 94–96, 98, 100, 108, 136, 148, 151, 153–54, 157, 181, 184–90
digital storytelling, 13–14, 34, 45, 67
digital technologies, 1, 3–6, 9–11, 13–17, 19–21, 23, 25, 28, 30, 35, 46–47, 50–51, 67–69, 76–79, 81–82, 98, 130, 133–34, 136, 147, 157, 159–60, 174, 183, 188, 192, 198
Disney (company), 64, 68
distribution, 25, 28, 50, 61, 69, 71, 80, 135, 148–49, 157, 173, 186, 190; distributor, 3, 37, 108, 147, 186
Dojeon Manhwa (Challenge Manhwa), 55, 160, 186
dramas, 7, 20, 28, 39–42, 45, 52, 66, 71, 85, 91–92, 96, 100, 103, 107–9, 114–19, 125, 129, 132, 134, 141, 144–45, 148–49, 163–64, 171, 175, 177; drama series, 7, 41, 66, 109, 113–15; Korean dramas, 116, 143, 163; melodramas, 119, 125, 141; television dramas, xii, 1, 3, 6, 20, 24, 39, 41, 61, 66, 71–73, 79, 81, 88, 100, 102, 105, 107, 109, 115–16, 118–19, 129–30, 134, 148–49, 164, 176, 179, 181, 188–89, 191, 193; webtoon-based dramas, 44, 72, 108–9, *110–11*, 115

earnings, webtoon companies, 53–54, *54, 55*
East Asia, 8, 66, 134, 137, 172
Emergency Landing, 163, 198
entertainment, 17, 20, 64, 91, 95, 101; entertainment business, 65; entertainment company, 3, 67; entertainment content, 45, 140; entertainment industry, 10, 19, 101, 130, 196; entertainment products, 23; entertainment program, 108; entertainment sector, 16, 145, 181; entertainment television programs, 107; media/entertainment platform environment, 141; web entertainment 85; web-entertainment material, 40
Eorin, 105, 164, 198
exploitation, 84, 96, 153, 187, 188
exports of Korean cultural products, 137, *138*

Facebook, 44, 68, 76, 93, 187, 196
fan labor, 153–54
fandom, 45, 73, 86, 151; anime fandom community, 86; fandom culture, 153–54, 159
fantasy, 28, 64, 91, 93, 101, 109, 119, 129, 141–42, 146, 155, 184, 192; fantasy worlds, 159
Fashion King, 106
feminism, 43, feminists, 43–44, 46
films, xii, 1, 3, 6–7, 10, 12–14. 16–17, 19–20, 24, 28–29, 39–41, 45, 46, 51–52, 60, 66–67, 70–71, 73, 81, 84–85, 88, 100, 102, 105, 107, 109, 115, 119, *120*, 122–23, 125, 127–30, 132–34, 136–37, 148–49, 154, 158–59, 163, 180, 188–89, 191, 193; film companies, 76, 131, 175. *See also* movies
financial crisis of 1997, 34, 46
France, xi, 3, 25, 139
Freaking Romance, 92
free labor, 153–54
freemium, 61; freemium game, 61, 66, 97; freemium model, 58, 60–62, 79, 88–90, 94, 98, 187

gag (webtoon genre), 28, 106, 156
Game of Thrones, 91
Gangnam leftists, 177, 199n5
Gangnam Style, xi
Generation Z, 2, 9, 19, 78, 89, 94, 98, 103, 185, 195

Germany, 25, 173
Ghost Lights, 92
Gian84 (webtoonist), 59, 106
Global North, xi, 3, 7–8, 142
Global South, 3, 7–8, 133, 142
global youth, xi, 4, 7, 14, 78–79, 84, 90, 94–95, 97, 103, 151, 158, 183, 185–86, 192–93. *See also* youth culture
globalization, xi, 15, 64, 68, 70, 133, 135, 139, *140*. 148, 155, 158, 172–73
glocalization, 133, 152, 154, 192
God of High School, The, 142
Google (company), 68, 187; Google Play, 146; Google Translate, 198. *See also* Android (operating system)
Greetings! Earthling!, 91

Hagwon, 119, 192, 198
Hallyu, xii, 7, 19, 116, 133–36, 141–43, 145, 147, 153–54, 157–58
He Is a High School Girl, 91
Heir's Game, 92
Hell Is Other People, 72
Helmond, Anne, 50, 187
History of Jji-jil, The, 107
Hollywood, 189; Hollywood movies, 20, 141
Hulu, 90, 95
Hur Young Man (cartoonist), 166–67, 198
hybridity, 129, 133–36, 155, 157–58
hybridization, 10, 134–35, 142, 152, 155, 190
Hyundai (company), 60

I Hate Love, 64
I Love Yoo, 92
ICO (initial coin offering), 179
Ikki, 152, 162, 167. *See also Moss*
il-sang (webtoon genre), 28 101, 119, 136, 156, 192; *il-sang-toon*, 32, 35, 45
income, webtoonist annual, 56–59, *57*
Indonesia, xi, 3, 64, 137, 139–40, 145; Indonesian market, 64
Inside Men, 41, 162, 164, 176–77
Instagram, 44, 196
intellectual property. *See* IP (intellectual property)

internet portals, 3, 18, 21, 26, 34–36, 46–47, 49, 58, 81, 157, 187; digital portal, 130; Korean web portal, 33; mega portal, 131; portal platform, 52; portal site, 36, 197
Invincible Hong Assistant Manager, 33
iOS, 66, 68, 140. *See also* Apple (company)
IP (intellectual property), 8, 49, 56, 59–60, 64–66, 68, 70–73, 75–76, 143, 145–46, 148–50, 158–59, 170, 182, 187; intellectual property rights, 12; IP-based global reach, 9; IP-based Hallyu, 158; IP-based revenue, 67; IP-based transmedia, 18, 48, 60 158; IP-based transmedia storytelling, 8, 54, 66, 71, 158; IP-based transnational transmedia, 150; IP-based webtoons, 149
Iron Girl, 148
Itaewon Class, 6, 62, 101, 109, *111, 112,* 113, 115–18, 126, 128, 155, 191

Japan, xi, 2–5, 16, 23, 25, 42, 51, 64–66, 68, 82, 103, 131, 134–35, 137, 139, 141–42, 147, 149, 155, 172–73, 181, 189, 197; Japanese colonial government, 23; Japanese comics market, 141; Japanese market, 65; Japanese movies, 6; Japaneseness, 135; Japanese youth, 141–42
Jenkins, Henry, 6, 15, 80, 95, 101, 128
Joo Ho-min (webtoonist), 107, 163
JTBC (general cable television channel), 108–9
Jump, 163
Justoon (webtoon platform), 26, 163

Kakao, 3, 4, 26–27, 44, 51–52, 54–55, *55, 63*–65, *65,* 68–70, 72–73, 77, 84, 90, 96, 136, 139, 148, 155, 157, 169, 187, 190, 197; Kakao Corp., 26; Kakao Entertainment, 65; Kakao Japan, 64, *65;* Kakao M, 65; Kakao Talk, 26, 82, 83; Kakao TV, 44
Kakao Page, 18, 26–27, 48, 54, 56, 59, 61, 63–65, *65,* 70, 72–73, 76–77, 79, 84–85, 88–90, 94, 105, 109, 130, 133, 141, 149, 155, 186, 196–98

Kang Full (webtoonist), 35–36, *36*, 38–39, 163, 167, 171, 173
KBS (Korea Broadcasting System), 108–9
Killed My Wife, 119
Kim Poong (webtoonist), 167
Kingdom, 143–45, 155–56, 159, 182, 191, 198
Korea Creative Content Agency, 11, 40, 57
Korea Telecom, 147–48
Korea Manhwa Contents Agency (KOMACON), 5, 30, 137
Korean Cartoon Association, 163
Korean Ministry of Culture, Sports, and Tourism, 24
Korean Ministry of Education, 52
Korean Wave, xi, 1, 7–8, 11, 18–19, 43, 45, 68, 132–34, 137, 140, 145, 148, 151, 157–58, 182
Korean youth, xi, 3, 101, 103, 106, 109, 113, 181, 184–85, 197
Koreanness, 10, 155–56, 191–92
K-pop, xi, 1, 3, 10, 24, 29, 45, 116, 132–34, 137, 142, 151, 153–54, 158–59, 189, 191, 197
KTOON (web site), 148
Kubera, 153
Kwang-su Thinking, 31, 35, 196

Lady and Her Butler, The, 156, 191
Lan Kwai Fong Group, 147–48
Lee Mal-nyeon (webtoonist), 105–7
Lee Mal-nyeon Series, 105
Legendary Moonlight Sculptor, The, 73
Lezhin Comics, 26, 42, 44, 55, 139, 156, 169–70, 173, 197
LG (company), 49
LGBTQ, 43, 44, 46, 115
Line, 27, 51, 65–66, 68, 139; Line Corp., 142; Line Digital Frontier, 68; Line Manga, 66, 142, 198; Line Webtoon, 2, 7, 42, 45, 66, 68, 140–41, 147
localization, 20, 141, 155
Lookism, 142, 151, 152
loser, 103, 105, 107, 113, 115–16, 185; loser syndrome, 103, 105, 107
Lost in Transition, 91
Lumine, 92

magazines, 2, 32, 33, 82, 87, 163, 165–67, 180
manga, 2, 4–6, 16, 42, 45, 66, 82, 134–35, 142, 147–48, 159, 189, 197–98; Japanese manga, 2, 16, 37, 47, 100, 130–31, 134, 139, 141–42, 155, 178, 185, 189, 193, 197; manga industry, 3
manhwa, 2, 3–4, 7, 11, 14, 22–25, 27–33, 35–36, 40, 43, 46–49, 53, 55, 59, 86, 88, 98, 102, 107, 126, 137, 141, 157–58, 160–63, 165–67, 169–70, 172–74, 177–78, 180, 183, 188, 193, 195–96, 198; American manhwa, 10; Chinese manhwa, 173; global manhwa market, 8, 137; global manhwa sphere, 3; internet manhwa service, 30, 32; Korean manhwa, 2, 20, 30; Korean manhwa market 5
manhwa industry, 5, 9, 17, 19–20, 22, 24–25, 35, 45, 50, 87, 90, 97, 137, 157, 164–65, 170, 182; online manhwa, 30, 33, 193
manhwabang, 23, *24*, 87, 88
Marine Blues, 33–35
Marvel (company), 17, 64; Marvel Comics, 64, 141, 149, 189; Marvel movies, 64, 178; Marvel Universe, 149
MBC (Munhwa Broadcasting Corporation), 106–9
MBN (general cable television channel), 108
media ecology, 5, 8, 9, 13, 21–22, 25, 51, 108, 113, 185, 187–88
media flow, 10; transmedia flow, 71
Memorist, 109
Men are Men, 107
Millennials, 2, 9, 19, 78, 89, 94, 98, 103, 185
Misaeng, 6, 40–41, *41*, 101, 103, 105, 107, 109, 129, 160, 162, 164–65, 169–70, 172, 176–77
mobile games, 1, 61, 63, 73, 81–82, 85, 142, 146, 184, 198
mobility, 14, 79, 81–82, 118, 184–85, 198
monetization, 58, 61, 62–63, 73, 96–98
monopolization, 70, 96
Moss, 41, 162, 164, 165, 167, *168*, 169, 171. See also *Ikki*

movies, 6–7, 17, 19–20, 39, 41, 54, 61, 64, 66, 81, 86, 107, 109, 118–19, 122–26, 128, 141, 149–50, 164, 171, 175–179, 182, 197; Korean movies, 191; movie clips, 106; movie companies, 100, 169, 176; movie directors, 171, 177; movie industry, 119; movie trailers, 122; moviegoers 122; webtoon-based movies, 119–26, *120–21*, *123*, 188. *See also* films
MrBlue, 26, 42, 55
multimedia, 13–14, 34, 38, 157; 3G mobile multimedia content service, 80; multimedia manhwa service, 32
Muted, 91
My Giant Nerd Boyfriend, 91
My ID Is Gangnam Beauty, 6, 109 *111*
My Little Television, 106
Myeoneuragi, 44–45
mysteries, 101, 109, 142
Mystic Pop-up Bar, 109
Mytoon (company), 107

N4 (internet portal site), 36
Naver, 3–4, 26, 35, 47–49, 51–53, 55, 58, 60–61, 65–72, 77, 81, 84, 90, 96, 119, 130, 139, 142, 152, 157, 169–70, 172, 175, 187, 190, 195–97; Naver Japan, 65; Naver Webtoon, 7, 18, 26, 27, 45, 48–49, 53–56, *54*, 59, 61, 65–68, 70, 72, 76–77, 79, 84, 89, 90, 93, 107, 119, 133, 140–41, 151, 160, 186, 197; Webtoon Entertainment, 68
Navillera: Like a Butterfly, 102–3, *104*
NeoBazar (webtoon platform), 64, *65*
Netflix, 6–8, 10, 59, 68, 72, 76, 85–87, 89–92, 95–96, 108–9, 115, 130, 132, 143–46, 148–49, 155–56, 159, 182, 185–87, 189, 198
new media, 7–9, 15, 22, 169, 174, 193
NHN Entertainment, 139
Nieborg, David, 50, 187
Noblesse, 142, 147, 153
Now at Our School, 145
Nulook Media, 20, 198; Nulook, 163

OCN (cable television channel), 72, 108–9, *110*
openness, 79, 179, 196
OSMU (one-source, multi-use), 17, 148, 182
OST (original soundtrack), 116
OTT (over-the-top), 6, 72, 95, 130, 185; OTT platform, 8, 10, 96, 97, 143, 157; OTT service platform, 6, 87, 113, 133, 143, 159, 187

Pandora's Choice, 91
Papepopo Memories, 33
PC (personal computer), 37, 142, 196; PC bang (internet café), 23, 31, 37, 175, 183
Pegasus Market, 72
Personalization, 94–95, 184
Piccoma (platform), 64, 141–42, 198
platformization, xii, 8, 9, 12, 18, 48–51, 60, 63, 67–73, 76–77, 82, 148, 153, 183, 185–88, 196
Poell, Thomas, 50
political economy, xi, 10–11, 18, 49, 73
popular culture, 1, 6–7, 9, 11, 14, 17, 19, 23, 40, 44, 47, 50, 67–68, 70, 72, 78–79, 81, 84, 86, 88, 92, 94–95, 98, 132–37, 141, 143, 147–48, 150, 183
PPS (Page Profit Share), 58
PR (public relations), 60
Psy, xi

Quartz Weekly Obsession, 2

Reddit, 92, 141
Relife, 139
Rise from Ashes, 91
romance (webtoon genre), 35, 42–43, 91, 93, 101, 107, 109, 118–19, 141, 156, 189, 197
romantic comedy, 35, 64, 109
Rugal, 109

Samsung (company), 49, 60; Samsung Galaxy, 40
Save Me, 92
SBS (Seoul Broadcasting System), 108–9, 169, 198

Scholar Who Walks the Night, 109
science fiction, 101
Secretly, Greatly, 6, 171
Seungriho (Space Sweepers), 182
Shaman Girl, 64
Showbox (company), 109
smartphone, 1–4, 6–7, 9, 14, 18–19, 21, 25, 32, 35, 37–38, 40–42, 46, 48–49, 59, 62, 67–68, 78–80, 81–85, 88, 95, 98, 101, 133–34, 142, 157, 159, 171–72, 174–75, 180–81, 183–84, 186, 193
snack culture, 5–10, 13, 14, 18–19, 33–34, 40, 46, 62, 78–85, 95–96, 98–101, 183–84, 193, 197
Snow Cat, 33
social media, 11, 14, 38, 44–46, 50, 80, 91–94, 102, 132, 196; social media platforms, 14, 66, 153, 186–87
soft power, 3, 76, 195
Sola Entertainment, 147
Solo Leveling, 141, 155
Something about US, 91
Southeast Asia, 64, 137
Space Sweepers, 119, 121, 149, 182. See also *Seungriho*
speed culture, 9–10, 79, 82–84
sports, 28
Spotify, 59, 186
Star X Fanboy, 42, 44
Steinberg, Marc, 51, 66, 76, 149, 193
Student A, 119
Studio N (Naver subsidiary), 66, 67, 71
sunjeong (webtoon genre), 28, 35, 43, 47, 119, 141, 192
Sunjeong Manhwa, 28, 35, 39
Sweet Home, 72, 92, 109
Swimming Lessons for a Mermaid, 91

Telecom Animation Film (company), 147
television, xii, 6, 12, 17, 20, 45, 85–87, 89, 94, 143, 150; mobile television platforms, 44; television anime, 139; television channels, 108, 131; television dramas, xii, 1, 6, 20, 24, 39, 41, 52, 61, 71–73, 79, 81, 88, 100, 102, 105, 107, 109, 115–16, 118–19, 129, 130, 132, 134, 148–49, 164, 176, 179, 181, 188–89, 191, 193; television industry, 17; television monitors, 7; television producers, 7, 16, 19, 39, 41, 100, 102, 119, 130, 169, 170, 175; television programs, 1, 6, 10, 17, 29, 39, 51, 59–60, 70, 88, 102, 107, 133–34, 136, 154, 158–59, 169, 180, 188–89; television series, 12, 41, 72, 116, 144, 197; television shows, 19, 71, 94, 96
Tencent (company), 64; Tencent DongMan (webtoon and animation platform), 64
They Say I Was Born a King's Daughter, 73, 74
thriller, 10, 28, 101, 119, 156, 162, 189; action thriller, 64
TOOMICS (webtoon platform), 26, *63*, *140*
TOPTOON (webtoon platform), 26, *63*
Totally Captivated, 43
Touch Your Heart, 72
Tower of God, 91, 92, 141, 142, 146, 147, 153, 182
ToYou's Dream (webtoon agency), 5, 6
transmedia storytelling, xii–xiii, 3, 8, 11–21, 28, 30, 34, 38–40, 44, 54, 72–73, 75, 101–2, 108, 115, 126–31, 133, 143, 145, 148–49, 159, 161, 169, 171, 174–75, 177, 179, 182, 188–90; digital transmedia storytelling, 13, 19, 20; IP-based transmedia storytelling, 8, 54, 66, 71, 158; transnational transmedia, 143, 148, 155; transnational transmedia storytelling, 18, 143, 157, 159, 189, 193; webtoon-based transmedia storytelling, 6, 9, 19, 40, 101, 108, 113, 118, 127, 129, 130–31, 171, 180, 182, 189
transmediality, 8, 11–12, 17–18, 35, 72, 75, 103, 127, 187–88, 192; transnational transmediality, 16, 188; webtoon-based transmediality, 17, 113, 128
transnationality, xi, 12, 183; transnational cultural phenomenon, 7; transnational culture, 7, 11; transnational popular culture, 1

transnationalization, xi, 10, 44, 73, 127, 133–34, 136, 139, 148, 150, 154, 180
True Beauty, 91–92, 141–42
TV Chosun, 108
tvN (television network), 41, 72–73, 102, 108–9, 116, 169, 177
Twitch.tv, 106
Twitter, 44, 93, 187, 196

United States, 1–4, 17, 20, 25, 55, 61, 68, 70, 86, 106, 129, 136, 140–143, 147, 156, 181, 197; American comics, 2, 156, 185; American distributors, 147; American dollars, 152; American market, 2; American pop culture, 46; American readers, 198; American series, 91; American websites, 92, 93
universe, 149; IP universe, 149; transmedia universes, 182
unOrdinary, 91

V.DO (AI startup), 67
van Dijck, José, 50, 94
vertical integration, 49, 64, *65,* 71
vertical layout, 35–38, 45, 98, 184, 196
Vietnam, 117, 139
villains, 144

Wassup Man, 106
Wattpad (company), 67
web 2.0, 80, 98
web dramas, 40, 83, 85
web novels, 40, 56, 59, 62, 66, 71–73, 83, 85, 90, 95, 188
webcomics, 1, 3, 4, 6, 20, 31, 34, 106, 143; webcomic market, 20, 141
webtoon agency, 54, 56, 67, 72
webtoon genres, 18, 19, 25, 28, *29,* 42–44, 47, 119
webtoon industry, xii, 18, 25, *26, 27,* 38, 48–49, 52, *53, 54,* 62–63, 77, 141, 157–58, 161, 172–73, 177–80, 182, 189, 192, 196

webtoon market, 28, 55, 62, 69, 76–77, 97, *140,* 141, 155, 171, 174, 187, 192, 197
webtoon platforms, 6, 9, 11, 18, 19, 25–27, *27,* 35, 37–38, 41–42, 45, 48, 49, 52–56, 58–60, *63,* 63–64, 67, 69–72, 75–80, 84–85, 88, 90–91, 94–99, 101, 115, 129, 133, 139, 141, 149–160, 163, 169–71, 173, 177, 180, 182–83, 185–88, 190–92, 197
webtoon portals, 32, 35, 49, *63,* 89
Webtoon Translate (webtoon translation web site), 152–53
webtoonists, 4, 16–18, 20, 22, 25, 32, 34–35, 37–39, 41, 43–45, 48–55, *57,* 57–60, 70, 72–73, 75–78, 80, 93, 101–3, 106–7, 115, 128–31, 139, 141–42, 155–56, 159–63, 165–67, 169–180, 182, 186, 188–89, 191–93; Korean webtoonists, 47, 161, 178
Welcome, 109
What's Wrong with Secretary Kim?, 72
Wind Breaker, 153
Winter Woods, 91
Wisdom House (company), 163
Work Man, 106
worldview, 148, 149, 155, 184, 191, 192

Yaoi, 42
Yaongyi (webtoonist), 141
Yeondam (webtoon agency), 56
YLAB (company), 56, 143, 149
Yoon Tae-ho, 11, 20, 41, 103, *110, 120, 121,* 152, 161, *162, 168,* 162–179
youth culture, xii, 3, 6, 10, 18, 21–22, 25, 33, 40, 43, 46, 79, 85, 88–89, 97, 99, 101, 183, 185, 191; digital youth culture, xii–xiii, 5, 8, 33, 98, 193; global youth culture, 4, 97, 151, 183, 186; Korean youth culture, 113, 197; transnational youth culture, 18, 20, 43
YouTube, 14, 59, 106, 115, 143, 186, 189, 190

zombies, 102, 143, 144, 145, 146

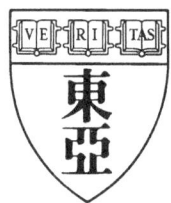

Harvard East Asian Monographs
(most recent titles)

414. Chieko Nakajima, *Body, Society, and Nation: The Creation of Public Health and Urban Culture in Shanghai*
415. Pu Wang, *The Translatability of Revolution: Guo Moruo and Twentieth-Century Chinese Culture*
416. Hwansoo Ilmee Kim, *The Korean Buddhist Empire: A Transnational History, 1910–1945*
417. Joshua Hill, *Voting as a Rite: A History of Elections in Modern China*
418. Kirsten L. Ziomek, *Lost Histories: Recovering the Lives of Japan's Colonial Peoples*
419. Claudine Ang, *Poetic Transformations: Eighteenth-Century Cultural Projects on the Mekong Plains*
420. Evan N. Dawley, *Becoming Taiwanese: Ethnogenesis in a Colonial City, 1880s–1950s*
421. James McMullen, *The Worship of Confucius in Japan*
422. Nobuko Toyosawa, *Imaginative Mapping: Landscape and Japanese Identity in the Tokugawa and Meiji Eras*
423. Pierre Fuller, *Famine Relief in Warlord China*
424. Diane Wei Lewis, *Powers of the Real: Cinema, Gender, and Emotion in Interwar Japan*
425. Maram Epstein, *Orthodox Passions: Narrating Filial Love during the High Qing*
426. Margaret Wan, *Regional Literature and the Transmission of Culture: Chinese Drum Ballads, 1800–1937*
427. Takeshi Watanabe, *Flowering Tales: Women Exorcising History in Heian Japan*
428. Jürgen P. Melzer, *Wings for the Rising Sun: A Transnational History of Japanese Aviation*
429. Edith Sarra, *Unreal Houses: Character, Gender, and Genealogy in the* Tale of Genji
430. Yi Gu, *Chinese Ways of Seeing and Open-Air Painting*
431. Robert Cliver, *Red Silk: Class, Gender, and Revolution in China's Yangzi Delta Silk Industry*
432. Kenneth J. Ruoff, *Japan's Imperial House in the Postwar Era, 1945–2019*
433. Erin L. Brightwell, *Reflecting the Past: Place, Language, and Principle in Japan's Medieval Mirror Genre*
434. Janet Borland, *Earthquake Children: Building Resilience from the Ruins of Tokyo*
435. Susan Blakely Klein, *Dancing the Dharma: Religious and Political Allegory in Japanese Noh Theater*

436. Yukyung Yeo, *Varieties of State Regulation: How China Regulates Its Socialist Market Economy*
437. Robert Goree, *Printing Landmarks: Popular Geography and* Meisho zue *in Late Tokugawa Japan*
438. Lawrence C. Reardon, *A Third Way: The Origins of China's Current Economic Development Strategy*
439. Eyck Freymann, *One Belt One Road: Chinese Power Meets the World*
440. Yung Chul Park, Joon Kyung Kim, and Hail Park, *Financial Liberalization and Economic Development in Korea, 1980–2020*
441. Steven B. Miles, *Opportunity in Crisis: Cantonese Migrants and the State in Late Qing China*
442. Grace Huang, *Chiang Kai-shek's Politics of Shame: Leadership, Legacy, and National Identity*
443. Adam Lyons, *Karma and Punishment: Prison Chaplaincy in Japan*
444. Craig A. Smith, *Chinese Asianism, 1894–1945*
445. Sachiko Kawai, *Uncertain Powers: Sen'yōmon and Landownership by Royal Women in Early Medieval Japan*
446. Juliane Noth, *Transmedial Landscapes and Modern Chinese Painting*
447. Susan Westhafer Furukawa, *The Afterlife of Toyotomi Hideyoshi: Historical Fiction and Popular Culture in Japan*
448. Nongji Zhang, *Legal Scholars and Scholarship in the People's Republic of China: The First Generation (1949–1992)*
449. Han Sang Kim, *Cine-Mobility: Twentieth-Century Transformations in Korea's Film and Transportation*
450. Brian Hurley, *Confluence and Conflict: Reading Transwar Japanese Literature and Thought*
451. Simon Avenell, *Asia and Postwar Japan: Deimperialization, Civic Activism, and National Identity*
452. Maura Dykstra, *Empire of Routine: The Administrative Revolution of the Eighteenth-Century Qing State*
453. Marnie S. Anderson, *In Close Association: Local Activist Networks in the Making of Japanese Modernity, 1868–1920*
454. John D. Wong, *Hong Kong Takes Flight: Commercial Aviation and the Making of a Global Hub, 1930s–1998*
455. Martin K. Whyte and Mary C. Brinton, compilers, *Remembering Ezra Vogel*
456. Lawrence Zhang, *Power for a Price: The Purchase of Appointments in Qing China*
457. J. Megan Greene, *Building a Nation at War: Transnational Knowledge Networks and the Development of China during and after World War II*
458. Miya Qiong Xie, *Territorializing Manchuria: The Transnational Frontier and Literatures of East Asia*
459. Dal Yong Jin, *Understanding Korean Webtoon Culture: Transmedia Storytelling, Digital Platforms, and Genres*
460. Takahiro Yamamoto, *Demarcating Japan: Imperialism, Islanders, and Mobility, 1855–1884*
461. Elad Alyagon, *Inked: Tattooed Soldiers and the Song Empire's Penal-Military Complex*
462. Borje Ljunggren and Dwight H. Perkins, eds., *Vietnam: Navigating a Rapidly Changing Economy, Society, and Political Order*